HTML for Fun and Profit

Grace Tai

Mary E. S. Morris

SunSoft Press
A Prentice Hall Title

HTML for Fun and Profit

Contents

≡

HTML for Fun and Profit

Figures

≡

HTML for Fun and Profit

Tables

≡

HTML for Fun and Profit

Code Examples

Preface

HyperText Markup Language (HTML) is the language of the World Wide Web, the fastest growing part of a very quickly evolving phenomena called the Internet. *HTML for Fun and Profit* covers basic HTML authoring and emphasizes the use of CGI scripts and forms to create customized and interactive web pages. The book also touches on some of the newest features, like tables, that bring HTML into the real publishing world.

Signature Edition Preface

The Signature edition now includes a Microsoft Windows 3.1 web server.

Who Should Use This Book

If you want to make a home page to list your musical preferences, this book is for you. If you want to make a high-tech career out of building storefronts for the newest commercial ventures, this book is also for you. No matter what your ambitions, if you want to be a producer of information instead of just a consumer on the Web, this book will help you learn HTML.

How This Book Is Organized

Chapter 1, "Getting Started" provides an overview of the software and explains how to set up a server so that your tour of HTML can be a hands-on experience.

Chapter 2, "The Basics" introduces the concept of a tag and demonstrates the use of simple tags.

Chapter 3, "Hypertext — Linking Documents," describes hypertext and document interaction in HTML.

Chapter 4, "Multimedia — Going Beyond Text," explains the full range of data beyond plain text and shows how to incorporate multimedia into your web creations.

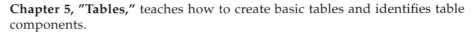

Chapter 5, "Tables," teaches how to create basic tables and identifies table components.

Chapter 6, "Using the Common Gateway Interface (CGI)," introduces the Common Gateway interface, which enables developers to tie scripts to web pages.

Chapter 7, "Server Includes," demonstrates the use of commands that are included or embedded in web pages to customize web pages.

Chapter 8, "Creating Forms," details the variety of form elements and implements several forms.

Chapter 9, "Processing Data from Forms," discusses input and output handling from the CGI and implements a feedback form.

Chapter 10, "Style Guide," outlines common sense guidelines to make web pages more intuitive to use and more appealing to all audiences.

Chapter 11, "Work-Saving Tools," explains the classes of available tools that make HTML authoring less tedious.

Chapter 12, "Putting Data on the Internet," discusses the issues involved in putting your data out for public consumption.

Chapter 13, "Future Directions," highlights the trends and directions of the World Wide Web.

Appendixes A, B, and C describe Mosaic™ for X-Windows™, Microsoft® Windows™, and Macintosh® systems, respectively.

Appendix D, "References," provides a complete list of the tags, environment variables, and special characters listed throughout the book.

Appendix E, "More Information," lists pointers to additional resources.

Typographic Conventions

Table PR-1 describes the typographic conventions used in this book.

Table PR-1 Typographic Conventions

Typeface or Style	Description	Example
AaBbCc123	The names of commands, files, tag attributes, and directories; on-screen computer output	Edit your `.login` file. Use `ls -a` to list all files. `system% You have mail.`
AaBbCc123	What you type, contrasted with on-screen computer output	`system%` **`su`** `password:`
AaBbCc123	Command-line placeholder: replace with a real name or value	To delete a file, type `rm` *filename*.
AaBbCc123	Book titles, new words or terms, or words to be emphasized	Read Chapter 6 in *User's Guide*. These are called *class* options. You *must* be root to do this.

HTML for Fun and Profit

Introduction ≡

My experiences in learning HTML have led me down many strange and unusual paths. I have spent many hours reading news groups and mailing lists to just find starting points for my learning. Until recently, such learning has had the bootstrapping problem that you must have at least a browser in order to find most documentation on the subject, and you *must* be on the Internet to get anything. Needless to say, no bedtime perusing for me.

I found documentation in some of the most unusual sources, *including* source itself. It has now become a habit for me now to `grep` or search all source code that I get for `http`. The tutorials for HTML are spread across the Internet. It is the nature of the Web that people publish locally and a few souls then publish hotlists or lists of pointers to items of interest on a topic. Unfortunately, there is no single master list, so many hours are spent following dozens or hundreds of links in the hope of finding new material or a different perspective on design. I hope to change this state and give HTML authoring a new beginning.

Begin at the Beginning

The story of HTML is the story of the medium that uses it, the World Wide Web. Then again, the story of the World Wide Web is a story about the evolution of tools to manage the vast sea of data that is the Internet.

The Internet

The Internet was born sometime in the early 1980s after a 14-year gestation period as the research and development network called ARPAnet. Its growth has equalled that of a child by almost doubling in size every year. So far this child shows no sign of slowing its rampant growth.

The data available to casual users on the Internet has grown as fast as the Internet itself and measures in the terabytes. Products have been developed to manage the information about data and provide a way of finding the document, program, or, in general, the bytes that are wanted.

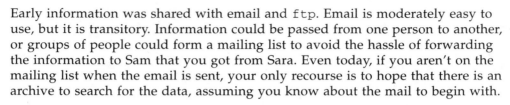

Early information was shared with email and `ftp`. Email is moderately easy to use, but it is transitory. Information could be passed from one person to another, or groups of people could form a mailing list to avoid the hassle of forwarding the information to Sam that you got from Sara. Even today, if you aren't on the mailing list when the email is sent, your only recourse is to hope that there is an archive to search for the data, assuming you know about the mail to begin with.

Originally email was just a text message; it didn't have the capability to include programs and data files. In some cases, this is still true. Data and programs were stored and retrieved by using additional features of the mail transfer software, `uucp`. FTP (File Transfer Protocol) was developed to move files from place to place on systems that didn't originally have `uucp`. Files were stored at anonymous FTP sites. *Anonymous* here refers to the fact that you don't have to be known to the FTP site to acquire the files—you can be anonymous. For those familiar with the command syntax, FTP provides an efficient method of acquiring data, with only one drawback—you have to know that the data exists and where it can be found.

A program called `archie` was then developed to canvass the anonymous FTP sites and create a database of what is available. This made for two-stop shopping: one stop at the `archie` server to locate the data, and another stop to pick up the data.

This method was fine for storing programs and information files at a site. However, the Internet is a little like the stone soup myth. One person contributes a script here, another offers some documentation there, and third offers a cute little add-on utility. Together these pieces make up the tools that the Internet offers. This development method does little for the two-stop shopping model.

Some enterprising students at the University of Minnesota created a tool that could tie together the pieces that make up a tool and make them accessible from a common menu-like access point. This humanly logical organizer was called `gopher` after the school's mascot. This was a significant breakthrough in ease of use. Now people could walk gopher trees to find related information stored at different sites.

For some people, even this level of organization wasn't enough. They wanted to be able make a document, not just one-line descriptions, complete with pointers to other papers, reference documents, and point to software when available. This concept had previously been baptized *hypertext*.

Hypertext

The following two paragraphs don't flow together very well, but they are both important ideas that should be conveyed. By linking the word hypertext in the first paragraph to the second paragraph, hypertext can be explained to those unfamiliar with it, without breaking the flow of the document for those who don't require the additional information.

> gopher menus resemble *hypertext* documents in that they are links to other information, but gopher menus are quick information blips instead of a document that presents a master theme or top-level discussion.

> The word hypertext was coined many years ago. In essence, hypertext documents are a set of documents where various parts of the text can be selected to follow a specific thread or concept other than the topic under discussion.

Document Publication

Once the concept of hypertext was born, people needed a language to describe hypertext documents. The publishing world produced a document-formatting language that could be consistently implemented on different platforms, called Standard Generalized Markup Language (SGML) to address this. SGML is unfortunately a large and complex language. The tools that were created to use this formatting language were also large and usually commercial. These factors have limited the use of SGML.

A few scientists at CERN in Switzerland needed to share their documents with cohorts in various places. They needed the platform variety that SGML promised, but they also needed something much less complex than SGML, something that could be distributed over wide areas, such as the Internet, and something that supported hypertext. These scientists designed a TCP/IP-based protocol to share hypertext information and called it http or *hypertext transmission protocol.* To write the documents for this tool, they developed an SGML-derivative language that used hypertext linking conventions and a reduced set of formatting codes that worked with the new hypertext protocol. This language became HyperText Markup Language, or HTML.

It is important to remember here that World Wide Web (WWW) was first and foremost a document-distribution application, and secondarily a document-publishing medium. This means that HTML is still developing some features, like tables, that most publishing systems have had for a long time.

Mosaic, the "Sexy App"

Early versions of World Wide Web tools were text-based just like `gopher`. The most common client tool or browser was Lynx. Methods were eventually developed to handle images externally for the times when the images could actually be viewed. This was only possible when using a windowing system.

Windowing systems or GUIs (Graphical User Interfaces) use point-and-click methods to enable the user to move around in a file. It didn't take too long before the wonders of the GUI were incorporated into a browser itself. NCSA, the National Center for Supercomputing Activities in Illinois, developed the next most popular browser, Mosaic. Mosaic has not only become a popular browsing tool, it has become the darling of the media, who christened it *the sexy app*. This popularity brought the World Wide Web to the attention of the general public.

Mosaic and other second-generation browsers that support HTML 2.0 conventions have brought the WWW community out of the library and document-handling world and into the interactive application realm with forms.

WWW is considered to be interactive because the user chooses what to view next by clicking on hypertext links. The current versions of HTML and the `http` servers have significantly extended that interactivity. Now, web pages can be customized and built on-the-fly. Other tools such as WAIS (Wide Area Information Servers) can be used to locate specific words within an entire document set, like an index for a book. Scripts can be used with databases as well. With the addition of these capabilities, not only can users choose their own path through the web, but a server can generate a custom path for that specific person's wishes. This extended level of interactivity creates even more versatile HTML applications, including help systems, cyberspace shopping malls, and surveys.

Future Directions

The next generation of HTML, HTML 3.0, returns to the library and document-production environments. HTML 3.0 focuses on the features that most document-publishing systems have but that WWW does not have. These features include tables, the ability to wrap text around images and figures, mathematical notation, text alignment, and more ways to format text to add structure to the information.

The users and developers who view WWW as an interactive application are not left out. NCSA is adding the Common Client Interface, or CCI. Many Web product developers are adding security features. However, most of these features are outside of the scope of HTML evolution and will only be touched on in Chapter 14, *Future Directions*.

WWW Miscellany

The World Wide Web is a generalist's dream, and a specialist's nightmare. The person who flourishes in producing for this environment is part technical professional, part writer, part layout designer, part information analyst, and part visionary. The information about WWW technology, culture, and tradition hasn't always been conveyed in the formal documentation. However, with the rich medium that WWW is becoming, it is time to place the oral tradition into print.

WWW Naming

Most multiple-word terms become acronyms. Unfortunately, taking the first letter of each word in World Wide Web yields WWW, which when spoken becomes *double-you double-you double-you*. In this case, the acronym is more of a mouthful than the term itself. Therefore, WWW is usually referred to as *double-you-three*, which is shorter than saying the letter three times. It is also sometimes written as W3.

WWW Culture

The Internet evolved a culture very different from the standard Western *in-your-face* and hype-based communications. A certain morality evolved that is now defined as *netiquette*. The basic concepts are to maintain a high signal-to-noise (or relevant-to-irrelevant information) ratio, conserve resources, and give back to the Internet community.

The WWW project contributed to these values by making a set of tools that served data in a stripped-down, text-based way that focused on content rather than on appearance and hype. WWW conserved resources by sending text instead of bulky, preformatted PostScript files. It provided the means for thousands of people to give back to the Internet the very lifeblood of the Internet—information.

The popularity of Mosaic has taken the Web away from its roots. Images now add flash, sex appeal, and bulk. In some cases the flash has led people astray from the concept of providing content. As long as the Web gives back to the Internet community and brings Internet access and understanding to more people, the shortcomings aren't all hopeless. But, it is important to understand the guiding principles of the Web and hopefully make a positive contribution.

Emotags

One of the most significant inroads that WWW has made into the Internet culture is the HTML-ization of emotags. Recent email has gone beyond the initial smiles and limited quantities of emoticons. Email now uses HTML-style emoticons, for example, <smirk> and </smirk>. Luckily, this type of communication was found on a WWW mail alias where it was recognized for what it was. This type will evolve to the point that <flame> and </flame> will become as common as *flame on* and *flame off* warnings. If only the browser developers would figure out how to format emotags, we may yet find a way to add new depth to the information that is being published.

Page Formatting Philosophy

For many years the term WYSIWYG (What You See Is What You Get) has dominated the desktop publishing world. This usually means that there is different software for each hardware platform. The only thing that these Desktop Publishing, or DTP, systems had in common was paper. HTML was not designed to be a WYSIWYG publishing tool. It was designed to be a universal, document distribution and publishing medium.

Users can stretch the window until it fills up the entire screen. They can change and enlarge the fonts until even the near-blind can see. For this reason, the HTML author cannot currently say that all text will be right-justified or insert a page break here, because the author doesn't control the browser—the user does.

What the author does control is the conceptual organization. The author can still add *emphasis* when it is need.The words can be **strong** or **bold**. Titles, headings, and list structures can be defined. Many however feel that this is not enough. In actuality, many of the current structures are used in ways for which they weren't designed, such as using glossary or list definitions to make indented material. Where advanced HTML features have been implemented in the most common browser Mosaic, they are heavily used.

Perhaps the current HTML isn't enough. Perhaps HTML+, aka HTML 3.0, will solve the need for more format control. This book covers only those items that are currently available, so, since HTML 3.0 isn't quite ready for prime time, little of HTML 3.0 is covered.

People

WWW document management and creation is a new field. The people doing this now wear many hats. One day the person may be a technical writer, the next a programmer, and that night become a system administrator when the server logs overflow.

Many of the uninitiated are looking for HTML programmers, which is something of a misnomer. HTML is not a programming language, it is a formatting language. However, the use of scripts along with the documents requires a generalist instead of the technical specialists who can't reach beyond their specific field.

Within the Web community, *webmaster* is the term commonly used to refer to the person who manages the technical administration and integrates new web pages. Since most webmasters previously wrote the information on the server, a title hasn't been created for the writer of HTML material. I propose that the title become *HTML Author*.

Getting Started 1≣

This chapter describes how to install the server for your specific platform. In order to use the examples, you need a client browser. The primary browser listed in the examples is the Mosaic browser, which is discussed in Appendixes A, B, and C for UNIX®, Microsoft® Windows™, and Macintosh®, respectively. Most of the book refers to the tools from the CD-ROM included with this book, so a correct setup is a top priority. In addition to the server and the client browser, several applications and scripts are included. Many of these utilities come with the original server packages.

A Tour of the CD-ROM

This book comes with a CD-ROM that contains programs, tools, and sample HTML and perl scripts. The CD-ROM can be used for most UNIX systems, Microsoft Windows NT™, Microsoft Windows 3.1 and Macintosh.

Tools

Quite a few programs are available for creating a web server, automating functions, and customizing your web site. Most of the basic tools for getting started are on the CD-ROM included with the book. These tools are upgraded frequently; Appendix E, *More Information*, lists sources for the latest version of a specific program and also lists many tools not included on the CD-ROM.

http Server

The server is the component that responds to http (Hypertext Transfer Protocol) requests. On UNIX systems, this program is called a daemon and is named httpd. On Windows NT, the program is called a service and is named https. The server works with each platform's networking software to constantly monitor traffic.

1

Authoring Tools

This book covers the manual way to write HTML. However, HTML is not easy to remember and syntax is important. There are tools that provide the author a screen-oriented editor similar to current WYSIWYG word processing programs. These tools are new and green; they can make your life easier, but you may need to go back and do additional work to finalize your documents.

Filters

You may have legacy documents that exist in one form or another. It is more efficient to use filters to convert current documents to HTML than to rekey the data. Filters are discussed in Chapter 11, *Work-Saving Tools*.

perl for Scripting

There is a wide range of scripting options, and few are available on all platforms mentioned in this book. One that is available across all platforms covered in this book is the perl scripting language. Script examples in this book are perl scripts because of this portability. Appendix E, *More Information*, includes pointers to additional perl information.

WAIS Search Engine

Wide Area Information Servers (WAIS) is a standard tool for indexing and doing full text searches. It has become the de facto standard indexing tool for use with WWW.

Directory Structure

The CD-ROM has a top-level directory for each of the platforms, Solaris® 1.x (SunOS™ 4.x), Solaris 2.x (SunOS 5.x), Windows NT, Microsoft Windows 3.1 and Macintosh, called sol1, sol2, WINNT, WINDOWS, and mac, respectively. The top level also has two additional directories, src and docs, that contain the source code to compile the software on additional platforms and general information document, respectively. The unix directory contains a copy of the HTML examples and scripts for use when compiling the software for a new platform.

In each platform directory are three directories, examples, scripts, and programs. Because Microsoft Windows 3.1 and Windows NT limits filenames to eight-character names and three-character extensions, an additional directory, example8, and a file, names.txt, are provided to convert the long names used in this book to the short DOS names found in the example8 directory.

Types of Software Licensing

The software on the CD comes from many sources. Each of these sources has determined what type of licensing or use their software can be used for. It is important to read the information that comes with each piece of software and use or license it accordingly. Software can be categorized as follows:

* **Freeware** — Available without cost, now or in the future. It provides no support agreement or recourse if the software fails in any way. Use this software at your own risk.

* **Shareware** — Software that you may use for a period of time for evaluation. If you intend to use this software after that period of time, you should pay the author of the product. Details for doing so are usually given in the documentation included with each file.

* **Restricted Use** — A new category of software, which is showing its face on the Internet. This software can be used without cost in some circumstances, whereas in other cases, a license may be required; for example, a software package that can be used by educational institutions. This type of licensing can be very confusing for corporate and small business users. It is important to contact the author and determine how the software can be used.

* **Licensed or Purchased** — Software that must be purchased either individually or by a group license.

Latest Version of Software

Software on the Internet evolves very quickly. It is very difficult to keep the latest versions on a CD-ROM. Pointers to all of the software packages are included in Appendix E, *More Information*. It is a good idea to check for the latest version of software.

Setting Up **httpd** from CERN for UNIX

Installing the Files

You need to create a place to hold the executable binaries, the configuration files, the log files, the scripts, and the HTML documents. You can name the directory whatever you choose. We recommend placing the files in a single tree for ease in upgrading. For the example below, the directory tree /usr/local/WWW is used.

1

1. **Mount the CD-ROM.**

2. **Create the directory structure.**

   ```
   mkdir -p /usr/local/WWW
   cd /usr/local/WWW
   mkdir bin conf icons logs cgi-bin docs
   ```

3. **Copy the server binary to the new** bin **directory.**

   ```
   cp -p /mnt/sol{x}/programs/cern_httpd_3.0/httpd /usr/local/WWW/bin
   ```

4. **Copy the configuration files to the newly created** conf **directory.**

   ```
   cp -rp /mnt/sol{x}/programs/cern_httpd_3.0/config/*
   /usr/local/WWW/conf
   ```

5. **Copy the scripts and programs to the** cgi-bin **directory.**
   The products on the CD-ROM are grouped as you would find them on the
   Internet. The cgi-common directory is a compilation of the NCSA and CERN
   cgi-bin directories and the script samples in this book.

   ```
   cp -p /mnt/sol{x}/programs/cgi-common/* /usr/local/WWW/cgi-bin
   ```

6. **Copy the examples to the** docs **directory.**

   ```
   cp -rp /mnt/sol{x}/examples /usr/local/WWW/docs
   ```

7. **Copy the icons to the** icon **directory.**

   ```
   cp -rp /mnt/sol{x}/programs/cern_httpd_3.0/icons
   /usr/local/WWW/icons
   ```

Configuring the httpd Daemon

Http traffic is directed to a specific software address called a port. In some cases,
the networking software monitors requests and starts the http program when
information addressed for that port is received. This is primarily done on UNIX
systems with the inetd daemon. This method is referred to as "running the
daemon as *inetd*." In other cases, the program is resident in memory at all times
and monitors the port itself. This method is referred to as "running *standalone*."
With the inetd method, you can define a maximum number of connections that
httpd can use at any given time. You can use this high-water mark to start
rejecting connections.

Note – There are several tunable directives for caching and proxying in the other
`.conf` files in this directory. Leave these values as default or refer to a book on
the details of web server administration when modifying these directives.

1. **Change to the directory in which you placed the configuration files**
   (`/usr/local/WWW/conf` **for the installation above).**

2. **Edit** `httpd.conf`.

3. *(Optional)* **Change the port number.**
   `httpd` daemons normally use port 80. You may wish to change this if you
   want to retain anonymity or use port 80 for some other service. If port 80 is
   not used, the next most common port is 8000. To change the port, modify the
   line:

   ```
   Port 80
   ```

4. **Change the ServerRoot variable to reflect the root of your WWW files.**
   To change the port, modify the *ServerRoot* definition line to resemble the
   following:

   ```
   ServerRoot/usr/local/WWW
   ```

5. *(Optional)* **Change the User / Group.**
   The standard user is Nobody (uid -1) with a nonexistent group of -1. Use a
   pound (#) sign to indicate when you are using the uid or gid instead of a
   name. To change the user and group, modify the lines, as shown in
   Code Example 1-1.

Code Example 1-1   Changing User/Group

```
UserId nobody
GroupId #-1
```

6. *(Optional)* **Enable logging.**
   The `httpd-log` and `httpd-errors` are two important logging files. The
   `httpd-log` file can grow to be quite large. Plan on the `httpd-log` file
   growing about 4 Mbytes for every 30,000 file accesses or *hits*. Remember that a
   web page with five different inline images for special bullets and two images
   will have eight hits every time someone loads the page. The `httpd-errors`

file tends not to grow very large, but it should be kept in the same place as the `httpd-log` for ease of administration. To enable logging, uncomment the following lines and specify a directory in which to store the logs.

Code Example 1-2   Enabling Logging

```
# AccessLog/where/ever/httpd-log
# ErrorLog/where/ever/httpd-errors
```

7. **(Optional)- Change the HTML subdirectory for use with a user's home directory.**
You can enable users to serve files from a subdirectory under their home directory via the ~ character in the URL. To define the directory to use, modify the line:

```
UserDir public_html
```

8. **Define the root of your document tree (sometimes referred to as the DocumentRoot).**
To define the directory, modify the Pass line to reflect the following:

```
Pass/*  /usr/local/WWW/docs/*
```

9. **(Optional) Remap directories for special directory trees.**
The physical directory structure can be remapped to create a logical directory structure consistent with the structure of the information on the server. The Pass directive modifies this structure.

Add an alias definition for /Stuff/ that points to the directory hidden/Stuff/ under the regular *DocumentRoot* directory. This definition is used in Chapter 3, *Hypertext — Linking Documents*. The alias entries should now look like Code Example 1-3.

Code Example 1-3   Remapped Directories

```
Pass /icons/* /usr/local/WWW/icons/*
Pass /Stuff/* /usr/local/WWW/docs/hidden/Stuff/*
```

10. **Map a directory as executable for running programs and scripts.**
Define the directory trees that can hold executable scripts by modifying the Exec line:

```
Exec    /cgi-bin/*      /usr/local/WWW/cgi-bin/*
```

11. Configure either for standalone use or for inetd use.

a. Configuring for standalone use
To use the server in a standalone manner, start the daemon from a startup script at boot time. Since startup scripts vary from platform to platform, refer to system administration manuals for information on starting a daemon at boot time.

b. Configuring for `inetd` use
To configure the system to start a daemon when `inetd` receives a request, add the following lines to the `/etc/inetd.conf` and `/etc/services` files, respectively.

To `inetd.conf`:

```
http    stream  tcp nowait  nobody  /usr/local/www/httpd
/usr/local/www/httpd
```

To `services`:

```
http 80/tcp
```

12. Reboot the system.

Setting Up httpd from NCSA for UNIX

The NCSA `httpd` server files can be found on the CD-ROM under `sol1/programs/NCSA_httpd`.

Installing the Files

You need to create a place to hold the executable binaries, the configuration files, the log files, the scripts, and the HTML documents. You can name the directory whatever you choose. We recommend placing the files in a single tree for ease in upgrading. For the example below, the directory tree `/usr/local/WWW` is used.

1. Mount the CD-ROM.

2. Create the directory structure.

```
mkdir -p /usr/local/WWW
cd /usr/local/WWW
mkdir bin conf icons logs cgi-bin docs
```

3. Copy the server binary to the new bin directory.

```
cp -p /mnt/sol{x}/programs/NCSA_httpd/httpd /usr/local/WWW/bin
```

4. **Copy the configuration files to the newly created** `conf` **directory.**

```
cp /mnt/sol{x}/programs/NCSA_httpd/conf/* /usr/local/WWW/conf
```

5. **Copy the scripts and programs to the** `cgi-bin` **directory.**
The products on the CD-ROM are grouped as you would find them on the
Internet. The `cgi-common` directory is a compilation of the NCSA and CERN
`cgi-bin` directories and the script samples in this book.

```
cp -p /mnt/sol{x}/programs/cgi-common/* /usr/local/WWW/cgi-bin
```

6. **Copy the examples to the** `docs` **directory.**

```
cp -rp /mnt/sol{x}/examples /usr/local/WWW/docs
```

7. **Copy the icons to the** `icon` **directory.**

```
cp /mnt/sol{x}/programs/NCSA_httpd/icons /usr/local/WWW/icons
```

Configuring the `httpd` Daemon

The configuration files must be updated for the directory tree that you used and
for the method of running the `httpd` (`inetd` or standalone). Other configuration
can be modified at this time as well.

Http traffic is directed to a specific software address called a port. In some cases,
the networking software monitors requests and starts the `http` program when
information addressed for that port is received. This is primarily done on UNIX
systems with the `inetd` daemon. This method is referred to as "running the
daemon as *inetd*." In other cases, the program is resident in memory at all times
and monitors the port itself. This method is referred to as "running *standalone*."
With the `inetd` method, you can define a maximum number of connections that
`httpd` can use at any given time. You can use this high-water mark to start
rejecting connections.

1. **Change to the directory where you placed the configuration files**
(`/usr/local/WWW/conf` **for the installation above).**

2. **Edit** `httpd.conf-dist`.

3. *(Optional)* **Change the daemon to run from** `inetd`.
To change this, modify the line:

```
ServerType standalone
```

4. **(Optional) Change the port number.**

   `httpd` daemons normally use port 80. You may wish to change this if you want to retain anonymity or use port 80 for some other service. If port 80 is not used, the next most common port is 8000. To change the port, modify the line:

   ```
   Port 80
   ```

5. **(Optional) Change the User / Group.**

   The standard user is Nobody (uid -1) with a nonexistent group of -1. Use the pound (#) sign to indicate when you are using the uid or gid instead of a name. To change the user and group, modify the lines, as shown in Code Example 1-4.

Code Example 1-4   Changing the User/Group

```
User nobody
Group #-1
```

6. **Change the ServerAdmin.**

   Change the ServerAdmin definition to the email address of the webmaster for the system. Since email may come from anywhere on the Internet, use a fully qualified address. To change the email address, modify the line:

   ```
   ServerAdmin you@your.address
   ```

7. **(Optional) Change the location of logs.**

   The `access_log` and `error_log` are two important logging files. The `access_log` file can grow to be quite large. Plan on the `access_log` file growing about 4 Mbytes for every 30,000 file accesses or *hits*. Remember that a web page with five inline images for special bullets and two images will have eight hits every time someone loads the page. The `error_log` tends not to grow very large, but it should be kept in the same place as the `access_log` for ease of administration. These log files are placed by default in the `logs` subdirectory under the path defined by the `ServerRoot` directive. To change the location of logging, modify the lines to use an absolute path starting with `/`:

Code Example 1-5   Changing the Location of Logs

```
ErrorLog logs/error_log

TransferLog logs/access_log
```

8. **Save the changes and exit.**

9. **Edit** `srm.conf`.

10. **Change the ServerRoot directive to reflect the root of your WWW files.**
    To change the port, modify the line:

    ```
    ServerRoot/usr/local/WWW
    ```

11. **Change the DocumentRoot directive to reflect the root of your document tree.**
    To change the directive, modify the line:

    ```
    DocumentRoot/usr/local/WWW/docs
    ```

    If you copied the examples in the previous section to
    `/usr/local/WWW/docs`, set this line to:

    ```
    DocumentRoot /usr/local/WWW/docs
    ```

12. *(Optional)* **Change the HTML subdirectory for use with a user's home directory.**
    You can enable users to serve files from a subdirectory under their home directory via the ~ character in the URL. To define the directory to use, modify the line:

    ```
    UserDir public_html
    ```

13. *(Optional)* **Change the default file returned.**
    When a user loads a directory instead of a file, the server searches for a default filename, usually `index.html`. If this file isn't found, then a list of the contents of the directory is displayed. Originally, it was assumed that the `index.html` file would be a listing of the directory with additional comments. The `index.html` file can be placed in a directory where the contents of the directory should be hidden. To change the file returned, modify the line:

    ```
    DirectoryIndex index.html
    ```

Note – There are several configurable directives for serving directories in the
`srm.conf`. Leave these values as default or refer to a book on the details of web
server administration when modifying these directives.

---

14. *(Optional)* **Change the access control list filename.**

When access is restricted on a directory-by-directory basis, the `.htaccess` file indicates who has permission to access the directory in which the `.htaccess` file resides. To change the name of the file that is used for recording access control, modify the line:

```
AccessFileName .htaccess
```

15. *Not Recommended*: **Change the default Multipurpose Internet Mail Extensions (MIME) type.**

The server needs to indicate the content of the data that it is returning to the browser. This is primarily determined by comparing the file's extension to the `mime.types` file found in the *ServerRoot*/`conf` directory. If the content cannot be determined by the extension, a guessing routine in the server attempts to determine the content by examining the beginning of the file. If the content still cannot be determined, a default MIME type is assigned to the file. The *DefaultType* directive determines the MIME type to assign to the file. Ideally, the default MIME type should always be `text/plaintext`, since undefined data on every system is usually ASCII text. To change the default MIME type, modify the line:

```
DefaultTypetext/plaintext
```

16. *Optional - **Add aliases for special directory trees.**

Aliases are a method of using directory trees beyond the DocumentRoot directory tree. To add more aliases, add an alias definition in the form of:

```
Alias AliasNameFullPathOnTheSystem
```

Add an alias definition for `/Stuff/` that points to the directory `hidden/Stuff/` under the regular *DocumentRoot* directory. This will be used in Chapter 3, *Hypertext — Linking Documents*. The alias entries should now look like Code Example 1-6.

Code Example 1-6   Alias Entries

```
Alias /icons/ /usr/local/WWW/icons/
Alias /Stuff/ /usr/local/WWW/docs/hidden/Stuff/
```

17. **Save the changes and exit.**

18. **Configure either for standalone use or for `inetd` use.**

1

a. Configuring for standalone use

To use the server in a standalone manner, start the daemon from a startup script at boot time. Since startup scripts vary from platform to platform, refer to system administration manuals for information on starting a daemon at boot time.

b. Configuring for `inetd` use

To configure the system to start a daemon when `inetd` receives a request, add the following lines to the `/etc/inetd.conf` and `/etc/services` files, respectively.

To `inetd.conf`:

```
http    stream  tcp nowait  nobody  /usr/local/www/httpd
/usr/local/www/httpd
```

To `services`:

```
http 80/tcp
```

19. Reboot the system to verify that all changes are read in.
Ideally, `kill -1 {inetd_pid}` should cause `httpd` to read changes, but it doesn't always do so. When in doubt, reboot the system.

Setting Up a Windows NT Server — `https`

Setting up a Windows NT server consists of unpacking the files and configuring `https`.

Unpacking the Files

1. **Create a directory for your server programs.**
   The example directory is `e:\winnt\apps\server`.

2. **Copy `hsi386.zip` from the `\WINNT\PROGRAMS\SERVER` directory on the CD-ROM to the directory that you created.**

3. **Unzip the files.**

   ```
   pkunzip hsi386.zip
   ```

Configuring `https`

1. **Copy `https.cpl` to the `\winnt\system32` directory on the disk that holds your Windows NT OS files.**

2. Verify that the IP address of your system is correct.

https Example 1-7   Verifying IP Address

```
E:\winnt\apps\server> https -ipaddress
Name:  crosstime.finesse.com
Address:140.174.171.130
```

3. Install the `https` **server into the Windows NT services.**

https Example 1-8   Installing the Server

```
E:\winnt\apps\server> https -install
HTTP Server installed successfully
```

4. Open the Control Panel for Windows NT.
Note that the HTTP Server icon is now displayed.

5. Double-click on the Services icon.
This is a list of all of the services that your Windows NT server handles. The HTTP Server Service should be listed with a blank status and Manual listed in the Startup field.

6. Double-click on the HTTP Server.

7. Click on Automatic.
This step automatically starts up the server on boot.

8. Change the account that `https` **uses.**

  a. Click on This Account.
  The name LocalSystem is displayed on the account line and a button with … on it is also displayed.

  b. Click on the … button.
  To summon the Add User Window.

  c. Select an account and click on Add.
  For this example, we use the Guest account, which places the line {*systemname*}\Guest onto the Add Name line at the bottom of the window.

  d. Click on OK.
  This step returns the HTTP Server Service window.

9. **Click on OK to approve all changes.**
   A pop-up window is displayed with the message: The account
   {systemname}\Guest has been granted the Log On As A Service right. Click on
   OK to clear this message.

10. **Click on Start to start the HTTP Service.**
    A window with a clock is displayed with the message: Attempting to start the
    HTTP Server service on *{systemname}*.

11. **Click on Close to close the Services window.**

12. **Click on the HTTP Server icon.**
    This brings up the HTTP Server window.

13. **Change the Data Directory.**
    Change the pathname to the root of the directory tree where you will store
    your documents. Examples in this book are based on setting the pathname to
    e:\http. If you set the pathname to something else, be sure to note it for
    future reference.

14. *(Optional)* **Change the port number.**
    http services (aka daemons in UNIX) normally use port 80. You may want to
    change this if you want to retain anonymity or use port 80 for some other
    service.

15. *(Optional)* **Change the Multipurpose Internet Mail Extensions (MIME)
    mappings.**
    You can change the MIME mappings that are configured here. For this
    example, we are going to leave them as they are.

16. **Click on the Log HTTP transactions check box.**
    This step starts transaction logging. This is important to do.

17. *(Optional)* **Click on the Permit directory browsing check box.**
    This step allows users to view a directory of files when a default file isn't
    available.

18. **Click on OK to update these changes.**
    A pop-up window displays the message: You have changed the configuration
    of the HTTP Server. For the change to take effect, you must stop and restart
    the service. Click on OK to clear the window.

19. **Stop and start the service.**

Note – The `\winnt\programs\server\egscript.zip` file contains additional `cgi-bin` samples to review. They will not be referenced in this book.

Setting Up a Microsoft Windows Server

Winhttpd14 is a new server that was programmed to work around the fact that Microsoft Windows was designed as a user-centric operating system. This server is available for evaluation. Please take time to read the enclosed license.

Unpacking the Files

1. **Create a directory for your server programs.**
   The example directory is `e:\apps\server`.

2. **Copy** `WHTTPD14.ZIP` **from the** `WINDOWS\PROGRAMS\SERVER` **directory on the CD-ROM to the directory that you created.**

3. **Unzip the files with the** -d **option.**

   ```
   pkunzip -d WHTTPD14.ZIP
   ```

4. **Copy all files from the** `WINDOWS\SCRIPTS` **directory to the newly created** `CGI-BIN` **directory.**

5. **Copy the** `WINDOWS\EXAMPLES` **directories to the newly created** `HTDOCS` **directory.**

6. **Create a new program item by pulling down the File menu and selecting the New option.**

7. **Select** Program Item **and click OK.**

8. **Fill in the** Description **line.**

9. **On the command line enter** *pathname*/httpd.exe -d *pathname*, **where** *pathname* **is the disk and directory that the program files were extracted into.** In the example above the pathname is `e:\apps\server`.

10. **With a text editor change the file SRM.CNF in the CONF directory.**

11. **Change the line:**

    ```
    # DocumentRoot c:/httpd/htdocs
    ```

    to

```
DocumentRoot pathname
```

12. With a text editor change the file HTTPD.CNF in the CONF directory.

13. Change the line:

```
# ServerRoot c:/httpd
```

to

```
ServerRoot pathname
```

14. Double-click on the new icon to start the server.

Setting Up a Macintosh Server

MacHTTP was created and continues to be updated by Chuck Shotton. The software is available to you for evaluation. Please take the time to read the README.html file and the licensing information about this product.

Installing the Files

1. **Insert the CD-ROM.**

2. **Open the mac folder on the CD-ROM.**

3. **Open the programs folder under the Mac folder.**

4. **Create a destination folder on the hard drive.**
   For this example, we created a folder called Http on the top level of the hard drive.

5. **Open the folder that you just created.**

6. **Drag the machttp.sit file on the CD-ROM to the Http folder on the hard drive.**

7. **Uncompress the file by starting StuffIt Expander.**

Note – StuffIt Expander 3.0.7 or newer is required. You can acquire the latest version via anonymous ftp from ftp.aladdinsys.com.

---

8. **Pull down the File menu and select Expand.**
   Select machttp.sit from the file dialog box and click Expand.

9. **(Optional) If you want the server to start every time you boot the system, do the following:**

a. **Open the** `MacHTTP 1.3` **folder.**

b. **Open the** `MacHTTP Software` **folder.**

c. **Select the** `MacHTTP` **icon by single-clicking on it.**

d. **Pull down the** File **menu and select** Make Alias.
   A second icon that overlaps the first is displayed. The second icon, which is darker than the original icon, is the alias.

e. **Open the** `System` **folder.**

f. **Open the** `Startup Items` **folder.**

g. **Drag the alias icon to the** `Startup Items` **folder.**
   Note that the alias icon is darker than the regular icon. Be sure to drag the alias icon, not the regular icon.

Configuring the Server

1. **Open the following folders:** `Http` -> `MacHTTP 1.3` -> `MacHTTP Software`.

2. **Drag the** `cgi-bin` **folder on the CD-ROM to the** MacHTTP Software **folder.**

3. **Open the** `MacHTTP.config` **file.**

4. **Change the default text type from:**

   `DEFAULT TEXT text/html`

   to

   `DEFAULT TEXT text/plain`

5. *(Optional)* **Change the Multipurpose Internet Mail Extensions (MIME) type mappings.**
   You can change the MIME type mappings here. Only 20 mappings can be defined at any given time. We will leave these alone for now.

6. *(Optional)* **Change the logging.**
   MacHTTP logs error messages, access information, and access failure information to `Error.html`, `MacHTTP.log`, and `NoAccess.html`, respectively. By default, these files reside in the same directory as the

MacHTTP program. The error and access failure lists can stay where they are. However, the access log can grow to be quite large. If you choose to move it, change the pathname now to reflect the new location.

Code Example 1-9   Changing the Logging

```
ERROR  :Error.html
LOG    :MacHTTP.log
NOACCESS :NoAccess.html
```

7. *(Optional)* **Change the default web page.**
   When a user specifies a directory instead of a file, the server searches for a default filename. To change the file returned, modify the line:

```
INDEX  :Default.html
```

8. *(Optional)* **- Change the number of users or connections.**
   More than one client may try to connect to your server at any given time. It is important to control how many clients can access at the same time. If you allow too many connections, your system slows down and may hang. If you allow too few connections, users must wait for their data. The default is 8. It is a good idea to start with the default and adjust it when you notice connection waits. This number can go as high as 1000.

```
MAXUSERS 8
```

9. *(Optional)* **Change the number of listening processes.**
   When you configured the MAXUSERS variable (Step 7), you specified how many connections could be active. A process must listen for a connection before the connection is accepted and processed. The MAXLISTENS variable specifies how many processes listen for connections. When more clients try to get a connection than there are processes listening for requests, you receive "Unable to connect" error messages on the client.

```
MAXLISTENS 3
```

10. *(Optional)* **Change the port number.**
   Http services (aka daemons in UNIX) normally use port 80. You may want to change this if you want to retain anonymity or if you will use port 80 for some other service.

```
PORT 80
```

11. Uncomment the HIDEWINDOW line by removing the # (pound) sign.
   The `config` file line should resemble the line below:

```
HIDEWINDOW
```

The Basics 2 ≡

In the previous chapter, you set up a server for your working environment; you will need to choose a client browser as well. Appendixes A, B, and C give a quick overview of installation and caveats for the Mosaic browsers that are used for most of the examples in this book. You will be using this environment for the exercises in this chapter.

This chapter assumes the use of the Solaris 2.x `httpd` daemon and Mosaic from NCSA as the basic environment. Where there are differences between platforms, these differences are noted.

The chapter covers formatting basics, including formatting paragraphs, section headings, titles, italics, bold text, special characters (8-bit letters), other formatting codes, indenting, blocking text, and creating both numbered and unnumbered lists.

Starting Out

Word processing programs are actually a combination of the text that you see and hidden formatting commands. With most WYSIWYG word processors, you never see the formatting codes. WYSIWYG HTML editors are still in startup mode and are covered in Chapter 11, *Work-Saving Tools*. First, become acquainted with WYSIWYG displays and the HTML-equivalent formatting codes, which are called elements or tags.

Formatting Text in Word Processing

Some word processing products break formatting into classes such as character or paragraph formatting. *Character formatting* refers to formatting that is applied to a single character or set of characters such as a word. *Paragraph formatting* refers to formatting of all text in the same group or paragraph. Usually, paragraphs are ended by a carriage return.

If you were to look behind the scenes of a word processor, it would look like the following:

Example 2-1   *Behind the Scenes—Formatting Text with a Word Processor*

> *(formatting information - 8pt Helvetica type)* `This is the text of the document itself.`
> `It is important to remember that you normally only see the text here. The`
> *(formatting information - start italics)* `format` *(formatting information - end italics)* `of this`
> `document is not usually displayed for you to see.` *(Carriage Return)*

In the above example, the formatting information about *italicizing* the word format has a start format block and an end format block. This is called a *container* in HTML. On the other hand, the paragraph information *8pt Helvetica* doesn't have an end format block to match the start format block. This is called an *empty element* since it doesn't have an end instruction to match the start instruction. In HTML, these strings of format information are called *tags*.

Opening the First Document

This book extensively uses the examples included on the CD-ROM. Chapter 1, *Getting Started*, configures the server to use the examples provided as the initial documents that the server serves.

When you are instructed to open `http://{server}/Chapter2/example1.html`, for *server* substitute the name of the server on which you installed the documents.

When you are instructed to open *{Document_Root}*/`Chapter2/example1.html`, use a text editor to open the file found in the server and directory that you configured as your document area in Chapter 1, *Getting Started*.

1. **Start up the** `http` **server and client browser that you configured in the previous chapter.**

2. **Open the document** `http://{server}/Chapter2/example1.html`**, which should look like the document in Figure 2-1.**
   Notice that it is all text, and nothing but text. When displayed, it is one long paragraph without headings or breaks between ideas and concepts. This is the raw material; by addition of HTML formatting, a finished product will be created.

Note – If you loaded this document as `http://{server}/Chapter2/example1.html/`, the Mosaic displays the document as it is typed in. This is a problem with documents that are improperly, or incompletely, marked as HTML documents. Document identification is described in *Naming the Document*, later in this chapter.

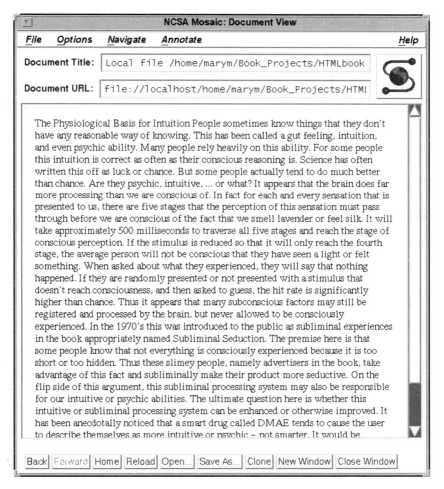

Figure 2-1   A Document As One Continuous Block

3. Start up a text editor for your specific platform. Load the file
{*Document_Root*}/`Chapter2/example1.html`.
Notice that the actual text has carriage returns all over the place. The WWW browser, which in this case is Mosaic, ignores the carriage returns in the actual text and inserts a carriage return where the line should wrap on that specific display.

HTML Example 2-2 Text of First HTML Example

```
The Physiological Basis for Intuition
People sometimes know things that they don't have any reasonable
way of knowing. This has been called a gut feeling, intuition,
and even psychic
ability.
Many people
rely heavily on this ability. For some people this
intuition
is correct as
often as their conscious reasoning is.
Science has often written this off as luck or chance. But some people
actually tend to do much better than chance. Are they psychic,
intuitive, ... or what?
It appears that the brain does far more processing than we are conscious
of. In fact for each and every sensation that is presented to us, there
are five stages that the perception of this sensation must pass through
before we are conscious of the fact that we smell lavender or feel
silk. It will take approximately 500 milliseconds to traverse all
five stages and reach the stage of conscious perception. If
the stimulus is reduced so that it will only reach the fourth
stage, the average person will not be conscious that they have
seen a light or felt something. When asked about what they experienced,
they will say that nothing happened. If they are randomly presented
or not presented with a stimulus that doesn't reach consciousness,
and then asked to guess, the hit rate is significantly higher than
chance.
Thus it appears that many subconscious factors may still be
registered and processed by the brain, but never allowed to be
consciously experienced. In the 1970's this was introduced
to the public as subliminal experiences in the book appropriately
named Subliminal Seduction. The premise here is that some people
know that not everything is consciously experienced because it is
too short or too hidden. Thus these slimy people, namely advertisers
in the book, take advantage of this fact and subliminally
make their product more seductive.
On the flip side of this argument, this subliminal processing system
may also be responsible for our intuitive or psychic abilities.
The ultimate question here is whether this intuitive or subliminal
processing system can be enhanced or otherwise improved.
It has been anecdotally noticed that a smart drug called DMAE tends
to cause the user to describe themselves as more intuitive or
psychic - not smarter. It would be interesting to test DMAE in
subliminal awareness experiments.
```

HTML Example 2-2 Text of First HTML Example (Continued)

```
The Physiological Basis for Intuition

Maybe what makes us smarter isn't always what we can consciously reason
out.

This page is maintained by
Mary Morris
marym@finesse.com
```

4. **Change the font size on the client display to** Times Large.
   In Mosaic, the font type and size are modified with Options-->Fonts-->Times Large. If you are using a different WWW browser, refer to the documentation for that browser for changing the size of the font. Notice that when the text became larger, the lines wrapped at different places. WWW browsers are not WYSIWYG. They display the document differently, depending on the display configuration of the browser.

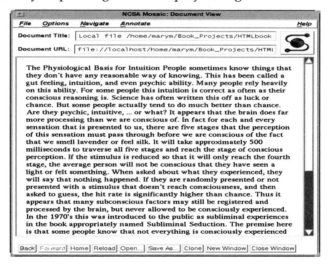

Figure 2-2   Different Fonts with the Same Continuous Block

Adding Paragraphs — A Start Tag Without an End Tag

HTML tags are formatting codes surrounded by < > (less than and greater than signs). For example, the tag <p> tells the WWW display client to start a new paragraph.

In word processing, paragraphs are broken into reasonably sized ideas, those items have titles or headers for each group of concepts, and important items are made to stand out by either bold or italicized text. In the exercise below, you will add tags to format the text in the document, example1.html.

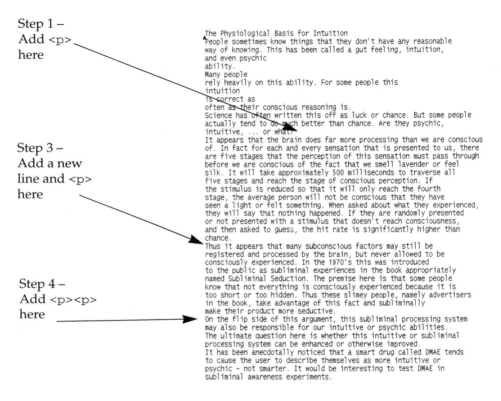

Figure 2-3   First Steps in Creating Paragraphs

1. **Add the paragraph formatting code <p> to the text so that it resembles step 1 of Figure 2-3.**

2. **Save the changes to your document; update your changes to the document by pressing** reload **in the Mosaic viewer. If you are using a different WWW browser, refer to the appropriate documentation for equivalent instructions.**

   Most browsers cache a few documents locally to save the time of retrieving a new copy. To update your changes, you must force a reload of the document.

3. **Now add `<p>` on a line by itself, as noted in step 3 of Figure 2-3. Save and reload the image.**

There is no difference between placing the `<p>` code in the middle of the document and placing it on a line by itself. For the `troff` literate, this is a notable item.

4. **Add `<p><p>` as noted in step 4 of Figure 2-3. Save and reload the image.**

Note that there is no difference between one or more `<p>` codes. This is *not* the way to add more than one blank line.

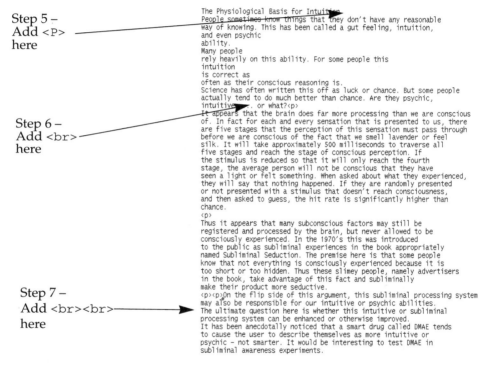

Step 5 –
Add `<P>`
here

Step 6 –
Add `<br>`
here

Step 7 –
Add `<br><br>`
here

```
The Physiological Basis for Intuition
People sometimes know things that they don't have any reasonable
way of knowing. This has been called a gut feeling, intuition,
and even psychic
ability.
Many people
rely heavily on this ability. For some people this
intuition
is correct as
often as their conscious reasoning is.
Science has often written this off as luck or chance. But some people
actually tend to do much better than chance. Are they psychic,
intuitive, or what?<p>
It appears that the brain does far more processing than we are conscious
of. In fact for each and every sensation that is presented to us, there
are five stages that the perception of this sensation must pass through
before we are conscious of the fact that we smell lavender or feel
silk. It will take approximately 500 milliseconds to traverse all
five stages and reach the stage of conscious perception. If
the stimulus is reduced so that it will only reach the fourth
stage, the average person will not be conscious that they have
seen a light or felt something. When asked about what they experienced,
they will say that nothing happened. If they are randomly presented
or not presented with a stimulus that doesn't reach consciousness,
and then asked to guess, the hit rate is significantly higher than
chance.
<p>
Thus it appears that many subconscious factors may still be
registered and processed by the brain, but never allowed to be
consciously experienced. In the 1970's this was introduced
to the public as subliminal experiences in the book appropriately
named Subliminal Seduction. The premise here is that some people
know that not everything is consciously experienced because it is
too short or too hidden. Thus these slimey people, namely advertisers
in the book, take advantage of this fact and subliminally
make their product more seductive.
<p><p>On the flip side of this argument, this subliminal processing system
may also be responsible for our intuitive or psychic abilities.
The ultimate question here is whether this intuitive or subliminal
processing system can be enhanced or otherwise improved.
It has been anecdotally noticed that a smart drug called DMAE tends
to cause the user to describe themselves as more intuitive or
psychic - not smarter. It would be interesting to test DMAE in
subliminal awareness experiments.
```

Figure 2-4   Next Steps in Formatting Paragraphs

5. **Add `<P>` as noted in step 5 of Figure 2-4. Save and reload the image.**

There is no difference between lower and upper case tags.

6. **Add `<br>` as noted in step 6 of Figure 2-4. Save and reload the image.**

Note that `<br>` starts a new line but doesn't place a blank line between images.

7. **Add `<br><br>` as noted in step 7 of Figure 2-4. Save and reload the image.**

Two `<br>` tags in a row equal a `<p>` tag.

2

Adding Italics - A Start and End Tag Pair

Where the formatting information needs a definite start and end place as in the example of italics below, there are two tags: a start tag and an end tag. The start tag is the formatting command between < >. The end tag is a slash placed before the command, </ >. An example of this is <i> and </i> for italics.

Step 8 –
Add
here

Step 8 –
Add
here

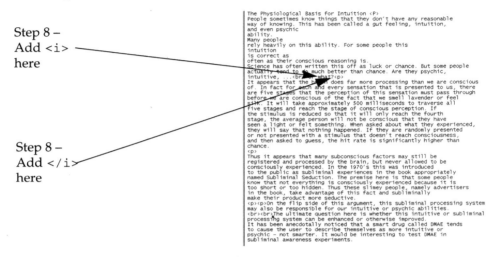

Figure 2-5   Adding Italics

8. **Add the paragraph formatting codes <i> and </i> to the text so that it resembles step 8 of Figure 2-5. Save and reload the image.**
   Note that the end tag is the same as the start tag except for the addition of the / .

Now that you have learned how to add tags, it is time to learn what the tags do. There are tags for many purposes. As shown above, some tags create breaks in text, but there is no page break. These are only a sample of the tags available for formatting text. In addition, there are yet other tags to define the different parts of an HTML document.

Sections of a Document —Tour of an HTML Document

A document is usually broken down into parts. First, the document should be defined as an HTML document. Then, the head to the document includes a *title* and a *body* that can be broken into subtopics with different levels of headings. Comments and other nondisplayable information can be included in a document. Finally, it is always good practice to sign your documents at the bottom.

Parts of a Page

The following sections describe the basic tags that a document should have. Ten steps in "Parts of a Page" help you visualize and experiment with an HTML page.
HTML Example 2-3 shows a template that can be used when designing new documents.

HTML Example 2-3 `template.html` *for Designing New Documents*

```
<html>
<head>
<title>

</title>
</head>
<!-- this is a comment -->
<body>

<address>

</address>
</body>
</html>
```

Naming the Document

WWW browsers differ in how they determine what to do with incoming data. Some browsers look at the extension (characters of a filename after the last .) of the file to determine what type it is. The Xmosaic browser uses the extension of a file and the `.mailcap` file to determine the viewer or display system to use. A list of file types and their associated extensions can be found in Chapter 4, *Multimedia—Going Beyond Text*.

In the first example of this chapter, if the document that was opened had a trailing /, it wasn't recognized as an HTML document, even with the `.html` extension. This problem was introduced into the NCSA server when the / became an optional character. Since the document wasn't known as an HTML document by its extension, the document itself was checked for clues as to what type of document it was.

1. **Load** `http://{server}/Chapter2/example1.html/`.

2. **View the HTML text by pulling down the File menu and selecting View Source.**
   This view shows the actual text with formatting characters. The original document did not have any formatting information. However, the HTML source shows a `<PLAINTEXT>` formatting tag. The server added the tag to the document before sending it to the client, because the server didn't identify the document as being of a specific type.

Another way to determine what the data type is, is to look for information at the start of the data to see if it matches a recognizable pattern. Since you can't control what browsers will be used, it is always a good idea to label your documents as HTML inside the document itself by placing the <html> and </html> tags at the start and the end of a document.

Note – It is important to label your documents fully to avoid having the server *guess* at the data type. Most browsers have routines that try to guess what document type a web page is if the page doesn't have an obvious type. Pure 7-bit text pages will be declared <PLAINTEXT>, but multipart pages, such as multimedia pages, can contain 8-bit references. If the web page cannot be identified, it is treated as a binary file and the user is offered the option of saving the file to disk. This treatment is referred to as *dropping* or *falling into the magic bucket*.

Defining the Head

HTML documents should have a clearly defined head and body. Many of the documents on line today label the body of a document, but not the head. This practice works for most browsers, but it is usually better to define the head of a document as well as the body.

The head of a document is shown by the <head> and </head> tags. Ideally, the head of a document will contain information about the document, such as the title and an index if used. This information is not displayed as part of the document itself. The title is actually displayed only in the Title window of a browser. One part of the head that will be displayed in the browser is an index. If the <ISINDEX> tag is used, then an index prompt is presented at the top of the page. Indexes are covered in Chapter 9, *Processing Data From Forms* in the section, *Search For Data*.

Adding the Title

As noted, the title of a document doesn't appear in the body of a document. It is displayed in the Title window and in the hotlist. It is a good idea to title your documents, so that if someone makes a hotlist link to your page, their hotlist will show a reasonable name. If the document is left untitled, the Universal Resource Location (URL) of the document appears in the hotlist instead. How many people are going to remember that they wanted to go back to http://www.somewhere.com/NeatStuf/Ocean/Scubagear/NoGutsNoGlory.htm, especially if the URL doesn't show completely in the hotlist window?

The title should be plain text. Format information such as bold and italics doesn't appear on browsers. The title is indicated by the <title> and </title> tags.

Defining the Body

The body of a document contains all the displayed information for a document. Unlike the head, the body of a document *can* contain format information. The body is indicated by <body> and </body> tags. Some of the key components of the body of the document are the text of the document itself, section titles or *headings*, and an address or author-contact information.

Headings

HTML supports six levels of headings. It is important to note that headings are actually logical formatting directives; that is, each browser implements the headings as appropriate for that platform. What may be 14-point Helvetica Bold on one system may be 20-point TimesRomanBold on another platform. Headings are indicated by <h#> and </h#>, where # is the level of the heading. For example, heading-level three is <h3> and </h3>.

Note – The text in heading levels five and six is actually smaller than standard text in the document on Mosaic and several other GUI browsers. Many authors tend to take advantage of this font size difference by designating footer information as heading six. According to CERN, heading-level five should have emphasis or be in italics. This stipulation hasn't proven to be true on the Mosaic browser, but there may be some browsers where this actually is the case.

By convention, heading-level one is usually a repeat of the title line (with <h1> and </h1> codes,) so that a document actually has a title visible in the document. This is important if you are writing documents that may be printed at a future date.

Figure 2-6 shows a good example of what each heading looks like on Mosaic.

This is what Heading 1 Looks Like

This is text in between.

This is what Heading 2 Looks Like

This is text in between.

This is what Heading 3 Looks Like

This is text in between.

This is what Heading 4 Looks Like

This is text in between.

This is what Heading 5 Looks Like

This is text in between.

This is what Heading 6 Looks Like

This is text in between.

Figure 2-6   Samples of Headings

3. **Load** `http://{server}/Chapter2/heading_examples.html`.
   See what the different headings look like on your display.

Adding Comments

There may be times when you need to insert a comment that you don't want the end user to see. There is no specific HTML comment line, but the SGML comment line can be used with most browsers. A comment line looks like:

```
<!--text here-->
```

Adding the Author/Responsible Party

It is a good practice to list a contact who maintains the page. In many cases, this is the author. However, many companies are now setting up web servers on the Internet. Since a large corporate server usually contains work from several people, and still other people may provide administration services, the term *webmaster* has come into use. The webmaster is the person or group of people ultimately responsible for keeping the web server running, integrating new work, and farming problems back to the original author of the page.

Regardless of whether you maintain the pages yourself or whether a corporate entity does that work, every page *should* have an address to contact for both questions and problems. The author or contact for the page is identified with the `<address>` and `</address>` tags.

Adding Document Tags to the Example

Now that you have seen the basic tags for all documents, use a text editor to put the tags into `example1.html`.

4. **Add the start and end tags that define this document to be type HTML.**

5. **Label the head and body of the document with the appropriate tags.**

6. **Label the title of the document**
   The line that reads *The Physiological Basis for Intuition* was meant to be the title of the document. Label it as such.

7. **Make a level-one heading that matches the title.**

8. **Identify the author's address in the document. Reload the document.**

9. **Compare your results to** `http://{server}/Chapter2/example1d.html`.

10. Reload your newly formatted document
`http://{server}/Chapter2/example1.html/`.

Your document now looks the same regardless of the name used to load it because HTML tags were recognized in the document itself. You have fixed the problem noted on *page 28*. On the Mosaic browser, the page looks like this:

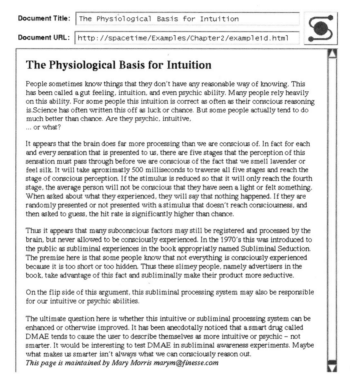

Figure 2-7   A Finished Product

Paragraph Formatting

Whitespace, such as carriage returns, tabs, and multiple spaces is ignored by browsers. Special types of tags create and control whitespace. These tags include headers, list elements, address elements, and blockquotes.

HTML allows different browsers to display the information to the best of their ability. A browser that is sized to display only 30 columns of text cannot display text with the same layout as a browser sized to display 60 columns. Consider the following two lines of text. When the lines are entered by a command-line editor, they appear to be about the same length.

Example 2-4   *Monospace Font Display*

```
mmmmmmmmmmmmmmmmmmmmmmmmmmmmmmmmmmmmmmmmmmmmmmmmmmmmmmmmmmmmmmm
iiiiiiiiiiiiiiiiiiiiiiiiiiiiiiiiiiiiiiiiiiiiiiiiiiiiiiiiiiiiii
```

However, when these lines are displayed using a kerned or proportional font, as most GUI displays do, the second line is only half the length of the first.

Example 2-5   *Kerned Font Display*

```
mmmmmmmmmmmmmmmmmmmmmmmmmmmmmmmmmmmmmmmmmmmmmmmmmmmmmmmmmmmmmmm
iiiiiiiiiiiiiiiiiiiiiiiiiiiiiiiiiiiiiiiiiiiiiiiiiiiiiiiii
```

This example illustrates that text can't be consistently formatted for both GUI and text-based displays if the formatting is controlled in the text. Therefore, HTML leaves the determination of where lines should wrap to the browser. That is, the text must have tags to indicate where carriage returns and other mandatory whitespace formatting should be used. These tags are as follows:

- **Paragraph** – <p> — This tag was introduced in the initial example in this chapter. The paragraph starts a new line, and places a blank line between the text before the tag and the text after the tag.

- **Break** –
 — This tag was also introduced in the initial example. Like the paragraph, this tag starts a new line, but it does not place a blank line between the two sections of text.

- **Horizontal Rule** – <hr> — This tag starts a new line and places a horizontal graphic line between the sections of text instead of a blank line.

- **Preformatted Text** – <pre> and </pre>— This set of tags defines a section of text that must be presented as it is typed in. Such definition is the only way to make tabs and other whitespace characters appear. Until HTML 3.0 is supported on all browsers, use this set of tags to make tables.

- **Blocktext** – <blockquote> and </blockquote> — This set of tags indents the text as if it were a quotation. This is a logical formatting method. Alternative methods for indenting text are discussed in the *Lists* section of this chapter. These methods were not designed for indent formatting and offend many of the HTML purists. They are, however, widely used.

Refer to Figure 2-8 to see how each of the formatting codes looks on a Mosaic browser.

1. **Load** `http://{server}/Chapter2/paragraph_format_examples.html`
   to see how the different headings look on your display.

2. **View the HTML text by pulling down the File menu and selecting View Source.**
   Note that only the preformatted text retains the whitespacing of the original material.

This is text that is terminated by a paragraph. What does that mean? The text will wrap on it own. Whitespace is not maintained. Notice how much space is between this text and the next line.

This is text that is terminated by a line break. What does that mean? The text will wrap on it own. Whitespace is not maintained. Notice how much space is between this text and the next line.
This is text that is terminated by a horizontal rule. What does that mean? The text will wrap on it own. Whitespace is not maintained. Notice how much space is between this text and the next line.

This is text that is in block quote. What does that mean? will the text wrap on its own? Will the text be in a specific format? Are tab and other whitespace characters conserved?

```
This is text that is in pre. What does that mean?
will the text wrap on its own? Will the text be in a specific format?
     Are tab and other whitespace characters conserved?
```

Figure 2-8   Samples of Various Paragraph Formats

Character Formatting

If you haven't read *Page Formatting Philosophy* in the *Introduction*, please do so. It is important to remember that HTML is not designed to be a WYSIWYG document system. HTML was designed for logical formatting. For example, if you define a section to be code, the browser will use some type of formatting to set off the text from other types of formatting. It *will probably* make the code monospace type, but if the browser is already monospace type, that won't be setting the code off from regular text, so the text marked as code may become bold instead. With physical formatting, the browser renders the text exactly as you specify, if it can. With logical formatting, the browser renders the text based on the modifications that it can make for the environment that it is in.

There are significantly more character-formatting tags for the logical formatting of text. Format tags accommodate people who want to physically force **bold** or *italics* on a document.

Note – HTML provides methods for both physical and logical formatting. In physical formatting, text is specified as being in italics. Logical formatting would declare the text to have *emphasis*. On Mosaic and some GUI-based browser, this means the same thing.

However, a text-based browser doesn't have the display capabilities, so it is good practice to use logical formatting instead of physical formatting. Then, a wider range of client browsers can see the special formatting.

Font Changes

The initial example in this chapter showed how to put text in italics by surrounding the text with the start and stop tags `<i>` and `</i>`. All character formatting is done in the same way, only the tags are changed. The chart below outlines the different types of character formatting.

1. **load** `http://{server}/Chapter2/char_ex.html`.
   Compare your results with Figure 2-9, which is a sample of how each of these formatting tags looks on a Mosaic browser.

This text is emphasized

This text is italics

This text is variable

This text is citation

This text is strong

This text is bold

`This text is teletype`

`This text is code`

`This text is sample`

`This text is keyboard entry`

This text is keyword

This text is dfn

This is regular text.

Figure 2-9   Samples of Character Formats

Note – When characters are formatted by themselves, they will still wrap when they reach the end of a line. Only paragraph formatting with `<pre>` can keep text on the same line if the line is too long.

Table 2-1 lists HTML character tags.

Table 2-1 HTML Character Tags

Name	Start Tag	Stop Tag	Logical or Physical
citation	`<cite>`	`</cite>`	Logical
code	`<code>`	`</code>`	Logical
definition	`<dfn>`	`</dfn>`	Logical
emphasized	`<em>`	`</em>`	Logical
keyboard entry	`<kbd>`	`</kbd>`	Logical
keyword	`<key>`	`</key>`	Logical
sample	`<samp>`	`</samp>`	Logical
strong	`<strong>`	`</strong>`	Logical
variable	`<var>`	`</var>`	Logical
bold	`<b>`	`</b>`	Physical
italics	`<i>`	`</i>`	Physical
strike-through	`<strike>`	`</strike>`	Physical
teletype	`<tt>`	`</tt>`	Physical

8-bit Characters

Everything covered so far deals with English and the 7-bit per character ASCII that is used to make each letter. Because 7-bit ASCII is insufficient for many languages, an alternative is available to display most of the standard Latin-1 characters.

The ampersand (&) character indicates that the characters following it are evaluated as a single entity. The semicolon (;) prevents concatenation of several characters into a single character. For example, Á is written as `&Aacute;` and Ü is written as `&Uuml;`. A space can also be used to terminate a string, but the space will be displayed. Therefore, a semicolon must be used within a word.

There is a second method of indicating these characters. The ampersand character starts the string, followed directly by the pound, or number, character (#), and the numerical ASCII value of the character. This method doesn't use the semicolon; instead, the numerical value will always be a value between 128 and 256.

2. Load `http://{server}/Chapter2/eightbit.html`.
This example shows the word Ádios twice.

3. View the HTML text by pulling down the File menu and selecting View Source.
This example shows the two different methods of displaying 8-bit characters. On the Mosaic browser, it looks like the menu shown in Figure 2-10.

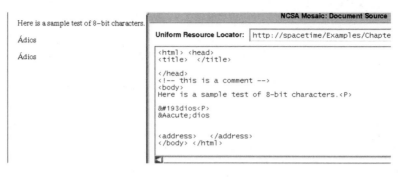

Figure 2-10   Sample of 8-bit Characters

A complete list of characters, their 8-bit ASCII value, and string values can be found in *8-bit ASCII Characters* on page 252.

This method doesn't meet the needs of the Cyrillic, Greek, Hebrew, Chinese, Japanese and Korean languages. To display these languages, you need a special Mosaic-L10N browser. Information about the latest L10N browser can be found on the `www-mling` email alias listed in Appendix E, *More Information*. Details about the browser are beyond the scope of book.

Other Special Characters

Since the characters <, >, and & indicate formatting, they are considered to be metacharacters and cannot be printed directly in the text itself. They also cannot be *escaped*, which in UNIX parlance means that you cannot use a metacharacter to indicate that some other metacharacter should be treated as a regular character instead of its *special* designation. HTML metacharacters are composed by using the &*string* method discussed above. Some browsers also implement the 8-bit numerical ASCII rendering of these characters. However, Mosaic does not do so, and since Mosaic is one of the most commonly used browsers at present (according to the usage survey by Georgia Tech), use of the 8-bit numerical ASCII values for metacharacters is not recommended.

One other special character, the nonbreaking space, can be composed in this manner. This character is only sporadically implemented in the various browsers and not implemented in Mosaic 2.4. It is noted here for reference only. Table 2-2 summarizes special characters.

Table 2-2   Metacharacters

Character	8-bit ASCII	String Name
<	<	<

Table 2-2   Metacharacters (Continued)

Character	8-bit ASCII	String Name
>	&#062;	&gt;
&	&#038;	&amp;
nonbreaking space	&#032;	

4. **Load** `http://{server}/Chapter2/special.html`.
   This page demonstrates what is implemented on your browser and what is not implemented.

5. **View the HTML text by pulling down the File menu and selecting View Source.**
   This example shows the different methods of displaying special characters.

Lists

People tend to organize things into lists. These may be numbered lists or bulleted lists or even lists of lists. The formatting covered so far is not enough to make lists. In HTML a special set of formatting tags is devoted to making lists. Eight steps in this section illustrate the use of tags in formatting lists.

Regular Lists

Until now, all formatting has been either a single tag or a start and end tag around the text to be operated on. Lists have a slightly more complex form. The list itself is defined with a start and stop tag. Then each list item is defined separately. There is no stop tag for each list item. The format is:

HTML Example 2-6 List Formatting

`<ul>`	Start by defining the type of list that you want to use.
`<li> first item text`	Indicate that the following text is a *list item*.
`<li> second item text`	Indicate that the following text is another *list item*.
`</ul>`	Close the list.

The four types of lists are: unnumbered `<ul>`, ordered `<ol>` *(i.e. numbered)*, menu `<menu>`, and directory `<dir>`. Menu and directory lists have the same appearance as unnumbered lists and can be used interchangeably on most browsers.

1. **Load** `http://{server}/Chapter2/list1.html`.

   This page shows the various types of lists and demonstrates the bullet styles associated with each list type. On Mosaic, this format looks like the display on the left side of Figure 2-11.

   - This is the first list item for an unnumbered list.
   - This is the second list item for an unnumbered list.
   - This is the third list item for an unnumbered list.
   - This is the fourth list item for an unnumbered list.

   1. This is the first list item for an ordered list.
   2. This is the second list item for an ordered list.
   3. This is the third list item for an ordered list.
   4. This is the fourth list item for an ordered list.

   - This is the first list item for an menu list.
   - This is the second list item for an menu list.
   - This is the third list item for an menu list.
   - This is the fourth list item for an menu list.

   - This is the first list item for an dir list.
   - This is the second list item for an dir list.
   - This is the third list item for an dir list.
   - This is the fourth list item for an dir list.

   - This is the first list item for an unnumbered list.
     - This is the first list item for an dir list nested in a unnumbered list.
     - This is the second list item for an dir list nested in a unnumbered list.
     - This is the third list item for an dir list nested in a unnumbered list.
     - This is the fourth list item for an dir list nested in a unnumbered list.
   - This is the second list item for an unnumbered list.
     - This is the first list item for an unnumbered list nested in a unnumbered list.
     - This is the second list item for an unnumbered list nested in a unnumbered list.
     - This is the third list item for an unnumbered list nested in a unnumbered list.
     - This is the fourth list item for an unnumbered list nested in a unnumbered list.
   - This is the third list item for an unnumbered list.
     1. This is the first list item for an ordered list nested in a unnumbered list.
     2. This is the second list item for an ordered list nested in a unnumbered list.
     3. This is the third list item for an ordered list nested in a unnumbered list.
     4. This is the fourth list item for an ordered list nested in a unnumbered list.
   - This is the fourth list item for an unnumbered list.
     - This is the first list item for an menu list nested in a unnumbered list.
     - This is the second list item for an menu list nested in a unnumbered list.
     - This is the third list item for an menu list nested in a unnumbered list.
     - This is the fourth list item for an menu list nested in a unnumbered list.

   1. This is the first list item for an ordered list.
      - This is the first list item for an dir list nested in a ordered list.
      - This is the second list item for an dir list nested in a ordered list.
      - This is the third list item for an dir list nested in a ordered list.
      - This is the fourth list item for an dir list nested in a ordered list.
   2. This is the second list item for an ordered list.
      - This is the first list item for an unnumbered list nested in a ordered list.
      - This is the second list item for an unnumbered list nested in a ordered list.
      - This is the third list item for an unnumbered list nested in a ordered list.
      - This is the fourth list item for an unnumbered list nested in a ordered list.

Figure 2-11   List Samples

2. **Load** `http://{server}/Chapter2/list2.html`.

   The list items are nested within one another in this example. Note that when unnumbered, menu, and directory lists are nested, a different bullet character is used for each level. Ordered lists merely start over from 1 every time. On Mosaic, this format looks like the display on the right side of Figure 2-11.

3. **Load** `http://{server}/Chapter2/list3.html`.

   Different characters are used as the bullet symbol for the first three nested layers. Starting with the fourth layer, the bullets keep the same shape. On Mosaic, this format looks like the display on the left side of Figure 2-12.

This is a sample of nesting lists

- The first list item – one deep.
  - The first list item – two deep.
    - The first list item – three deep.
      - The first list item – four deep.
        - The first list item – five deep.
        - The second list item – five deep.
        - The third list item – five deep.
        - The fourth list item – five deep.
      - The second list item – four deep.
      - The third list item – four deep.
      - The fourth list item – four deep.
    - The second list item – three deep.
    - The third list item – three deep.
    - The fourth list item – three deep.
  - The second list item – two deep.
  - The third list item – two deep.
  - The fourth list item – two deep.
- The second list item – one deep.
- The third list item – one deep.
- The fourth list item – one deep.

This is a sample of nesting lists

The first list item – one deep.

The first list item – two deep.

The first list item – three deep.

The first list item – four deep.

The first list item – five deep.

The second list item – five deep.

The third list item – five deep.

The fourth list item – five deep.

The second list item – four deep.

The third list item – four deep.

The fourth list item – four deep.

The second list item – three deep.

The third list item – three deep.

The fourth list item – three deep.

The second list item – two deep.

The third list item – two deep.

The fourth list item – two deep.

The second list item – one deep.

Figure 2-12   Nested Lists

4. **Load** `http://{server}/Chapter2/list4.html`.
   Using list start and end tags without using the list item tags provides indenting without having a defined bullet character. This technique allows nesting of indents. On Mosaic, this format looks like the display on the right side of Figure 2-12

5. **View the HTML text by pulling down the File menu and selecting View Source.**
   Notice that the tag `<li>` doesn't appear anywhere.

Description Lists

HTML also has a special kind of list called a *description* list. This list is usually used for a glossary or list of items and associated descriptions. It follows the same formatting conventions as above with a start `<DL>` and end definition `</DL>`. However it has two different list items inside the list, a *data term* `<DT>` and a *data description* `<DD>`.

A sample of a description list is:

HTML Example 2-7 Description List Sample

`<DL>`	Start by defining the type of list that you want to use.
`<DT> Book`	Indicate that the following text is a *data term*.
`<DD> Tree-killer copy of on-line documentation`	Indicate that the following text is a *data description*.
`</DL>`	Close the list.

6. **Load** `http://{server}/Chapter2/dlist1.html`.
A description list indents the data description, while leaving the data term at the left margin, as seen in Figure 2-13.

> This is a data term
>> This is a data description.
> Book – This is a data term
>> Tree-killer copy of a document. – This is a data description.

Figure 2-13 Sample Description List

7. **Load** `http://{server}/Chapter2/dlist2.html`.
By use of multiple description-list start tags, data terms can be indented and data descriptions can be indented even farther. Description-list components can be used to provide additional indenting capabilities above and beyond the `<blockquote>` and `<pre>` paragraph formatting methods noted previously.

8. **Load** `http://{server}/Chapter2/dlist3.html`.
A new paragraph can be started and indented as long as the last tag was a `<DD>`, as seen in Figure 2-14.

> This is a data term
>> This is a data description.
>
>> I would like to continue the data description with a new paragraph that is still indented.

Figure 2-14 Variation in a Description List

Summary

In this chapter you learned:

- What tags are and how to use them.

- How to add the tags that provide the underlying structure to an HTML document.

- Tags for formatting paragraphs of text.

- Tags for formatting individual characters.

- How to create 8-bit and special characters.

- How to make lists.

- When the document is not defined as HTML with the appropriate tag, the default font is a fixed-width font.

You have just learned the basics for creating an individual document. In the next chapter you learn how to tie individual documents together to make hypertext.

Looking Forward

The HTML 3.0 standards are expected to enhance some of the tags listed in this chapter. The most notable changes will be in the paragraph-formatting tags. Currently, <P> and <BR> merely indicate a break in the text. In the future these tags will probably change from empty elements to containers. The text within a container can then have more formatting applied to it. One example is <P ALIGN="center"> stuff </P> to center text. Enhancements to lists are being discussed as well, since many people create custom lists with graphic bullets and alternative numbering systems.

Netscape Communications has jumped the gun and proposed to include some changes in the not-yet-final HTML 2.0 specifications. The most notable Netscape modification is the creation of a <CENTER> tag to center text. The rationale for this tag is that the <P ALIGN="center"> tag breaks some current browsers. It remains to be seen how many of Netscape's enhancements will be incorporated in the HTML 2.0 specifications.

Tags Used in This Chapter

Name and Description	Start Tag	Stop Tag
Document Formatting		
HTML document indicator	<html>	</html>
Document head	<head>	</head>
Document body	<body>	</body>

Name and Description	Start Tag	Stop Tag
Owner/contact	`<address>`	`</address>`
Headings	`<h1>...<h6>`	`</h1>...</h6>`
Title	`<title>`	`</title>`
Comment	`<!-- -->`	
Character Formatting		
emphasized	`<em>`	`</em>`
variable	`<var>`	`</var>`
citation	`<cite>`	`</cite>`
italics	`<i>`	`</i>`
strong	`<strong>`	`</strong>`
bold	`<b>`	`</b>`
code	`<code>`	`</code>`
sample	`<samp>`	`</samp>`
keyboard entry	`<kbd>`	`</kbd>`
teletype	`<tt>`	`</tt>`
keyword	`<key>`	`</key>`
dfm	`<dfn>`	`</dfn>`
strikethrough	`<strike>`	`</strike>`
Paragraph Formatting		
blockquote	`<blockquote>`	`</blockquote>`
paragraph	`<p>`	
line break	` `	
horizontal rule (horizontal line)	`<hr>`	
preformatted text	`<pre>`	`</pre>`
List Formatting		
list item	`<li>`	
unnumbered list	`<ul>`	`</ul>`
ordered list	`<ol>`	`</ol>`
menu list	`<menu>`	`</menu>`
dir list	`<dir>`	`</dir>`
description list	`<dl>`	`</dl>`
data term	`<dt>`	
data description	`<dd>`	

Hypertext—Linking Documents   3

The documents created in the previous chapter stand by themselves. WWW is a hypertext document system, linking pertinent data from different documents. If you want to know more about what is being said before continuing to the next topic, you can select a link shown in highlighted text and read about it. This chapter describes how to create such links, both between documents and within documents.

Elements of Hypertext

It would be nice to tie together information, for example, a document that discusses apple growing and a second document that shows what fruits are best grown across the state of Colorado. Hypertext is the medium that made this joining of information, called a *link*, common. In WWW this link is made by placing an *anchor* around the referenced text and referring to the other document.

Since WWW works across multiple platforms, the naming convention for doing so needed to be universally recognized. The *Universal Resource Locator*, or *URL*, naming scheme was proposed to create a standard naming convention. URLs are the method by which links are named in WWW.

Universal Resource Locator (URL)

URL components are shown in Figure 3-1 and described below.

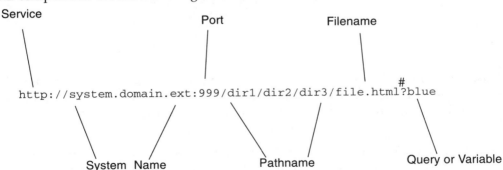

Figure 3-1   URL Components

51

- **Service type** — *A required part of a URL*. The service tells the client browser how to contact the server for the requested data. For most of the examples here, HyperText Transport Protocol or `http` is used. WWW can handle several other services including `gopher`, `wais`, `ftp`, `netnews`, and `telnet` and can be extended to handle new ones.

- **System name** — *A required part of a URL*. The system is the fully qualified domain name of the server of the data being requested. Partially qualified domain names should be used only for documents that won't leave your domain. It is always good practice to use fully qualified domain names.

- **Port** — *An optional part of a URL*. Ports are the network socket addresses for specific protocols. By default, `http` connects at port 80. In some cases, the default port is not used by the server. This may be for several different reasons: the server may be a proxy server; or a nonstandard port discourages robots and crackers from polling the system; or some other service is already using that port. This number comes after the `:` and before the first `/` of the directory name. This part of a URL is needed only when the server doesn't communicate on the default port for that service.

- **Directory path** — *A required part of a URL*. Once connected to the system in question, a path to the file must be specified. It is important to note here that the directory path listed in the URL may *not* exactly match the path to the file on the system itself. There are several ways to shorten the pathnames, including aliasing. Each level of the directory tree is delimited by a `/`. The directory is also separated from the filename with a `/`.

- **Filename** — *An optional part of a URL*. The filename is the data file itself. The server can be configured so that if a filename isn't specified, a default file or directory listing will be returned.

- **Search components or variables** — *An optional part of a URL*. If the URL is a request to search a database, the query can be embedded in the URL. This is the text after the `?` or `#` in a URL. In the case of forms, the URL can return the information collected from a form in this area.

Adding Links

Links between documents and points within documents are created by placing anchors in the text. These anchors are of two types, *reference anchors* and *named anchors*. The reference anchor points to the destination of that hypertext link. The named anchor defines a name or place marker for a specific place in a document.

Many hypertext references are links to other pages, not specific points on a page. In this case, the named anchor isn't required. Named anchors are used primarily when the hypertext link points to a specific portion of a document instead of pointing to the document as a whole.

Reference Anchors

The concepts of a start and end tag that were discussed in the previous chapter are taken one step further. A link is created when the anchor tags <a> and </a> are placed around the text. What is new about this is that the anchor needs additional information to be valid. The <a> has added information that identifies the destination of the link in question. This additional information is called an *attribute* of the tag. The attribute is enclosed in the <> with the tag, and a value can be assigned to the attribute by using the equals sign (=).

Note – It is a good idea to always enclose attribute values in double quotes (" ").

The anchor tag <a> has the `href` or *hypertext reference* attribute added to it. An appropriate anchor tag is:

```
<a href="http://system/dir/file.html/"> Some Text </a>
```

1. **Load** `http://{server}/Chapter3/apples.html`.
   This document contains a link in the section **Growing Apples**. In Mosaic, the anchored text is displayed in a different color with a line underneath it.

2. **Pull down the File menu and select View Source.**
   Another window is opened in which the HTML source for that document is displayed. There is an anchor around the text Growing Apples in Colorado.

3. **Click on the Growing Apples in Colorado link.**
   The name on the Document URL name line of the browser now indicates that `http://{server}Chapter3/colorado-fruits.html` is being displayed.

4. **Click on the Back button at the bottom of the browser to return to the** Apples **document.**
   Notice that the anchored text has changed colors and the link is now underlined with dashes instead of a solid line, indicating that this link has already been traversed.

Named Anchors

An anchor doesn't have to be a pointer to other data. It can be a place mark for other data to point to. For example, the **Growing Apples** document points to **Fruit Growing Areas of Colorado**. It isn't fair to make the user read through all of the information about peaches and pears to get to the information about apples, so an anchor can be created at the start of the apple-growing information. The anchor is then *named* by using the NAME attribute with the <a> tag. An example is:

```
<a NAME="apple"> Apple Growing Areas </a>.
```

Notice that the anchor has no `href` variable in it: The anchor isn't pointing to anything else, it is being pointed to.

To reference this specific point, the reference anchor uses a # sign to indicate the named pointer within the document. For example, the reference anchor looks like:

```
<a href="http://{server}/colorado-fruits.html#apple> are grown in Co. </a>
```

In the case of a long document, pointers should be made to other sections of the same document to save scrolling through large bodies of data.

Note – If the above anchor is used, the file is reloaded prior to moving to the new place in the document. Use a *relative* URL, that is, a URL that contains only the differences in the URL to move without reloading. This procedure is discussed in detail in *Using Addressing Relative to Files* on page 55.

A relative reference anchor looks like:

```
<a href="#apples"> apples </a>
```

In this case, since the document name is the same, the only part of the href that changes is the pointer to the name. The # is prepended to indicate a named reference in which everything before the # is the same.

Addressing Variations

So far in this chapter, the URLs have been complete strings of *service*://*system*/*dir*/*file*, which is quite a bit to type. It is also inconvenient to have the entire URL hardcoded into a document or set of documents when the documents are moved to a new location on the same server or when the data is moved to another server. Therefore, you can specify relative or partial URLs.

Remember that the browser does not send a partial URL when it requests data. The browser takes a predetermined URL base and appends the relative URL listed in the `href=` attribute to that base. The initial character of the href determines how much of the current URL is parsed to obtain the base URL for the new document.

The URL base can also be modified by the use of the <BASE> tag and by directory aliasing by the server. This process can be very confusing, so step slowly through the details below.

Using Addressing Relative to Files

Absolute addressing uses absolutely everything. Relative addressing uses the difference between the current document or reference point and the desired destination. Each of the required parts of a URL has a unique delimiter character.

To create a relative URL, start the relative URL with the desired delimiter character. The current URL is used to obtain the rest of the information. Everything to the left of that delimiter character in the current URL is kept. Everything to the right of that delimiter character is replaced by the new relative URL. For example, if the full URL is `http://www.finesse.com/Examples/toomuch.html`, use:

- A `:` to indicate that the service stays the same and everything else changes. For example, `://www.sun.com/` loads the server www.sun.com with the same service, http.

- A `#` to indicate that the service, server, path, and filename stay the same, but the place within the document changes. For example, `#halfway` searches for the named anchor halfway through the file and displays that part of the document.

- A `/` to indicate that the service and the server stay the same but the entire pathname changes. For example, `/Chapters/Chapter1.html` loads `Chapter1.html` from the directory `Chapters` on the server `www.finesse.com`.

- No delimiting character to indicate that only the filename changes.

Since a pathname is treated as a single unit, the method for using a partial path is the same as using a relative path on a UNIX or MS-DOS system. A relative path can be specified, using the directory of the current document as a starting point instead of a fixed portion of the URL.

Note – The following examples depend on the proper configuration that was completed in Chapter 1, "Getting Started."

Files in Relative Directories

1. **Load the** `http://{server}/Chapter3/rel.html` **document.**
   Notice that the full URL name is listed in the Document URL line at the top of the browser.

2. **Use View Source to view the HTML specified in the document.**

It looks like::

Code Example 3-1   Relative Path Example

```
<html> <head>

<title> Relative Paths Exercise
</title>
</head>

<body>
<a href="file1.html"> filename only </a>

<p><a href="../file1.html"> file in parent </a>

<p><a href="down/file2.html"> file in subdirectory</a>

<p><a href="file2.html"> second filename only</a>
<address> me
</address>
</body>
</html>
```

3. **Select the item, filename only, which in the source is a filename without anything around it.**
   In this case, the browser removed the filename from the URL in the Document URL window and appended the new filename to this base URL. Loading this document was successful because the requested document was in the same directory.

4. **Click on Back to return to the original page.**

5. **Select the item, file in parent, which is a filename one directory up from the current file.**
   In this case, the browser removed the filename from the URL in the Document URL window and appended the new pathname, including the . . / to this base URL. Loading this document was successful because the requested document was in the directory above the current one.

6. **Click on Back to return to the original page.**

7. **Select the item, file in subdirectory, which is a filename in the directory below the current file.**
   In this case, the browser removed the filename from the URL in the Document URL window, and appended the new subdirectory and filename to this base URL. Loading this document was successful because the requested document was in the directory below the current.

8. **Click on Back to return to the original page.**

9. **Select the item,** second filename only, **which is a filename without anything around it.**
   In this case, the browser removed the filename from the URL in the Document URL window and appended the new filename to this base URL. Loading this document was not successful because the requested document was in the directory below—not in the current directory.

Partial URLs can be followed if they look like standard UNIX or DOS path movements. Use only the filename and place the files in the same directory or in directories relative to the current working directory.

The next exercise is about loading files that are on the same server, but not always in the same directory tree. Use the examples below if you are using the NCSA version of httpd. If you are using the CERN version, go to *Deriving Physical Directories from Virtual Directories with CERN's httpd*on page 59 and work through the exercises there.If you are using another server, go to *Using the <BASE> Tag for Relative Links* on page 64.

Deriving Physical Directories from Root and Alias Declarations with NCSA httpd

If a file is loaded from a protocol, such as file or ftp, the pathname is the actual pathname on the server. If a file is loaded via http, the httpd daemon remaps directories, based on the *Document_Root* and *Alias* definitions in the srm.conf file, which holds the configuration information for the httpd daemon.

Document_Root

NCSA uses the variable *Document_Root* in the srm.conf to determine what the root or / directory is for the httpd daemon. In the following examples, substitute your definition for *Document_Root* in the srm.conf for *Document_Root*.

1. **Load** file://*{server}*/*{Document_Root}*/Chapter3/pathex.html.
   This file loaded successfully. In this case, the httpd daemon was not used to retrieve the data because the specified service is file. The data was directly accessed on the system itself.

2. **Load** http://*{server}*/*{Document_Root}*/Chapter3/pathex.html.
   This file did not load successfully. In this case, the httpd daemon was used to retrieve the data. According to the daemon, the root is at *{Document_Root}*, so the daemon searched for /*{Document_Root}*/*{Document_Root}*/Chapter3/pathex.html, which doesn't exist.

3. **Load** http://{*server*}/Chapter3/pathex.html.
   This file loaded successfully. In this case, the httpd daemon was used to retrieve the data. The daemon prepended the *Document_Root* directory to /Chapter3/pathexample.html and found the document.

Alias

The configuration instructions in Chapter 1 said to make an alias of /Stuff/ to /{*Document_Root*}/hidden/Stuff/. This alias is used in the next example.

4. **Display** *Document_Root*/Stuff/aliasex.html **with a text editor or with** more.
   Notice that the text here states that the path is *Document_Root*/Stuff/aliasex.html.

5. **Display** *Document_Root*/hidden/Stuff/aliasex.html **with a text editor or with** more.
   Notice that the text here states that the path is *Document_Root*/hidden/Stuff/aliasex.html.

6. **Load** http://{*server*}/Stuff/aliasex.html.
   Notice that the version that was loaded was the version pointed to by the /Stuff/ alias. When processing a pathname, the httpd daemon uses the alias.

User Directory (On UNIX Only)

The configuration instructions in Chapter 1 said to make a directory in your home directory called public_html. Next, you were instructed to copy a specific file into that directory.

7. **Load** http://{*server*}/~{*your username*}/userex.html.
   The file in public_html under your home directory was loaded. In this case, the httpd daemon looked up the home directory of {*username*}, then appended public_html to that directory, and looked in that directory for the file userex.html.

The ~ character originated in the UNIX environment's C shell as a method of accessing a user's home directory. The home directory is determined from the password information that is found on the server. This information comes from the /etc/passwd file or from a name service.

Combining Relative Addressing with Root and Alias Directory Mappings

You have seen how pathnames are accessed via the *Alias*, *UserDir*, and *Document_Root* variables. This information can be used in creating documents that use partial URLs in a new fashion. To access documents relative to the current document, the / character was *not* placed at the beginning of the URL. Starting a URL with a single / tells the browser to start at the *root* of the `httpd` server; the service type and the server name are retained, but the entire path to that document changes. This process is effective when developing an entire server setup and then migrating or mirroring the setup on another server.

8. **Select the first item in** `aliasex.html` **that was previously loaded.**
Notice that the URL name starts with a `/`. This was interpreted as: Keep the protocol and server, start at the *Document_Root*, and load `rootex.html`. The text of this page lists its location.

9. **Go back to the** `aliasex.html`. **Select the second item.**
Notice that the URL name starts with `/Stuff/`. This is interpreted as: Keep the protocol and server, start at the `/Stuff/` directory, and load `alias2ex.html`. The text of this page lists that location.

10. **Load** `http://{server}/`.
This URL loads a list of the files from a directory. These are the files in *Document_Root*.

11. **Load** `http://{server}/../`.
This URL loads a list of the files in a directory. These are *still* the files in *Document_Root*. According to the `httpd` daemon, there is nothing at a higher level than the root.

The above exercises demonstrate the use of full and partial URLs, based on starting at the root of the system. If you are working on a UNIX system, skip to the symbolic links exercise on page 64. Since symbolic links aren't available as part of Windows NT, the section is not valid for Windows NT clients. If you are working on a Windows NT-based system, skip to the section on page 64 describing the use of the `<BASE>` tag.

Deriving Physical Directories from Virtual Directories with CERN's `httpd`

The CERN `httpd` daemon determines the path by use of the *Pass*, *Map*, and *Fail* variables, called *rules*, that are configured in the `httpd.conf` file. A fourth rule, *Redirect*, is not described here.

The configuration instructions in Chapter 1 said to alter the following lines in the `httpd.conf` file.

httpd.conf Example 3-2 Altering Map, Fail, and Pass in a File

```
Change
    Pass     /*            /local/Web/*
To
    Map      */corp/*      /special/moredirs/corp/*/*
    Map      */people/*    */staff/info/*
    Map      /Stuff/*      /hidden/Stuff/*
```

httpd.conf Example 3-2   Altering Map, Fail, and Pass in a File (Continued)

```
Change
    Fail    /hidden/Stuff/database/*
    Pass    /special/*
    Pass    /*          /WWW/docs/*
```

Using Pass

There is no specific variable definition for the root of the document tree for CERN's `httpd`, as there is for NCSA. For common understanding, *Document_Root* refers to whatever was used for the **Pass /*** definition in the configuration file `httpd.conf`.

1. **Load** `file://{server}/{Document_Root}/Chapter3/pathex.html`.
   This file loaded successfully. The `httpd` daemon was *not* used to retrieve the data. The data was directly accessed on the system itself via the file service.

2. **Load** `http://{server}/{Document_Root}/Chapter3/pathex.html`.
   This file did not load successfully. In this case, the `httpd` daemon retrieved the data. According to the daemon, the root is at *{Document_Root}*, so the daemon searched for `/{Document_Root}/{Document_Root}/Chapter3/pathex.html`, which doesn't exist.

3. **Load** `http://{server}/Chapter3/pathex.html`.
   This file loaded successfully. In this case, the `httpd` daemon retrieved the data. The daemon appended the *Document_Root* directory to `/Chapter3/pathexample.html` and found the document.

If a file is loaded via `http`, the configuration information for the `httpd` daemon translates directories, based on the rules defined in the `httpd.conf` file. If the same file is loaded from another protocol, such as file or ftp, the pathname is the actual pathname on the server.

Using Map

The **Map /Stuff/*** definition, as entered in httpd.conf Example 3-2, is the equivalent of *Alias* in the NCSA `httpd` configuration. The use of *Map*, *Pass*, and *Fail* is more complex than a simple *Document_Root* and *Alias*. They are discussed in this exercise.

- The CERN `httpd` daemon reviews all *Map*, *Pass*, and *Fail* rules from the top to the bottom of the list.

- If the given URL matches the template description in the middle column, then the result in the right-hand column is substituted for the text in the middle column.

- If the rule that made the translation was a *Map* rule, then processing continues with the next URL translation rule.

- If the translation rule that did processing on a string was a *Pass* or *Fail* rule, then translation ceases and the resulting URL is looked up.

4. **Display** *Document_Root*/Stuff/aliasex.html **with a text editor or with** more.
   Notice that the text here states that the path is *Document_Root*/Stuff/aliasex.html.

5. **Display** *Document_Root*/hidden/Stuff/aliasex.html **with a text editor or with** more.
   Notice that the text here states that the path is:
   Document_Root/hidden/Stuff/aliasex.html.

6. **Load** http://*{server}*/Stuff/aliasex.html.
   Notice that the version that was loaded is the version pointed to by the /Stuff/ mapping. In this case, /Stuff/ matched, so /hidden/Stuff/ was substituted for it. Then the processing continued to compare the result /hidden/Stuff/aliasex.html until the **Pass /*** line was reached. At this point, /WWW/docs (or whatever your *Document_Root* is) replaced the starting /, making the URL read /*{Document_Root}*/hidden/Stuff/aliasex.html.

7. **Load** http://*{server}*/people/corp/maptest.html.
   Notice that this page is loaded from the file /special/moredirs/corp/staff/info/maptest.html.

   - In this case, corp resolved to /special/moredirs/corp. The asterisk before corp in the template became the first asterisk in the result. The asterisk after corp became the second asterisk in the result. After this translation, the URL path became /special/moredirs/corp/people/maptest.html. Since the rule doing the translation was a *Map* rule, processing continued on the URL.
   - The next template match is */people/*. At this point, /staff/info/ is substituted for /people/, making the URL path /special/moredirs/corp/staff/info/maptest.html. Again, the translation rule was a *Map* rule, so processing continues on the URL.
   - /special/* matches the first Pass rule. There is no result to match to the template, so the URL is accepted without changes. This translation rule is Pass, so translation stops and the file /special/moredirs/corp/staff/info/maptest.html is used.

The **Pass /special/*** stopped the processing before the **Pass /*** rule had a chance to change the / to /WWW/docs/, which is not what is wanted here. This type of mapping can be used in cases in which the tree structure must be set up one way and the physical layout is organized around a different structure. The above example would be effective in the arrangement shown in Figure 3-2.

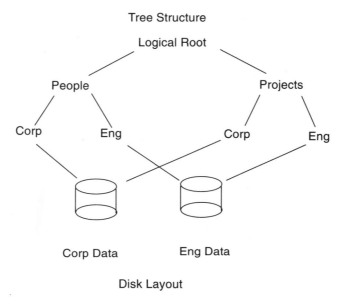

Tree Structure

Logical Root

People   Projects

Corp   Eng   Corp   Eng

Corp Data   Eng Data

Disk Layout

Figure 3-2   Tree Structure Versus Disk Layout in Pass Rule

Using Fail

Some times you want to use a complete directory structure. However, that structure may have one directory or a set of files that shouldn't be accessible to the user, for example, the data that is stored for indexes and mapped images. Other applications such as WAIS or CGI scripts can access this data, but the httpd daemon should be restricted from this data, making it secure from users. The *Fail* rule acts the same as the *Pass* rule. If the requested URL matches the template, then processing stops and the user receives a message that the request failed.

8. **Load** http://{*server*}/Stuff/database/data.html.
   /Stuff/ resolved to /hidden/Stuff/, which then matched the **Fail**
   /hidden/Stuff/database/* rule. At this point, processing stops and the failure is reported to the user.

User Directory (UNIX Only)

The configuration instructions in Chapter 1 said to make a directory in your home directory called public_html. Next, you were instructed to copy a specific file into that directory.

9. Load `http://{server}/~{your username}/userex.html`.
The file in `public_html` under your home directory was loaded. The `httpd` daemon looked up the home directory of *{username}*, then appended `public_html` to that directory, and looked in that directory for the file `userex.html`.

The ~ character originated in the UNIX environment's C shell as a method of accessing a user's home directory. The home directory is determined from the password information that is found on the server. This information comes from the `/etc/passwd` file or from NIS or NIS+.

Combining Relative Addressing with Virtual Directory Mappings

The above information is used in creating documents that use partial URLs in a new fashion. To access documents relative to the current document, the / character was *not* placed at the beginning of the URL. Starting a URL with a / tells the browser to start at *Document_Root*; the service type and the server name are retained, but the entire path to that document changes. This process is effective when developing an entire server setup and then migrating or mirroring the setup on another server.

10.Select the first item in `aliasex.html` **that was previously loaded.**
The URL name starts with a /. This was interpreted as: Keep the protocol and server, resolve /* to be `/WWW/docs`, and load `rootex.html`. The text of this page lists that location.

11.Go back to the `aliasex.html`. **Select the second item.**
The URL name starts with `/Stuff/`. This is interpreted as: Keep the protocol and server, translate `/Stuff/` to `/hidden/Stuff/` with the third *Map* rule, resolve /* to `/WWW/docs` with the *Pass* rule, and load `/WWW/docs/hidden/Stuff/alias2ex.html`. The text of this page lists that location.

12.Load `http://{server}/`.
This file loads a list of the files in the directory. Notice also that these are the files in *Document_Root*.

13.Load `http://{server}/../`.
This file causes an error message. Unlike the NCSA version of `httpd`, the CERN version recognizes that this is out of bounds.

The above exercises demonstrate the use of full and partial URLs in remapping virtual directories. If you are working on a UNIX system, continue with *Using Symbolic Links on UNIX Systems*. Since symbolic links aren't available as part of Windows NT, the section is not valid for Windows NT clients. If you are working on a Windows NT-based system, skip to *Using the <BASE> Tag for Relative Links*, which describes the use of the <BASE> tag.

Using Symbolic Links on UNIX Systems

Several examples about how to access directory trees were defined in the httpd configuration file for the specific daemon. Then, it was shown in the last example that data can't be accessed outside the defined directory trees. There is a way around this situation on the UNIX platform.

Most UNIX operating systems use links. A link, in this case, doesn't mean a pointer to other hypertext data, but is a special file that is a pointer to another file. There are two types of links, hard and symbolic. Hard links are restricted to the same physical partition on a disk. Hard links may have some good uses in other places, but they are limited in extending access to directories outside the configured httpd area. Symbolic links can be made to other partitions, other disks, and, with the automounter and NFS, these links can even be made to other systems.

As part of the configuration for this chapter, a file was placed in /junk.

1. **Load** file://{*server*}/junk/symlink.html.
   With the file service, this data is loaded easily.

2. **Load** http://{*server*}/junk/symlink.html.
   As was seen in the examples for each httpd daemon, this directory is not found in the *Document_Root* area, so the request fails.

3. **Make a symbolic link from** *Document_Root*/junk **to** /junk.
   Where *Document_Root* is /WWW/docs, the command line looks like:

   ```
   # ln -s /junk /WWW/docs/junk
   ```

4. **Load** http://{*server*}/junk/symlink.html.
   This time the document loaded. The httpd daemon is able to access the data because the operating system resolved the link and returned the data to the httpd daemon. It is important to note here that the httpd daemon did not go outside its known area. The operating system provided the file access once a pointer was within the known directory space.

Using the <BASE> Tag for Relative Links

Usually a document is not published alone in a hypertext environment. The related documents tend to stay in the same directory or general area. The base of a set of documents can be defined with the tag <BASE>. The <BASE> tag was originally designed to supply a base URL when the HTML document was taken out of context, such as when a document is emailed to someone.

However, since indiscriminate use of the <BASE> tag causes problems, limit its use. If <BASE> is defined, then, when the document is mailed, that value is retained instead of the actual base of the document. Defining <BASE> also causes the browser to list the value of <BASE> instead of the actual URL of the document in the hotlist and Document URL field of the browser. Thus, when a document is reloaded, the document will not be reloaded, but the <BASE> value is loaded instead. Use the <BASE> tag *only* when the documents will be routinely taken out of context.

Summary

Partial URLs are a boon to the developer of a complete set of documents. By use of these URL methods, documents do not require significant changes when moved. You can determine when to use each method, based on how the documents are to be maintained.

In this chapter you learned:

- When documents might be moved from one directory to another, the method of using relative pathnames is the most effective. Since full pathnames aren't listed in the document, changes aren't needed. This is one effective method for mirroring data on multiple servers.

- When documents are to be fixed to a formal directory structure, use the method of using pathnames relative to the root and aliases. This method compensates for the need to move documents to a new disk or path as the size of the document structure grows, by changing only the alias mapping for that directory structure. This is the other effective method for mirroring data on multiple servers.

- Symbolic links are a method of mimicking the behavior desired above. They work only for UNIX systems, and they exact a small overhead per request in following the symbolic link. Use symbolic links for moving document directories on-the-fly, when the daemon can't be reloaded, or for testing. Long-term use of symbolic links is not recommended.

- The <BASE> tag was originally designed to supply a base URL when the HTML document was taken out of context, such as when a document is emailed to someone. If a <BASE> is defined, it causes problems with standard browsing. Use the <BASE> tag *only* when the documents will be routinely taken out of context.

3

Tags Used in This Chapter

Tag	Attribute	Description
\<A\>		Anchors hyperlinks.
	HREF	Points to destination of link.
	NAME	Defines a named anchor so that a link can point to a place in a document, not just to the document itself.

Multimedia—Going Beyond Text

Most Internet tools are limited to one type of medium. In the case of netnews, `gopher`, IRC, and basic mail, this medium is text. A few tools, like the Internet Talk Radio, use sound or video as their medium. The one deciding characteristic of all of these applications is that they can only cope with one medium.

Using multiple media, or multimedia, in a document has become a requirement. Web pages aren't considered complete without at least one image. However, it is important to keep the audience in mind when developing multimedia documents. Many types of viewers have been ported to most platforms, but there still are some platform-specific formats. If the audience that you intend to reach is the Internet itself, use the standard formats outlined below.

Other audience characteristics to take into consideration when developing multimedia web pages include image quantity, image size, and page layout.

Multimedia

Email has been the catalyst for a whole new world of information transmission. In the late 1980s and early 1990s many email systems enabled two new options. The first option was to let the user send full 8-bit data instead of 7-bit ASCII by automatically converting the 8-bit data to and from a 7-bit version. The second new feature was the ability to attach a file to an email message. Since these files could now carry 8-bit converted data, a kind of sneaker net evolved where networking was still limited. The files could be dragged from the email message to folder and used without additional processing.

The next step in this evolution was the incorporation or binding of tools to the email readers that were specifically designed for viewing or playing the attached files. This allowed the files to be viewed directly within the email system, removing the steps of dragging to folder, starting the application, and loading the file.

4

It wasn't enough to be in touch with all of the other CCMail™ users or Internet-type mail users. People needed to communicate with everyone, and the email vendors provided gateways from one type of mail to another. This method was fine for text, but unsatisfactory on the attached data files. There weren't many common data formats in the beginning. Microsoft Windows used BMPs for images and WAVs for sound. SunOS and eventually Solaris 2.x used PostScript® or Sun Raster™ files for images and AU (audio) files for sound. The technology was ready for standards, and MIME (Multipurpose Internet Mail Extensions) was developed to meet that need.

MIME Formats

When configuring servers, MIME formats are associated with specific filename extensions. The browsers associate the filename extensions to MIME types and the MIME types to specific viewers.

- **GIF**™ — The Graphics Interchange Format© developed in 1987 by people from CompuServe. This bitmapped format came into being because people wanted to exchange images between different platforms. This format is now used on almost every platform that supports graphical applications. GIF format is not only a standard image type for WWW browsers, it is also the only image type that can be used for inline images on all platforms. The one drawback of GIF format is that it is limited to 256 colors.

  An extended standard called GIF89A was developed to add functionality for specific applications. The most notable use of this extended standard in web pages is the use of transparent backgrounds. Images can appear to float by making the background color the same as the background of the browser. However, browsers don't always come with the plain grey background, and the user can override the choice of background color. Therefore, designating a specific color as transparent compensates for the user's specific configuration.

- **TIFF** — The Tagged Image File Format designed by Microsoft and Aldus for use with scanners and desktop publishing programs. Most external viewers support this format.

- **JPEG** — A bitmap format with compression that was designed and named after the Joint Photographic Experts Group. JPEG isn't used as often as the other formats, but it is the basis for the most common moving image format, MPEG. In addition, the newest browser on the block, Netscape, now offers support for inline JPEG images.

- **Other Image Formats** — Several other image formats that are usually platform-specific. Unless you know that your audience will be limited to a specific platform, limit your graphics images to the above formats.

- **PostScript** — A document display language that originated from the need to display and print high-quality documents. Almost all platforms can print PostScript, but there are some holes in the ability to display PostScript.

- **PDF** — The format used for Adobe® Acrobat™ documents. Acrobat uses hypertext links within a document in a way similar to that in HTML. Version 2.0 Acrobat products also support links between documents. Acrobat viewers are only now being developed for many UNIX platforms.

- **MPEG** — An animated video standard format based on the JPEG methods. Like JPEG, the format received its name from the group that defined the standard, Motion Picture Experts Group. This is the most common movie format for WWW, primarily because viewers exist for all platforms.

- **AVI** — The movie format for Microsoft Windows. Use of this format isn't recommended until browsers for other platforms become common.

- **Basic Sound** — A sound that evolved on UNIX systems. There is a sound player for almost every platform. When in doubt of the audience, use this format.

- **WAV** — The sound files for Microsoft Windows. As with the AVI format, use of this format isn't recommended currently.

Adding Multimedia Links

A multimedia link doesn't look much different than a text link. The important thing to remember is to name the referenced file properly. The file should have an extension that declares what type of file it is. For example, if it is a GIF or GIF-89 type of file, the name would be *filename*.`gif`. Microsoft Windows servers can serve only files with a 3-character extension. Other platforms don't have this restriction. Table 4-1 lists common filename extensions for standard MIME types and the abbreviations for 3-character extensions where needed.

4

Table 4-1   Filename Extensions for MIME Types

MIME Type	Standard Extensions	3-Character/DOS Extensions
PostScript	.eps .ps	
Sound/Au (Basic)	.au .snd	
Sound/Wave	.wav	
Image/Gif	.gif	
Image/Jpeg	.jpeg	.jpg .jpe
Image/Tiff	.tiff	.tif
Text/HTML	.html	.htm
Video/Mpeg	.mpeg	.mpg .mpe
Video/AVI	.avi	

The link itself is a standard anchor with reference. An example is:

```
<a href="http://system/dir/file.gif/"> Some Image </a>
```

or

```
<a href="http://system/dir/file.mpeg/"> Some Movie </a>
```

1. **Load** `http://{system}/Chapter4/image1.html`.
   This document contains a link to a picture.

2. **Pull down the File menu and select View Source.**
   Notice that the only difference between a text link and the image link is the extension at the end of the name.

3. **Click on the link** Some Image.
   Notice that the image is downloaded; then, an external viewer is started to display the image.

Inline Images

All the external images, sounds, and movies that you add to your documents require an external viewer. GIF images can also be incorporated into the web page itself. By addition of images to the text, a web page resembles real books and documents.

Note – Specific browsers can incorporate other image types. However, GIF images are the only image type that can be viewed by all browsers, so stick to GIF.

70   *HTML for Fun and Profit*

Design Considerations

Some people feel that a document is not complete without a picture or two. Since a large percentage of the users do have image-capable browsers, this expectation isn't unreasonable. However, it is important to consider the audience when designing a web page. Clients with a slow connection, such as SLIP or PPP at 14.4K, don't like to download images because they take more time to load than the text.

Many of the browsers, including all versions of Mosaic, allow the user to delay image loading until it is convenient for them. Additionally, the browser will also supply a generic image if there is a problem with the image. The images shown in Figure 4-1 serve as placeholders for a delay image loading and as an image that was attempted but failed to be loaded.

Figure 4-1   Common Filler Images

Not all users are aware of the delay image-loading feature, and the filler images don't really add anything to a web page. If your audience isn't likely to load the images or if it will take more than a few seconds to load the images, keep them to a minimum or omit them entirely.

The standard bullets used in lists and horizontal line are pretty boring. Customized horizontal lines and colored bullets can be used to spruce up a page. However, when the images are delayed, the page layout can change. A custom horizontal rule will stretch across the page, whereas the filler image will not do so. If the average user is going to delay image loading, your customized page will not have the same impact.

An example of this philosophy is the Sun home page. Sun's clientele tend to be companies that already have significant network connections. Thus, their home page has quite a few images, as shown in Figure 4-2.

Figure 4-2   Sun Home Page

If the audience were primarily users with slow connections and delay image loading enabled, then the same image would look like Figure 4-3.

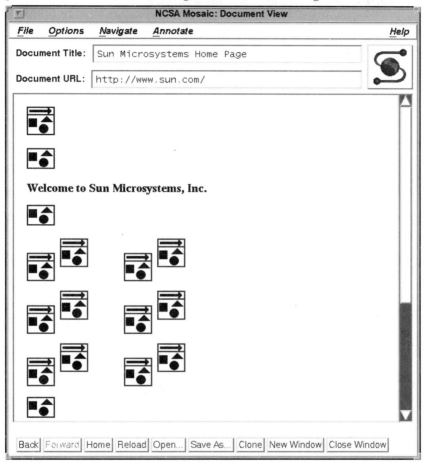

Figure 4-3   Sun Home Page with Delay Image Loading Enabled

The audience is the primary consideration when designing a page!!

Adding an Inline Image

An inline image is placed on a page with the <IMG> tag. The SRC=*href* attribute is required. An example of this is:

```
<IMG SRC="http://{system}/Chapter4/earth.gif">
```

1. **Load** http://{*system*}/Chapter4/iimage1.html.

2. **View the HTML source with File->View Source.**
   The page here has only one item, the inline image. Notice that when the image doesn't fill the line, text following the image is placed next to it.

3. **Load** http://{*system*}/Chapter4/iimage2.html.
   Notice that different alignment is specified for each image and notice how the text is laid out.

Images will be laid out side-by-side if there is space to accommodate them. To force an image to start below the previous one, start a new paragraph with the <P> tag.

Aligning an Image

In the previous example, the image took up only about half of the screen horizontally. Text showed up to the right of the image. The text started at the bottom of the image. The alignment of the first line of text can be changed by adding the ALIGN attribute with one of three options: top, middle, bottom. An example of this is:

```
<IMG ALIGN=top SRC="http://{system}/Chapter4/earth.gif">
```

The one problem with using alignments other than bottom is that only the first line of text is affected. All text after the first line appears under the image. Add the following step to the preceding ones:

4. **Load** http://{*system*}/Chapter4/iimage4.html.
   Notice that the text starts where the alignment is specified for each image, but the second line of text always starts at the bottom of the image.

Alternatives to Images

A few text-based browsers, for example, Lynx, cannot display the image. An attribute to the <IMG> tag, called ALT, accommodates these systems. The ALT attribute defines a text string to be put in place of the image for text-only browsers. Although there is some discussion of making graphical browsers use the ALT value instead of displaying a generic image for delayed image-loading, this requirement has not yet been implemented. An example of the use of this attribute is:

```
<IMG ALT="earth" SRC="http://{system}/Chapter4/earth.gif">
```

Another alternative is to create two sets of documents: one set with images and one without. Then, on the home page, you can offer the user the option of browsing with or without images. If you offer the choice of running without images, don't make references into pages with images. The user-specified preference should be respected.

Creating Transparent Backgrounds

By use of the transparent color definition used in GIF89A files, an image can appear to float above the web page. Transparent images are used in web pages in the same manner as regular inline images. The only difference is that the image needs to be processed so that it has a transparent color.

GIF images use a colormap or list of color values to manage the colors in an image. GIF images have a section in the header that identifies the number of colors in the colormap, and then goes on to list the RGB values for each color. For example, if the image had 256 colors, the header would have a table of 256 RGB values, even if the image used only 12 unique colors. Different programs use different methodologies for determining which colormap entry should be used for the transparent color. giftrans (UNIX and MS-DOS) can either take an index number in the colormap table and transform it to the transparent color or change a specific RGB value.

Note – A specific color is created on the screen by specification of a value for the amount of red in that color, the amount of blue, and the amount of green. For example, there is no red in black, so the red value is 0. The same applies to green and blue. Therefore, the RGB value is #000. The # sign indicates that the value is in hexadecimal, not decimal, notation.

In /{*Document_Root*}/Examples/Chapter4 is neat.gif. This is a fractal whose black background is a good candidate for conversion to a transparent background. However, the color black is not isolated to one cell of the colormap; it exists in 17 different colormap slots. Therefore, a program that changes the background by specific color would be a more optimal solution than changing the colormap slot by slot.

4

Setting Transparent Background by Color

A transparent color is defined with giftrans by defining the RGB value of the color in the -t option, using # to start the color definition. The -o option specifies a new output filename so that you don't write over your work in progress. It is a good idea to avoid writing over your work files. An example of using giftrans is:

```
giftrans -t #000 -o new.gif neat.gif
```

Setting Transparent Background by Colormap Cell

A transparent cell is defined with giftrans by defining the cell number of the color in the -t option. An example of this is:

```
giftrans -t 0 -o new2.gif neat.gif
```

Listing the Colormap of an Image

A list of the current color values can be obtained by using the -l option of giftrans.

```
giftrans -l new.gif
```

Adding Links to Images to Simulate Buttons

An inline image can be anchored just like text. Then, when the user clicks on the image, a new web page is brought up, giving the appearance of having buttons. An example of this is:

```
<a href="new.gif"> <img src="small_new.gif"> </a>
```

Summary

In this chapter, you learned about:

- MIME types — Several file formats can be used on multiple platforms to make web pages truly multimedia.

- Adding multimedia links — The only difference between links to other text and links to pictures, sounds, and images is that the pictures, sounds, and images will be downloaded and displayed on external viewers.

- Adding inline images — GIF images can be incorporated into the document itself.

- Creating transparent backgrounds — Images can appear to float on the web page by changing a color in the colormap to be transparent.

New Tags Used in This Chapter

Tag	Attribute	Description and Notes
<IMG>		Incorporates images in a document.
	SRC	The href for the image.
	ALIGN	Text can be aligned to start at the top, middle, or bottom of the side of an image.
	ALT	A name that can be displayed on browsers that don't have image capabilities.

4

Tables 5

The last few chapters covered HTML topics that have been around long enough to be officially included in the HTML 2.0 specifications. Tables, on the other hand, are a new feature that hasn't yet been formalized. Tables are the one area of formatting that is needed to make HTML a true publishing medium. For this reason, tables are included here, even in their infancy.

This chapter covers the basics of making tables, using the latest version of XMosaic and the new HTML 3.0 browser, Arena. Several proposed but not-yet-implemented items are also discussed. This chapter is about an evolving feature, so don't expect it to be completely factual for future releases of software.

Table Components

Only a few tags are common to all current table implementations. However, these tags are enough to make up simple tables.

- Tables are defined with the <TABLE> and </TABLE> tags.

- A table is made up of *cells* of data. A cell is defined by the *table data* <TD> and </TD> tags.

- The cells are grouped into rows with the *table row* <TR> tag. In some cases, the closing </TR> tag is used as well, but the most common use is the <TR> tag by itself.

The markup for a basic table is shown in HTML Example 5-1:

HTML Example 5-1 Table Markup Tags

```
<TABLE>
<td> a Column</td>
<td> another Column </td>
<td> yet another Column </td>
<tr>
<td> a Column </td>
```

HTML Example 5-1 Table Markup Tags (Continued)

```
<td> another Column </td>
<td> yet another Column </td>
</table>
```

Figure 5-1 shows the basic table rendered by the Arena and Mosaic browsers.

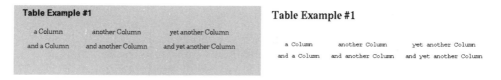

Figure 5-1   Basic Table in Arena (left) and Mosaic 2.5b2 (right) table1.html

Table Borders

In the table shown above, no lines separate the cells. In this case, there is plenty of space on a page, so the columns are well defined. In cases where it is important to visually segregate the data, the BORDER attribute can be added to the <TABLE> tag to add a border around each cell of the table. The full tag looks like:

HTML Example 5-2 Border Tag

```
<TABLE BORDER>
```

Figure 5-2 shows the result.

Table Example #2		
a Column	another Column	yet another Column
and a Column	and another Column	and yet another Column

Table Example #2		
a Column	another Column	yet another Column
and a Column	and another Column	and yet another Column

Figure 5-2 · Table with Borders in Arena (left) and Mosaic 2.5b2 (right) - table2.html

Table Headings

Headings were created to provide a different font for titles. This method has
continued with the creation of *table heading* cells, <TH> and </TH>. Table heading
cells act the same as table data cells in every other way. Ideally, table headings
will be in a different font than that for table data. An example of this is:

HTML Example 5-3 Table Heading Tag

```
<table border>
<th> a Column </th>
<th> another Column </th>
<th> yet another Column </th>
<tr>
<td> a Column </td>
<td> another Column </td>
<td> yet another Column </td>
</table>
```

Figure 5-3 shows the result.

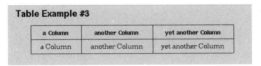

Figure 5-3   Table Heading Example in Arena - table3.html

Spanning Columns

In all the tables examined so far, each row has the same number of cells and thus
the same number of columns. The COLSPAN={*number*} attribute changes the
number of columns that a cell covers or spans. This attribute can be used on both
the <TD> and <TH> tags. An example of this is:

HTML Example 5-4 Cell Column-Spanning Attribute

```
<table border>
<th> a Column </th>
<th> another Column </th>
<th colspan=2> yet another Column </th>
<tr>
```

HTML Example 5-4 Cell Column-Spanning Attribute (Continued)

```
<td> a Column </td>
<td> another Column </td>
<td> yet another Column </td>
<td> yet another Column </td>
</table>
```

In this case, the heading has two, single-wide cells and a double-wide cell (COLSPAN=2), for a total of four cells wide. The next line down has four single-wide cells, also for a width of four cells. Figure 5-4 shows the resulting table.

Table Example #4			
a Column	another Column	yet another Column	
a Column	another Column	yet another Column	yet another Column

Table Example #4

a Column	another Column	yet another Column	
a Column	another Column	yet another Column	yet another Column

Figure 5-4   Spanning Columns with Arena (left) and Mosaic 3.5b2 (right) - table4.html

Spanning Rows

Just as a cell can be more than one column wide, it can also be more than one row high. The ROWSPAN={*number*} attribute to <TD> and <TH> tags accomplishes this. An example is:

HTML Example 5-5 Cell Row-Spanning Attribute

```
<table border>
<th rowspan=2> a Column </th>
<th> another Column </th>
<th> yet another Column </th>
<tr>
<th> another Column </th>
<th> yet another Column </th>
<tr>
<td> a Column </td>
<td> another Column </td>
<td> yet another Column </td>
</table>
```

In this case, the first column is two rows high; the second column is one row high; then, a new row is started. The new row starts in the second column, as shown in Figure 5-5.

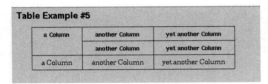

Table Example #5

a Column	another Column	yet another Column
	another Column	yet another Column
a Column	another Column	yet another Column

Figure 5-5   Spanning Rows with Arena (left) and Mosaic 2.5b2 (right) - table5.html

Counting Rows and Columns

It may seem unusual to count rows and columns, as was done in the two previous examples, but at this stage, it is necessary. A browser counts the number of columns in each row and uses the largest number that it gets when creating a table. If there is an additional cell on one row, as the <TD> line noted in bold in the following example, the entire table could be distorted.

HTML Example 5-6 Uneven Columns and Rows

```
<table border>
<th rowspan=2> a Column </th>
<th> another Column </th>
<th> yet another Column </th>
<tr>
<th> another Column </th>
<th> yet another Column </th>
<tr>
<td> a Column </td>
<td> another Column </td>
<td> yet another Column </td>
<td> yet another Column </td>
<tr>
</table>
```

Since the data row has one more cell than the heading rows, the table looks like that shown in Figure 5-6.

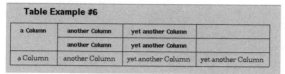

Table Example #6

a Column	another Column	yet another Column	
	another Column	yet another Column	
a Column	another Column	yet another Column	yet another Column

Figure 5-6   Sample of Unequal Columns in Arena (left) and Mosaic 2.5b2 (right) - table6.html

Notice one additional thing in the examples above. The table has a <TR> tag at the end, also noted in bold. On the Mosaic browser, this tag created an additional blank row. For consistency, do not finish a table with a <TR> tag.

Features in Transition

Some features aren't commonly implemented across browsers yet.

Word Wrapping

There has been very little text in each cell in the previous examples. Controlling word wrapping within columns is still new. The following example demonstrates how each browser does column layout when it must wrap the words.

HTML Example 5-7 Long Lines in a Table

```
<h1> Table Example #7 </h1>

<table border>
<td> This is a long set of table data to show how to make a page
that has 3 columns of text like a newspaper. </td>
<td> This column has very little data here. </td>
<td> This column will be longer than either the first or second
It will show that the 3 columns will end up
being the same height and have different widths. </td>
</table>
```

Figure 5-7 shows examples of word wrapping.

Table Example #7

This is a long set of table data to show how to make a page that has 3 columns of text like a newspaper.	This column has very little data here.	This column will be longer than either the first or second It will show that the 3 columns will end up being the same height and have different widths.

Table Example #7

This is a long set of table data to show how to make a page that has 3 columns of text like a newspaper.	This column has very little data here.	This column will be longer than either the first or second It will show that the 3 columns will end up being the same height and have different widths.

Figure 5-7   Examples of Word Wrapping in Arena (left) and Mosaic 2.5b2 (right) - table8.html

Notice that the columns are not the same size. Browsers are designed to lay out text by measuring the size of the text and making the best fit. Currently, the only way to get columns of the same size is to use the same text.

in the following example, the NOWRAP attribute is used in <TD> and <TH> tags on the Arena browser to force the columns to different widths:

HTML Example 5-8 Controlling Line Breaks with NOWRAP

```
<h1> Table Example #8 </h1>

<table border>
<td> This is a long set of table data to show how to make a page
that has 3 columns of text like a newspaper. </td>
<td nowrap> This column has very little data here. </td>
<td> This column will be longer than either the first or second
It will show that the 3 columns will end up
being the same height and have different widths. </td>
</table>
```

This creates a table that looks like that shown in Figure 5-8.

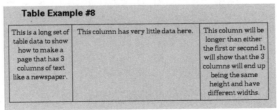

Figure 5-8   The NOWRAP Option in Arena

Using the NOWRAP option will not allow the browser to wrap the text at all. When you want to control where the words wrap, use the <BR> tag to force a new line.

Formatting Data in Cells

All the text in the examples above is left-justified on the Xmosaic example and centered on the Arena example. That is the default alignment for each browser. Alignment can be modified cell-by-cell with the ALIGN="*value*" attribute to the <TD> and <TH> tags. Alignment can be LEFT, RIGHT, or CENTER, as in the example below.

Code Example 5-9   Justifying the Text in Cells

```
<table border>
<td align="left"> This is a long set of table data to show how to
make a
page that has 3 columns of text like a newspaper. </td>
<td align="right"> This column has very little data here. </td>
<td> This column will be longer than either the first or second
It will show that the 3 columns will end up
being the same height and have different widths. </td>
</table>
```

Figure 5-9 shows the result.

Table Example #9		
This is a long set of table data to show how to make a page that has 3 columns of text like a newspaper.	This column has very little data here.	This column will be longer than either the first or second It will show that the 3 columns will end up being the same height and have different widths.

Figure 5-9   Justified Text

CENTER is the default display method for current browsers. Specifying CENTER may seem redundant now, but browsers aren't forced to use the same defaults. For a common appearance, specifically include ALIGN="CENTER."

Captions

Ideally, tables should have captions to label them. The <CAPTION> tag has been envisioned to fit this purpose, but at this time is not active.

Summary

In this chapter, you learned:

• How to make a table.

• How to make different-sized rows and columns.

• How to format the text within the cells.

Tags Used In This Chapter

Tag	Attribute	Description and Notes
`<TABLE>`		Defines the table.
	`BORDER`	Adds borders to separate rows and columns in tables.
`<TR>`		Marks the end/start of a table row.
`<TD>`		Encloses a cell of table data.
	`COLSPAN`	Modifies the number of columns a cell will span.
	`ROWSPAN`	Modifies the number of rows a cell will span.
	`ALIGN`	Defines the horizontal text alignment within a cell.
	`NOWRAP`	Declares that the cell text cannot be broken up to wrap from one line to the next.
`<TH>`		Encloses a cell of a table heading.
	`COLSPAN`	Modifies the number of columns a cell will span.
	`ROWSPAN`	Modifies the number of rows a cell will span.
	`ALIGN`	Defines the horizontal text alignment within a cell.
	`NOWRAP`	Declares that the cell text cannot be broken up to wrap from one line to the next.
`<CAPTION>`		Creates a title for the table, outside of the table.

5

HTML for Fun and Profit

Using the Common Gateway Interface (CGI) 6≡

Displaying information is a good start. However, it is even better to be able to customize the information that is sent to the client and to receive information from the client. The httpd daemon can execute scripts and programs on data that a client sends and can pass the results of these programs and scripts back to the client. Recently, external processing has been standardized with the Common Gateway Interface (CGI).

This chapter discusses how to configure CGI, basic CGI principles, and then demonstrates a CGI application, creating clickable imagemaps. The Macintosh server has three alternative programs for imagemap processing.

Platform Specifics

Scripting varies from platform to platform. For consistency, perl scripts are used for all script examples. To use the examples in this chapter, you must have perl installed on UNIX, Windows NT, Windows 3.1 and Macintosh systems.

UNIX

Since many of the concepts and methods evolved first on UNIX platforms, the UNIX methodology and terminology have become the de facto conventions. All exceptions to the UNIX conventions are noted.

Windows NT

All the examples in the documentation included with https use the name scripts for the directory that stores executable files. To retain commonality among platforms, this book uses cgi-bin as the directory.

The `https` server executes only programs with the `.exe` extension that are not GUI-based. Uncompiled batch files cannot be used. Run perl scripts by executing the `perl.exe` program and specifying the script name. When an executable program, such as `perl.exe` is called, the directory path for the script starts with the directory that the executable is in. Figure 6-1 illustrates an example.

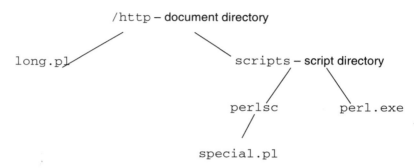

Figure 6-1   Example Directory Path for Perl Script Execution

In Figure 6-1, the `perl.exe` program resides in `/http/scripts`. It can execute other perl scripts found in `/http/scripts`. It can also execute perl scripts in the `/http/scripts/perlsc` directory. It cannot execute scripts found in the `/http` directory.

Note – Some features, such as file access control, long filenames, and some WAIS capabilities, can be employed only in an NTFS partition. Use of NTFS is recommended; the examples in this book are based on NTFS use.

Macintosh

The Macintosh server directly processes only AppleScript™ scripts. To enable the use of perl scripts, an AppleScript-to-perl interface, called PCGI, is used. MacPerl and the PCGI interface are currently being updated; download the new version of these tools from the location specified in Appendix E, *More Information.*

Configuring for CGI Use

Before running CGI scripts, your system must be configured to execute programs and the scripts and `perl` must be installed.

Configuration for UNIX `httpds`

With both UNIX httpd programs, any directory that will contain executable scripts and programs must be defined in the configuration file(s). Also, the scripts must be copied to the server and modified to reflect the path to `perl`.

Making a Directory Executable

- **NCSA** `httpd` **server** — For security, the `httpd` daemon is restricted to executing programs and scripts only in specific directories. These directories are defined by the *ScriptAlias* directive in the `srm.conf` configuration file. To make directories or directory trees where executable scripts and programs can reside, add the following line to the `srm.conf` file.

  ```
  ScriptAlias /cgi-bin/ /usr/local/WWW/cgi-bin/
  ```

- **CERN** `httpd` **server** — For security, the `httpd` daemon is restricted to executing programs and scripts only in specific directories. These directories are defined by the *Exec* directive in the directory mapping area in the `httpd.conf` configuration file. The *Exec* directive acts similarly to the *Pass* or *Fail* directives, in that directory substitution ceases and the path is processed if the *Exec* directive makes a match. To make directories or directory trees where executable scripts and programs can reside, add the following line to the `httpd.conf` file.

  ```
  Exec /cgi-bin/ /usr/local/WWW/cgi-bin/*
  ```

Installing the Scripts

If you didn't create and populate a `cgi-bin` directory in Chapter 1, do so now. If you previously created a `cgi-bin` directory, start with Step 5.

1. **Change to the** `/usr/local/WWW` **directory (or to whatever you named it).**

   ```
   cd /usr/local/WWW
   ```

2. **Make a directory called** `cgi-bin` **(or whatever you intend to call your scripts directory) and change to it.**

   ```
   mkdir cgi-bin
   cd cgi-bin
   ```

3. **Mount the CD-ROM.**

4. **Copy the UNIX script files to the newly created directory.**

   ```
   cp -rp {cdrom-mount point}:/{sol1 or sol2}/scripts/* .
   ```

5. **Copy** `perl` **to your common UNIX tools area (**`/usr/local/bin` **is used in this example).**

```
cp -rp {cdrom-mount point}:/{sol1 or sol2}/programs/perl
/usr/local/bin
```

6. **Edit the scripts in the** `cgi-bin` **directory.**
Modify the scripts to reflect the place in which you put the `perl` executable by changing

```
#!/opt/internet/bin/perl or #!/usr/local/bin/perl
```

to
    #!{path to perl}

Configuration for Windows NT `https`

Scripts can be run from `https` without specific server configuration. The `cgi-bin` directory must be created and populated with the scripts and programs from the CD-ROM. The following example assumes that you created your document area in `e:\http`.

Populating the `cgi-bin` Directory

1. **Change to the directory that was assigned to hold documents.**

```
e:
cd \http
```

2. **Make a directory called** `cgi-bin` **(or whatever you intend to call your scripts directory) and change to it.**

```
md cgi-bin
cd cgi-bin
```

3. **Load the CD-ROM.**

4. **Copy the Windows NT script files to the newly created directory.**

```
xcopy /s {cdrom-disk-letter}:\winnt\scripts\*.* .
```

5. **Copy the Windows NT perl program into the new scripts directory.**

```
xcopy {cdrom-disk-letter}:\winnt\programs\perl\*.* .
```

Unlike the case with UNIX-based servers, scripts and programs aren't isolated in specific directories to indicate that they are executable, so programs can be downloaded from the server. To prevent downloading, set the files to be execute-only with the following procedure.

▼ Setting Permissions on Files

Note – This procedure works only if the files are on an NTFS file system.

1. **Open** `FileManager` **as administrator.**
2. **Select the file(s) to be protected.**
3. **Pull down the** Security **menu.**
4. **Select** Permissions **from this menu.**
5. **In the dialog box, select the user that you defined to use with the** `https` **server.**
   The original instructions used the Guest account.
6. **Pull down the** Type of Access **menu and select** Special Access.
7. **Select** Execute[X] **and click on** OK.
8. **Select all other users and groups listed in the** File Permissions **pop-up window.**
9. **Set these users and groups to** No Access.

Configuration for the Macintosh `httpd`

The `httpd` program for the Macintosh interfaces directly with the AppleScript facilities of System 7. The configuration requires adding the scripting extensions to the appropriate folder and setting up MacPerl.

Adding Scripting Capabilities

1. **Insert the CD-ROM.**
2. **Open the** `program` **folder found in the** `mac` **folder on the CD-ROM.**
3. **Open the** `Apple's Scripting System` **folder found in the** `MacHTTP 1.3` **folder under the** `program` **folder on the CD-ROM.**
4. **Open the** `For Extensions folder` **folder.**

6

5. Open the `System` **folder on the Macintosh hard disk.**

6. Open the `Extensions` **folder found inside the** `System` **folder.**

7. **Drag the** `AppleScript` **icon from the** `For Extensions folder` **folder to the** `Extensions` **folder.**

8. **Drag the** `Frontmost Extension` **icon from the** `For Extensions folder` **folder to the** `Extensions` **folder.**

9. **Drag the** `Scripting Additions folder` **from the** `For Extensions folder` **folder to the** `Extensions` **folder.**

10. **Download the latest MacPerl and PCGI from the Internet.**

11. **Uncompress both archives.**

12. **Restart the system and rebuild the desktop.**

Note – When editing perl scripts, use the editor that comes with `MacPerl`, choose Save As, and specify MacHTTP CGI Script as the file type when saving.

CGI Basics

When a server parses a URL that it receives and determines that the URL is in the executable directory, the URL is passed to the CGI for execution. On UNIX systems, I/O is a simple affair. The standard input (stdin) and standard output (stdout) are used for I/O. On Microsoft Windows 3.1, Windows NT, and Macintosh systems, a similar I/O system is used.

One key item must be at the beginning of the output: the Content-type definition.

Substitute the path you configured above for the `cgi-bin` *path* in the examples below.

I/O Basics in CGI Scripts

1. **Load:**
   UNIX and Macintosh: `http://{server}/cgi-bin/date.pl/`

   Windows NT: `http://{server}/cgi-bin/perl.exe?date.bin`

   The current date and time on the server are returned in a fixed-width font. You can use the View Source option on the File menu to examine the entire output.

2. **Examine the file** */cgi-bin-path/*`date.pl` **with a text editor or with** `more`.
When executed, this script obtains the current date and time and displays
them. No output device is mentioned. When the destination is not defined, the
results of the script are passed directly back to the `httpd` and forwarded to the
requesting client.

3. **Load:**
UNIX and Macintosh: `http://{server}/cgi-bin/datenone.pl/`

Windows NT: `http://{server}/cgi-bin/perl.exe?datenone.pl`

Instead of the date, an error message is received.

4. **Examine the file** */cgi-bin-path/*`datenone.pl` **with text editor or with** `more`.
The only difference between the `datenone.pl` and the `date.pl` script is the
following line, found in the `date.pl` script:

```
print "Content-type: text/plain \n";
```

It is important to return the Content-type line before the data. The server has
problems with data when it doesn't know how to return that data to the client.

Environment Variables

A part of any scripting language is the use of environment variables. The CGI
implementation provides several preconfigured variables which vary slightly
from server to server. Refer to Table 6-1 on page 102 for a list of environment
variables for the platform.

5. **Load:**
UNIX and Macintosh: `http://{server}/cgi-bin/test-cgi.pl/`

Windows NT: `http://{server}/cgi-bin/perl.exe?test-cgi.bin`

This file displays all the environment variables and the initial values of each
variable.

Path Usage

The path of the `cgi-bin` script is important. The script need not necessarily be in
the root of the `cgi-bin` directory.

The URL that calls a CGI script or program may be longer than the path to the
script itself. This additional path information is stored in the `PATH_INFO` variable
and can be used by the script.

For example, in the URL —

```
http://{server}/cgi-bin/directory/script/additional/
```

— **http://{server}/cgi-bin** indicates that the remainder of the path is an executable program.

— **directory** is examined to see if it is a script or program to run. Since it is neither, it is examined to see if it is a directory, which it is. The CGI looks for script in the directory, directory.

— **script** is then examined to see if it is a script or program to run. Since it is a script, everything after script, namely additional, is placed into the PATH_INFO environment variable, and script is executed.

On Windows NT, the path is slightly different. In the example —

```
http://{server}/cgi-bin/perldir/perl.exe?scriptdir/script
/additional/
```

— **http://{server}/cgi-bin** indicates that the remainder of the path is an executable program.

— **perldir** is examined to see if it is a script or program to run. Since it is the perl program, the question mark follows it, and the examination process begins again for the string after the question mark.

— **scriptdir** is examined to see if it is a script or program to run. Since it is neither, it is examined to see if it is a directory, which it is. The CGI looks for script in the directory, directory.

— **script** is then examined to see if it is a script or program to run. Since it is a script, everything after script, namely additional, is placed into the PATH_INFO environment variable, and script is executed.

6. **Load:**
   UNIX and Macintosh: `http://{server}/cgi-bin/testing/test-cgi.pl/`

   Windows NT: `http://{server}/cgi-bin/perl.exe?testing/test-cgi.bin`

   Notice that scripts can be executed anywhere within the directory structure that has been defined as executable. Thus, scripts can be segregated to keep from being overwhelmed.

7. Load:

UNIX and Macintosh: `http://{server}/cgi-bin/test-cgi.pl/testing`

Windows NT: `http://{server}/cgi-bin/perl.exe?test-cgi.bin/testing`

In this case, the script is found at the top level. The path information after the command is still retained (`testing/`) and assigned to the `PATH_INFO` variable. This information can be used to call html files for customization before returning them to the client.

Passing Variables or Arguments

Variable information can be appended to the end of the URL and thus passed into the CGI script.

8. Load:

UNIX and Macintosh: `http://{server}/cgi-bin/test-cgi.pl?testing`

Windows NT: `http://{server}/cgi-bin/perl.exe?test-cgi.bin`

`http://{server}/cgi-bin/test-cgi.pl?testing`

In this case, the word "testing" becomes a command- line argument to the script. This information appears in both the `ARGV` data and in the variable `QUERY_STRING`. The question mark (?) originally indicated that the text after it was a query. Use of the question mark is now expanded for use by any CGI script.

9. Load:

UNIX and Macintosh: `http://{server}/cgi-bin/test-cgi.pl?testing+test1`

Windows NT: `http://{server}/cgi-bin/perl.exe?test-cgi.bin?testing+test1`

In this case, the `QUERY_STRING` variable appears to look the same as the input after the question mark. However, the `ARGV` line treats this as two arguments and places a space between them. The plus (+) character places spaces between strings.

10. Load:

UNIX and Macintosh: `http://{server}/cgi-bin/test-cgi.pl/?testing%2btest1`

Windows NT: `http://{server}/cgi-bin/perl.exe?test-cgi.bin?testing%2btest1`

In this case, there is only one argument, and it includes the + sign—2b is the ASCII equivalent of the + character. Because the ASCII value is used with a % sign in front of it, the + sign is carried through.

Another character that has special meaning in `QUERY_STRING` is the % character. The % character as used above returns the ASCII equivalent of a character that cannot be returned directly.

Note – Additional parsing items of note are covered in *Basic CGI Input and Output* in Chapter 9, *Processing Data From Forms*, where they are used.

Making Clickable Images

Pictures often contain interesting items whose information content is obtainable by clicking on the item. Such an image is called a *clickable image* and can be implemented with the CGI scripts. Clickable images are created by defining regions such as squares, circles, and other polygons around an item in the image. The coordinates of each region are then associated with a URL in a configuration file specific to that image, called an *imagemap*. On UNIX systems only, each imagemap file is then listed in a master image configuration file.

Note – Use `http://{server}/Chapter8/getpoints.html/` to determine the boundary values for your image regions. It is currently set up to use the image in the exercise below. Modify it with the name of your image and use it to obtain coordinates for images other than the example below. This page returns an *x,y* pair for each spot that you click on. Then, click on the Back button to return to the image to get values for the next point.

Steps in Making a Clickable Image

▼ Get a GIF image

The image must be in GIF format.

▼ Get coordinates of special areas.

1. **Load** `http://{server}/Chapter8/getpoints.html/`.
   For our example we will use the image `/Chapter6/web16.gif`. This image is loaded now.

   The first region to define is a square region around the dollar sign.

2. **Click on the upper left corner of the square with the dollar sign in it.**
   The x and y coordinates of the point that you selected are displayed on the screen. An example is:

Results Example 6-1 Coordinates for the Square Region

Query Results
You submitted the following name/value pairs:

X=456
y=87

The numbers that you get may be slightly different from the ones shown here. You are selecting a specific pixel in the image. On some screens you may not be precisely at the same spot.

3. **Record these numbers and then click on the Back button.**
   You still need to select one more point to define the square region.

4. **Select the lower right corner of the square with the dollar sign in it.**
   A square can be described by two points, upper left and lower right or upper right and lower left.

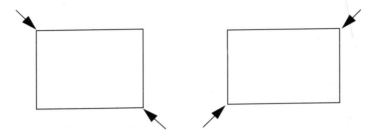

5. **Record these numbers and then click on the** Back **button.**
   You have the coordinates for the square.

A circle is defined by two points as well: the center point and a point anywhere along the edge of the circle.

6. **Click on the center of the circle.**
   The x and y coordinates of the point that you selected are displayed on the screen.

7. **Record these numbers and then click on the** Back **button.**
   You need to select one more point to define the square region.

8. **Select a point anywhere on the edge of the circle.**

A polygon is a shape with n points defining the edges. For example, a triangle is a polygon with three points defining the edges.

9. **Click on a point on the triangle.**
   Record these numbers and then click on the Back button.

   You need to select two more points to define the triangle region.

10. **Click on a second point on the triangle.**
    Record these numbers and then click on the Back button.

11. **Click on a third point on the triangle.**
    Record these numbers.

▼ **Make the imagemap file.**

The imagemap file will contain one line to define each area that is to be active. It will also contain a definition for default, so that the program won't fail if the user clicks outside of all defined regions. If the regions overlap, then the one that is defined first in the imagemap file is returned. An example is:

Code Example 6-2   Imagemap Specification

```
# Comments are indicated with a # sign
default    http://{system}/imagedefault.html
rectangle http://{system}/imagesquare.html 456,87510,54
circle     http://{system}/imagecircle.html222,46261,18
polygon    http://{system}/imagetriangle.html420,2233,8233,18
```

▼ **Make or add to the** imagemap.conf **file.**

This file goes in different directories for each UNIX server and doesn't exist for Windows NT servers. Specify the full pathname to the imagemap file, *not to the* httpd *modified path.* As with the imagemap file, use # to comment out text.

▼ **Create the HTML documents that are designated in the imagemap file.**

▼ **Create the HTML document that calls the** imagemap **program.**

To define an image to be a clickable image, create the image with the <IMG SRC=path> definition and surrounded with an anchor, just as when you converted an image to a button in Chapter 4, *Multimedia—Going Beyond Text.* There are two differences between creating that button and creating a clickable image.

- The anchor tag has an additional attribute, called ISMAP.
- The URL in the anchor points to the imagemap program for UNIX servers and to the imagemap file itself for the Windows NT server.

A UNIX example looks like:

Code Example 6-3   Creating a Clickable Image in UNIX Systems

```
<a href=http://{system}/cgi-bin/imagemap/demo>
<img src=http://Chapter8/web16.gif ismap>
</a>
```

In UNIX, the anchor should be a link to the `imagemap` program with the *name of the imagemap* after the `imagemap` command, so that it shows up in the `PATH_INFO` environment variable.

A Windows NT server example looks like:

Code Example 6-4   Creating a Clickable Image in Windows NT Systems

```
<a href=http://{system}/demo.map ISMAP>
<img src=http://Chapter6/web16.gif>
</a>
```

On a Windows NT system, the anchor references the imagemap file itself. The call to the `imagemap` program is not used.

Summary

In this chapter you learned:

• It is important to return a definition of the data that is coming back. Many browsers experience errors when the Content Type isn't defined.

Environment Variables

Note: Macintosh variables have different names in some cases. The new name is noted.

Table 6-1   Environment Variables on Various Platforms

Variable Name	NCSA	CERN	https	MacHTTP
AUTH_TYPE	Yes	Yes	No	No
CONTENT_TYPE	Yes	Yes	Yes	Yes
CONTENT_LENGTH	Yes	Yes	Yes	No

Table 6-1   Environment Variables on Various Platforms   (Continued)

Variable Name	NCSA	CERN	https	MacHTTP
DOCUMENT_ROOT	Yes	No	No	No
DOCUMENT_URI	Yes	No	No	No
DOCUMENT_NAME	Yes	No	No	No
DATE_LOCAL	Yes	No	No	No
DATE_GMT	Yes	No	No	No
GATEWAY_INTERFACE	Yes	Yes	Yes	No
HTTP_ACCEPT	No	Yes	Yes	No
LAST_MODIFIED	Yes	No	No	No
PATH_INFO	Yes	Yes	Yes	No
PATH_TRANSLATED	Yes	No	No	No
PATH	Yes	No	No	Yes
POST	No	No	No	Yes – equivalent to stdin
QUERY_STRING	Yes	Yes	Yes	No
QUERY_STRING_UNESCAPED	Yes	No	No	No
REMOTE_HOST	Yes	Yes	No	No
REMOTE_ADDR	Yes	Yes	Yes	address
REQUEST_METHOD	Yes	No	Yes	method
REMOTE_USER	Yes	Yes	No	user
REMOTE_IDENT	Yes	Yes	No	No
SEARCH	No	No	No	Yes
SERVER_PROTOCOL	Yes	Yes	Yes	No
SERVER_SOFTWARE	Yes	Yes	Yes	No
SERVER_NAME	Yes	Yes	Yes	Yes
SERVER_PORT	Yes	Yes	Yes	Yes
SERVER_ROOT	Yes	No	No	No
SCRIPT_NAME	Yes	Yes	Yes	Yes

6

HTML for Fun and Profit

Server Includes

Additional files, the contents of variables, and volatile information such as the modification date of any local HTML document can be included in a document returned by the server. This feature is called Server Includes or Server Side Includes. The current software supports only Server Includes with some UNIX-based `http` servers.

Server Includes are handy tools that can be used for a variety of purposes. However, they do incur more overhead than serving a plain HTML file. They should be used judiciously. In addition, Server Includes use the SGML comment line together with the # character to indicate the Server Include command to be processed. Comments should be used without the # sign to avoid confusion.

Configuring for Server Includes

The following instructions are for configuring the NCSA `httpd` server.

Configuring a New MIME Type

First, define the MIME type `text/x-server-parsed-html`. This MIME type indicates that a document uses Server Includes. To define this type, add the following line to the *ServerRoot*/`conf/srm.conf` file under the `AddType` comments.

```
AddType text/x-server-parsed-html .shtml
```

The most common extension is `.shtml`, as listed above. This extension is used for all examples in this chapter. Since every document with this extension will be examined for Server Include tags, it is a good idea to use this extension *only* for documents with Server Includes. If you were to configure the extension above to be `.html`, then every HTML document would be examined for Server Includes before the page was returned to the browser. That process would cause needless load on a server and so is not recommended.

7

Configuring Directory Permissions

Next, directory trees that are authorized to use Server Includes must be defined. There are two levels of permission for Server Includes, include and execution. The include level allows the web page to add additional information to the page. The execution level actually allows a script or program to run and includes the results. Since programs and scripts can be dangerous, it is a good idea to limit the web pages that have the execution permission. This is accomplished by adding one of the following sets of lines to the *ServerRoot*/conf/access.conf file. These definitions with other options should already exist for the *DocumentRoot* and *ServerRoot* directory structures. Add additional directory definitions below those two definitions.

Code Example 7-1   Configuring Directory Permissions

```
      <Directory directory_name>
      Options Includes
      </Directory>
  Or
      <Directory directory_name>
      Options IncludesNoExec
      </Directory>
```

In the above example, `Includes` is used for directory trees that have permission to both include and execute. `IncludesNoExec` is used for the directory trees that can include but not execute.

Including Other Files

It's tiresome to keep updating several documents with changing information. With Server Includes, the volatile data can be kept in one file and the pages that use it can be kept in another. This is a good method of maintaining a "What's New" page.

A file is included in a document with the `<!--#INCLUDE>` tag and either the `VIRTUAL` or the `FILE` attribute. The `FILE` attribute gives the filename of a file relative to the original document. An example of this is:

```
      <!--#INCLUDE FILE="earth.gif">
```

The `VIRTUAL` attribute defines a file relative to *DocumentRoot*. An example of this is:

```
      <!--#INCLUDE VIRTUAL="/Examples/Chapter7/earth.gif">
```

It would be nice to make a file for each news item and place the file in a directory as each item is created. The items could be deleted according to their age. Unfortunately, wildcards are not expanded in the `<!--#INCLUDE>` `ServerInclude`. To create this type of configuration, you will need to execute an external script. See *Executing Programs in Another Way* later in this chapter.

1. Load `http://{server}/Chapter7/siinc1.shtml`.

2. View the original file with a text editor or with the `more` **command.**
   The Server Include command is displayed here.

HTML Example 7-2 Including a File with the Virtual Attribute

```
<html> <head>
<title>    </title>
</head> <body>
<!-- this is a comment -->
This is a server include.<P>
<!--#include virtual="/Examples/Chapter11/include.html"--><P>
<address>

</address>
</body> </html>
```

3. View the HTML source with File->View Source.
   Notice that the form has regular text, without a Server Include instruction: The `httpd` daemon made the changes before returning the web page.

HTML Example 7-3 The HTML That the Browser Receives

```
<html> <head>
<title>    </title>
</head> <body>
<!-- this is a comment -->
This is a server include.<P>
<html> <head>
<title>    </title>
</head> <body>
<!-- this is a comment -->
This is the included text <P>
<address>

</address>
</body> </html>
```

7

4. Load `http://{server}/Chapter7/siinc2.shtml.`

5. View the original file with a text editor or `more`**.**
The same file was called with a different method, but the result is the same.

Adding Information About Files

When you are surfing on a slow connection, 14.4K, for example, it is really irritating to find that an interesting file turns out to take five minutes to download or is almost a year old. Place the size of a file or its modification date in the document that refers to it, so you can give people an idea of what to expect.

Adding File Sizes

The size of a specified file is listed in a document with the `<!--#FSIZE>` tag and either the `VIRTUAL` or the `FILE` attribute. As with the `<!--#INCLUDE>` tag, the `FILE` attribute gives the filename of a file relative to the original document. An example of this is:

```
<!--#FSIZE FILE="earth.gif">
```

The `VIRTUAL` attribute defines a file relative to *DocumentRoot*. An example of this is:

```
<!--#FSIZE VIRTUAL="/Examples/Chapter7/earth.gif">
```

1. Load `http://{server}/Chapter7/sisize1.shtml.`

2. View the original file with a text editor or with the `more` **command.**
The size is the same regardless of the method for referencing the file.

Changing Size Formats with `config`

In the examples above, the size is listed in Kbytes. There may be times when you want to change this formatting. The `<!--#CONFIG>` tag changes the formatting of the information returned from the `<!--#FSIZE>` tag. The `<!--#CONFIG>` tag must come before the Server Include tag on which it should modify the configuration.

The `SIZEFMT` attribute defines size formatting. It has two possible values: `BYTES`, which lists the size of the file in bytes; and `ABBREV`, which abbreviates the value to either Kbytes or Mbytes, depending on the size of the file. `ABBREV` is used by default.

```
<!--#CONFIG SIZEFMT="BYTES">
```

Or

```
<!--#CONFIG SIZEFMT="ABBREV">
```

1. Load `http://{server}/Chapter7/sisize2.shtml.`

> This is a server include.
>
> The size of include.hmtl is 142 bytes.
>
> The size of siinc2.shtml is 1K

2. View the original file with a text editor or with more.

HTML Example 7-4 Including and Formatting File Sizes

```
<html> <head>
<title>    </title>
</head> <body>
<!-- this is a comment -->
This is a server include.<P>
<!--#config sizefmt="bytes"-->
The size of include.hmtl is <!--#fsize file="include.html"-->
bytes.<P>
<!--#config sizefmt="abbrev"-->
The size of siinc2.shtml is <!--#fsize
virtual="/Examples/Chapter11/siinc2.shtml"-->
<address>

</address>
</body> </html>
```

Dating Document Changes

The last modification date of a specified file is listed in a document with the `<!--#FLASTMOD>` tag and either the `VIRTUAL` or the `FILE` attribute. As with the `<!--#INCLUDE>` tag, the `FILE` attribute gives the filename of a file relative to the original document. An example of this is:

```
<!--#FLASTMOD FILE="earth.gif">
```

The VIRTUAL attribute defines a file relative to *DocumentRoot,* the same way VIRTUAL is handled in the above two Server Includes. An example of this is:

```
<!--#FLASTMOD VIRTUAL="/Examples/Chapter7/earth.gif">
```

1. Load `http://{server}/Chapter7/sidate1.shtml.`

2. View the original file with a text editor or with more.
The date is returned for the file with both methods.

Changing Date Formats with config

In the examples above, the date is listed as *day-month-year-timeofday.* There may be times that you want to change this formatting. The <!--#CONFIG> tag changes the formatting of the information returned from the <!--#FLASTMOD> tag. The <!--#CONFIG> tag must come before the Server Include tag on which it should modify the configuration.

The TIMEFMT attribute changes date formatting. This format is very customizable because it relies on the strftime library on most UNIX systems. A percent sign and letter combination, such as %a, is used to indicate the date format. Some examples are:

```
<!--#CONFIG TIMEFMT="%a %b %e, %Y %l %M %S %p">
```

Code Example 7-5   Time and Date Formatting with TIMEFMT

%a is the abbreviated day of the week	%b is the abbreviated month name
%e is the day of the month	%Y is a four-digit year
%l is the hour (1-12 format)	%M is the minutes
%S is the seconds	%p is AM or PM

```
<!--#CONFIG TIMEFMT="%m/%d/%y %T %Z">
```

Use man strftime for a complete listing of the time format options.

Code Example 7-6   Time and Date Format Examples

%m is the number of the month	%d is the number of the day of the month
%y is the last two digits of the year	%T is the time on the system
%Z is the time zone	

1. Load `http://{server}/Chapter7/sidate2.shtml`.

> This is a server include.
>
> The modification date of include.hmtl is Sat Jul Sat Jul 09 15:37:09 1994
>
> The modification date of siinc2.shtml is Saturday

2. View the original file with a text editor or with more.
Notice the date format used in the Server Include tag.

HTML Example 7-7 Including and Formatting Dates

```
<html> <head>
<title>    </title>
</head> <body>
<!-- this is a comment -->
This is a server include.<P>
<!--#config timefmt="%a %b %c"-->
The modification date of include.hmtl is <!--#flastmod
file="include.html"--><P>
<!--#config timefmt="%A"-->
The modification date of siinc2.shtml is <!--#flastmod
virtual="/Examples/Chapter11/siinc2.shtml"-->
<address>

</address>
</body> </html>
```

Echoing Variables

Server Includes have access to all the environment variables that CGI has, and a few more. These variables can be included in a document with the `<!--#ECHO>` tag. The only attribute for this tag is VAR. An example is:

```
<!--#ECHO VAR="DOCUMENT_NAME">
```

1. Load `http://{server}/Chapter7/siecho1.shtml`.

2. View the original file with a text editor or with more.
Notice that the variable DOCUMENT_NAME is called here. This is a variable that isn't used with CGI.

3. Load `http://{server}/Chapter7/siecho2.shtml`.

This example lists the environment variables that can be used only with Server Includes.

HTML Example 7-8 Listing Environment Variables Used with Server Includes

```
<html> <head>
<title>    </title>
</head> <body>
<!-- this is a comment -->
This is a server include.<P>
Document Name: <!--#echo var="DOCUMENT_NAME"--><P>
Full Document Name: <!--#echo var="DOCUMENT_URI"--><P>
QueryString: <!--#echo var="QUERY_STRING_UNESCAPED"--><P>
Local Date: <!--#echo var="DATE_LOCAL"--><P>
Date (GMT): <!--#echo var="DATE_GMT"--><P>
Last modified on :<!--#echo var="LAST_MODIFIED"--><P>
<address>

</address>
</body> </html>
```

Executing Programs in Another Way

Scripts and programs can be run when an anchor to an executable file is accessed, when a form is submitted, and by using the Server Include tag, `<!--#EXEC>`. One advantage of using Server Includes is that more than one script can be run per page. One caveat about using Server Includes: Everything that is returned must have HTML formatting tags or it will be displayed as text formatted with `<PRE>`. There are two attributes, `CMD` and `CGI`, for the `<!--#EXEC>` tag.

The `CMD` attribute executes a program or script anywhere on the system, instead of being limited to specific directories that are configured as executable. An example is:

```
<!--#EXEC CMD="/usr/sbin/ping localhost">
```

1. Load `http://{server}/Chapter7/siexec1.shtml`.

2. View the original file with a text editor or with `more`.

The system load is returned by calling `uptime`, which isn't in an executable directory tree.

The CGI attribute executes a program or script found within any directory tree defined as executable and returns the results.

```
<!--#EXEC CGI="/cgi-bin/test-cgi.pl">
```

3. **Load** `http://{server}/Chapter7/siexec2.shtml`.
   Notice that the results returned here are unformatted.

4. **View the original file with a text editor or with** `more`.
   The Perl script is outputting a newline (\n) after each command. However, because the original page is an HTML page, the newlines are treated the same as all whitespace.

5. **Load** `http://{server}/Chapter7/siexec3.shtml`.
   This time a <P> is used instead of \n when formatting the document, and the layout appears correct.

6. **View the original file with a text editor or with the** `more` **command.**
   Verify that a <P> was used instead of a newline.

7. **Load** `http://{server}/Chapter7/siexec4.shtml`.
   This is the way to create a directory of items that you want to display and yet keep separate for easy cleanup.

Reporting Errors

If your document fails to read the included information, you won't get any error messages, but the added text won't be there either. Usually, once a web page is working, it stays working, and errors aren't very useful. In cases where users don't have permission to read the additional information, it is better to remain silent about what they cannot see than tell them that they don't have permission. For hackers, the lack of permission is a challenge. However, there are times when you may want to find out how often an intermittent problem occurs. It is possible to enable error reporting with the
<!--#CONFIG> tag and the ERRMSG attribute. This only reports that an error occurred. It doesn't specify the nature of the error, and you must supply the text of the error message. An example is:

```
<!--#CONFIG ERRMSG="Oops, something didn't happen here">
```

1. **Load** `http://{server}/Chapter7/sierr1.shtml`.

2. View the original file with a text editor or with more.

The system load should be returned by calling uptime; however, an incorrect pathname is specified, and the error message is returned.

Summary

In this chapter you learned:

- Pages can be made from including other pages.

- Pages can be customized with information about files.

- Pages can be generated on-the-fly with scripts and programs.

Tags Used in This Chapter

Tag	Attribute	Description and Notes
`<!--#CONFIG>`		Used in conjunction with the `<!--#FLASTMOD>` and `<!--#FSIZE>` to customize time and date displays. Also used alone to configure error messages.
	ERRMSG	Defines the error message string.
	TIMEFMT	Defines the date and time format returned.
	SIZEFMT	Defines the size format returned.
`<!--#ECHO>`		Returns a variable value.
	VAR	Defines the variable to return.
`<!--#EXEC>`		Executes a script or program.
	CMD	Defines the name of the program or script to be executed and that the program can be anywhere on the system.
	CGI	Defines the name of the program or script to be executed and that the program can only exist in an area defined as executable by the access.conf file.
`<!--#FLASTMOD>`		Displays the last modified date of a file.
	FILE	Defines the location of the document, based on the calling document.
	VIRTUAL	Defines the location of the document, based on the *DocRoot* variable.
`<!--#FSIZE>`		Displays the size of a file.

Tag	Attribute	Description and Notes
	FILE	Defines the location of the document, based on the calling document.
	VIRTUAL	Defines the location of the document, based on the *DocRoot* variable.
`<!--#INCLUDE>`		Adds the contents of a file to the document returned from the server.
	FILE	Defines the location of the document, based on the calling document
	VIRTUAL	Defines the location of the document, based on the *DocRoot* variable.

Environment Variables

- **DOCUMENT_NAME** — The name of the file.

- **DOCUMENT_URI** — The full Universal Resource Indicator. Unfortunately, this variable displays only the full document path, based on the definition of the server's *DocRoot* variable.

- **DATE_LOCAL**— The date and time, based on the local system time.

- **DATE_GMT** — The date and time, based on Greenwich Mean Time.

- **LAST_MODIFIED** — Returns only the modification date of the web page itself. Use the `<!--#FLASTMOD>` tag to obtain modification dates for other files.

7

HTML for Fun and Profit

√Creating Forms 8≣

One of the best reasons for having the Common Gateway Interface is that two-way communication is possible through the use of HTML. The client can enter information by selecting buttons, pulling down or scrolling through menus, and entering text into data entry boxes. These interactive building blocks can be brought together and defined as a *form*.

This chapter covers how to create forms, including text entry fields, default values, attributes, radio buttons, pull-down menus, and scrolling lists. The main exercise in this chapter is the creation of a survey tool.

Two Perl scripts, `query.pl` and `test-cgi.pl`, are used to display the results of the forms that are created. Chapter 9, *Processing Data From Forms* discusses how to manipulate the data after it has been gathered. There are quite a few sample HTML files for this chapter. These forms look different on UNIX, Window, and Macintosh. In addition, only sections of these files are reproduced in the text. It is a good idea to load these files and view the source. A sample of a full form on each platform is shown at the end of the chapter.

Form Creation and Submission

Creating a form is a simple process. The most basic form looks like HTML Example 8-1.

HTML Example 8-1 Basic HTML Form Template

```
<html><head>
<title>Form Template </title>
</head><body>

<FORM ACTION="http://localhost/cgi-bin/query.pl" METHOD="POST">
<INPUT TYPE="submit">
</FORM>
```

8

HTML Example 8-1 Basic HTML Form Template

```
<address>Me</address>
</body></html>
```

The basic form template consists of:

- **Basic HTML formatting** — Forms should have the five basic HTML tags: <HTML>, <HEAD>, <TITLE>, <BODY>, and <ADDRESS>. Not only is this a good practice, but some servers cannot handle forms if the document is not declared to be HTML with the <HTML> tag.

- **Form declaration** — A form is declared with the <FORM> and </FORM> tags.

- **Action definition** - The ACTION attribute of the <FORM> tag lists the URL of the program or script that will process the data collected by the form. The action must be a call to the http services, because the CGI interface used to execute the ACTION is available only through the http service. If anything other than http is used as the service, the script is returned to the browser instead of being executed.

- **Form method** — Forms can be accepted with either the GET or the POST method. The choice of method determines how the data is passed to the script or program defined by ACTION. If a form is returned with GET, then the data is placed in the QUERY_STRING environment variable. If a form is returned with POST, then the data is passed via the standard input method for each operating system, usually referred to as stdin.

  QUERY_STRING is actually a single list of the variable(s) and argument(s) that are collected from the client and passed to the ACTION script. Since the length of the string is limited, the length of the QUERY_STRING is also limited. Thus, POST is the method of choice for large forms.

Note – POST is actually the wave of the future for forms. This is a transition period when both methods are equally available and functional. Use the POST method for all new work.

- **Submission input definition** — The submission is most commonly an <INPUT> tag with the TYPE="submit" attribute. Forms can also be submitted with clickable images and single, text-box entries, as shown in *Clickable Images in Forms* and *Text Entry Fields*, respectively.

Note – When defining attributes, use double quotes, even if there are no spaces in the attribute.

1. **Load** `http://{server}/Chapter8/form1s.html`.
   This form has only one button that will submit the form to the server for processing. This form is the same as the template shown in HTML Example 8-1. The button looks like the example on the left of Figure 8-1.

2. **Submit the query by pressing the** Submit Query **button.**
   The results of this query are as sparse as the form itself. No values are listed under the comment You submitted the following name/value pairs:

Figure 8-1   Buttons on Xmosaic

3. **Load** `http://{server}/Chapter8/form2s.html`.
   The button is now labeled Push Me, instead of `Submit Query`. The button looks like the example on the right of Figure 8-1.

4. **View the HTML source with File->View Source.**
   The definition for the button changed from:

   ```
   <INPUT TYPE="submit">
   ```
   to
   ```
   <INPUT TYPE="submit" VALUE="Push Me">
   ```

   The label on the button was changed by addition of the VALUE attribute. Not all forms are for queries, and this is the way to change the Submit button label to accurately prompt the user.

HTML Example 8-1 is used as a template or starting point for most forms created in this chapter.

Clickable Images in Forms

A second method for submitting a form is with a clickable image. With a clickable image, the x and y coordinates of where the image was clicked are returned with the other form information. This is how `getpoints.html` delivered the coordinates for constructing the `imagemap` file in Chapter 6, *Using the Common Gateway Interface (CGI)*. This method also provides some artistic control over the submission button. On the downside, if users have Delay Image Loading set on their system, they will need to load the image before they can submit the form. This method should be used only for submission when images will be loaded all the time.

Note – The Windows- and Macintosh-based Mosaic browsers do not recognize this `<INPUT>` type. The Netscape (aka Mozilla) browsers do recognize this `<INPUT>` type, but the Mozilla browsers have reportedly had some forms-handling problems.

A clickable image is placed in a form with the `<INPUT>` tag. The `TYPE="image"` and `SRC=`*href* attributes are required. `NAME=`*value* is an optional attribute. The `NAME` attribute adds a variable name to the x and y coordinate data that is returned. This is useful when more than one clickable image is included in a form. Examples of this are:

```
<INPUT TYPE="image" SRC="http://{server}/Chapter10/earth.gif">
```

or:

```
<INPUT TYPE="image" SRC="earth.gif" NAME="First">
```

1. **Load** `http://{server}/Chapter8/form1i.html`.

2. **View the HTML source with File->View Source.**
   The `<INPUT>` definition here is the same as the first clickable image example above. The form here has only one input, the clickable image.

3. Click on the image.

The results of submitting the form are that the *x* and *y* coordinates of where the image was clicked are returned as x={*some number*} and y={*some number*}. These numbers are the x and y coordinates of the location on the image where you clicked. This form was used in Chapter 6, *Using the Common Gateway Interface (CGI)* in the section *Making Clickable Images*. Figure 8-2 illustrates the results.

Figure 8-2   Using an Image for Submission, the HTML Behind It, and the Results

4. Load http://{*server*}/Chapter8/form2i.html.

5. View the HTML source with File->View Source.

The <INPUT> tag has an additional attribute called NAME.

6. Click on the image.

By adding a NAME attribute the *x* and *y* coordinates of the image become *name.x* and *name.y*. The **x=**{*some number*} and **y=**{*some number*} shown in the first example now become **testing1.x=**{*some number*} and **testing1.y=**{*some number*}. Figure 8-3 illustrates this step.

Figure 8-3   Submitting an Image with a Name, the Page, HTML, and Results

Buttons

The previous forms were definitely simple. In order to collect data, however, some questions need to be asked.

Radio Buttons

Radio buttons are buttons that work together. Two or more radio buttons are used as a set when the question can have only one response. A typical example of this would be a yes *or* no question. Two buttons would be defined with the same NAME but different VALUE attributes. A radio button definition looks like:

```
<INPUT TYPE="radio" NAME="Question1" VALUE="yes">
```

For radio buttons, the attributes TYPE="radio" is used. NAME=*string* and VALUE=*definition* are required attributes. NAME defines a variable name for the input. Each piece of data from the form will come back in the form NAME=*value definition of selected button*. If the button in the above definition was selected by the client, the string returned is **Question1=yes**.

In some cases, data will not be returned.

- If a NAME isn't defined for that data, the data will not be returned, regardless of whether a button is checked.

- If the radio button isn't checked, data won't be returned. Since only one button out of a set can be selected, only one NAME=*value definition of selected button* string will be returned.

1. **Load** http://{*server*}/Chapter8/form1b.html.
   This form has a unique diamond-shaped button on a UNIX browser, as shown in Figure 8-4. On Windows and Macintosh browsers, the button appears as a circle. The **Submit** button is next to the radio button in both cases. Use the File->ViewSources option to verify that the new button line looks like the button definition listed above.

Figure 8-4   Sample Radio Buttons

2. **Load** http://{*server*}/Chapter8/form2b.html.
   Now this form has a button identified as **Of Course**. Radio buttons are labeled with regular text, instead of with the VALUE attribute. Use the File->ViewSources option to verify that the added text resembles the following:

   ```
   <INPUT TYPE="radio" NAME="Question1" VALUE="yes"> Of Course <P>
   ```

3. **Click on the Submit button.**
   The results of this form are still as blank as the original form. Since the radio button wasn't selected, it didn't get a value.

4. **Return to the previous screen by clicking on the Back button.**

5. **Click on the radio button to select it and click on Submit again.**
   Since the button was selected, it now has a value and data is returned.

8

Multiple Radio Buttons

A single radio button can record whether or not it was selected. Check boxes, which are covered in *Check Boxes* on page 125 can do the same thing. What makes radio buttons unique is this: If a group of radio buttons has the same name, they work together to return only one answer. Radio buttons are usually used alone for aesthetics only, for example, the unique diamond shape seen on the UNIX browser.

6. Load `http://{server}/Chapter8/form3b.html`.

This form now has two radio buttons with the same name but different values, as in the following example:

HTML Example 8-2 Multiple Radio Buttons

```
<INPUT TYPE="radio" NAME="Question1" VALUE="yes"> Of Course <P>
<INPUT TYPE="radio" NAME="Question1" VALUE="no"> No Way!!<P>
```

Only one of the buttons can be selected at any given time. Try clicking on one button and then the other and submitting the form. If the **Of Course** button is selected, then the results will be **Question1=yes**; if the **No Way!!** button is selected, then the results will be **Question1=no**. With radio buttons, only one answer can be returned for each NAME.

7. Load `http://{server}/Chapter8/form4b.html`.

This form has two questions with two radio buttons each, as in the following example:

HTML Example 8-3 Multiple NAME Values for Radio Buttons

```
Question 1:<P>
<INPUT TYPE="radio" NAME="Question1" VALUE="yes"> Of Course <P>
<INPUT TYPE="radio" NAME="Question1" VALUE="no"> No Way!!<P>
Question 2:<P>
<INPUT TYPE="radio" NAME="Question2" VALUE="yes"> Of Course <P>
<INPUT TYPE="radio" NAME="Question2" VALUE="no"> No Way!!<P>
```

Multiple buttons can be selected, but only one button can be selected for each question. The buttons function as a logical unit, based on the value of the NAME attribute. In this case, one answer is returned from **Question 1** and one answer from **Question 2**. Try various combinations of buttons to familiarize yourself with the way this works.

Check Boxes

Radio buttons are good to use when only one answer is needed. However, the world isn't just black or white; it's black *and* white *and* blue *and* red *and* green. Check boxes are the other type of button that can be used in a form. Multiple check boxes can be selected at time, and an answer will be returned for every selected check box. A check-box definition looks like the following:

```
<INPUT TYPE="checkbox" NAME="Question3" VALUE="UNIX">
```

For check boxes, the TYPE field is "checkbox." NAME and VALUE are required for check boxes, just as for radio buttons. NAME and VALUE in check boxes function similarly to radio buttons. If NAME isn't defined for that data, the data won't be returned; if the check box isn't checked, data won't be returned, either. The only significant difference is that more than one check box can be selected at a time, so NAME can have more than one value returned.

8. **Load** http://{server}/Chapter8/form5b.html.
   The check box uses a square instead of a diamond for the button on the UNIX browser only. Use the File->ViewSources option to verify that the new button line looks like the command listed above.

9. **Load** http://{server}/Chapter8/form6b.html.
   The form has three check boxes, as shown in the following example, that can all be selected at the same time.

HTML Example 8-4   Check Boxes Example

```
Question 3:<P>
<INPUT TYPE="checkbox" NAME="Question3" VALUE="UNIX"> UNIX<P>
<INPUT TYPE="checkbox" NAME="Question3" VALUE="DOS"> DOS<P>
<INPUT TYPE="checkbox" NAME="Question3" VALUE="WinNT"> WinNT<P>
```

10. **Select more than one check box and click on** Submit.

   If all the check boxes are selected, there are three results for the Question3 variable:
   • Question3=UNIX
   • Question3=DOS
   • Question3=WinNT

Setting Default and Initial Conditions

There may be times when an answer should always be returned. In these cases, a button can be set to a default value. The attribute CHECKED selects a specific button when initially displaying the screen. CHECKED doesn't have a value and can be used with both radio buttons and check boxes. A CHECKED definition looks like the following:

```
<INPUT TYPE="checkbox" NAME="Question3" VALUE="UNIX" CHECKED>
<INPUT TYPE="radio" NAME="Question2" VALUE="Of Course" CHECKED>
```

11.Load `http://{server}/Chapter8/form7b.html`.

Of Course is automatically selected for **Question1**, and **UNIX** is automatically selected for **Question3**. Use the File->ViewSources option to verify that the new attributes are the same as in the above example. Figure 8-5 illustrates this step.

Figure 8-5   Sample Buttons

12.Load `http://{server}/Chapter8/form8b.html`.

The **Question1** button definition lines should look like the following example:

HTML Example 8-5   Button Definition Lines

```
<INPUT TYPE="radio" NAME="Question1" VALUE="yes" CHECKED>Of Course <P>
<INPUT TYPE="radio" NAME="Question1" VALUE="no" CHECKED> No Way!!<P>
```

Notice that both buttons on **Question1** are CHECKED. Since a radio button can have only one answer, only one button can be selected when the form is displayed. The first occurrence of CHECKED is used, and the subsequent occurrences are ignored when the form is initially drawn. However, whatever the user selects does become the value that is returned.

Hiding Variables in Forms

There are times when it is important to record some information that isn't input by the user. This information might be data carried over from a previous form, special user identification or preferences, or a session-tracking number. Displaying this information to the client might be confusing and distract the user from filling in needed information. A *hidden variable* can hold this information in the form without the user seeing it.

A hidden variable is incorporated into a form with the <INPUT> tag and a TYPE of "hidden." The NAME and VALUE attributes are required. An example of this is:

```
<INPUT TYPE="hidden" NAME="hidden" VALUE="Big Brother">
```

1. **Load** http://{server}/Chapter8/form1h.html.
   This form appears to have only the submit button, **Push Me**.

2. **View the HTML source with File->View Source.**
   The source actually has the hidden value definition that matches the example above.

3. **Submit the form.**
   The results return hidden=Big Brother.

4. **Load** http://{server}/Chapter8/form2h.html.
   Again, this form appears to have only the submit button, **Push Me**.

5. **View the HTML source with File->View Source.**
   The source should be the same as the example below. It shows two hidden inputs. Both inputs have the same NAME but different VALUE definitions.

HTML Example 8-6   Two Hidden Variables with the Same NAME

```
<INPUT TYPE="hidden" NAME="hidden" VALUE="Big Brother">
<INPUT TYPE="hidden" NAME="hidden" VALUE="Big Sister">
```

6. Submit the form.
Both values for the name *hidden* are returned:

- hidden=Big Brother
- hidden=Big Sister

The hidden variable is like the check box, in that it can return an arbitrary number of values for a given name.

Text Entry Fields

Answering questions with buttons is very limiting. Therefore, text is an input type as well. Text entry works well when users are inputting their name, address, or a file to search for. A text box is placed in a form with the `<INPUT>` tag and a `TYPE="text."` Without a `NAME` for the text, the data will not be returned; thus, the `NAME` attribute is required. An example of this is:

HTML Example 8-7   Basic Text Entry Example

```
Full Name
<INPUT TYPE="text" NAME="Question4">
```

1. Load `http://{server}/Chapter8/form1t.html`.
This form has one text box, labeled Full Name, as shown in Figure 8-6.

Full Name [   ]

[submit]

Me

Figure 8-6   Sample Text Box

2. View the HTML source with File->View Source.
The text definition looks like the example above. Notice that the label Full Name for the text box is in regular HTML text, not part of the `<INPUT>` definition.

3. Enter a first and last name and submit the form.
The result is a string that includes the spaces that were typed in. If Mary Morris were typed in, the result would be **Question4=Mary Morris**.

Submitting Forms With a Text Box

The third way to submit a form is to have a form that contains a single text box. When data is entered into the text box and the user presses the Enter key, the form is submitted. This method is valid only if the form has *only* one text box.

4. **Load** http://*{server}*/Chapter8/form2t.html.
   There is no submit button shown on this form.

5. **View the HTML source with File->View Source.**
   This form has one text box labeled Name, as in the example below. No submit button is defined.

HTML Example 8-8   Using a Text Box to Submit a Form

```
<FORM ACTION="/cgi-bin/query.pl" METHOD="POST">
Name
<INPUT TYPE="text" NAME="Question4"><P>
</FORM>
```

6. **Enter a name and press Enter to submit the form.**
   The form is processed, and the text that you entered is returned as
   Question4={*text typed in*} without a submit button being clicked on.

7. **Load** http://*{server}*/Chapter8/form3t.html.
   This form has one text box labeled Name and a check box labeled Check Me. There is no submit button on this form.

8. **View the HTML source with File->View Source.**
   This form, shown in the example below, doesn't have a submit button.

HTML Example 8-9 Second Example of Using a Text Box to Submit a Form.

```
<FORM ACTION="/cgi-bin/query.pl" METHOD="POST">
Name
<INPUT TYPE="text" NAME="Question4"><P>
Check Me
<INPUT TYPE="checkbox" NAME="Question4" VALUE="checked"><P>
</FORM>
```

9. **Check the box, enter a name, and press Enter to submit the form.**
   The form is processed. The results are:

   • Question4= (the text box was blank)
   • Question4=checked (the check box was checked)

10. **Load** `http://{server}/Chapter8/form4t.html`.
    This form has two text boxes. Again, there is no submit button on this form.

11. **View the HTML source with File->View Source.**
    This form, shown in the example below, again doesn't have a submit button, but it has more than one text box.

HTML Example 8-10 How NOT to Submit a Form with Text Boxes

```
<FORM ACTION="/cgi-bin/query.pl" METHOD="POST">
Name
<INPUT TYPE="text" NAME="Question4"><P>
Address
<INPUT TYPE="text" NAME="Question5"><P>
</FORM>
```

12. **Fill in both fields and press Enter.**
    This time the form is *not* submitted by pressing Enter.

Setting a Default Value for Text

There may be times when a text box should be preset to a default value. The attribute VALUE stores the initial text that is displayed in the text box. An example of this is:

```
<INPUT TYPE="text" NAME="address" VALUE="Some Value">
```

13. **Load** `http://{server}/Chapter8/form5t.html`.
    This form has one text box labeled Name. The text already exists in the text box.

14. View the HTML source with File->View Source.

Figure 8-7 shows how the text definition looks.

Figure 8-7   Sample Text Box with Default Text

15. Submit the form without any modifications.

The form is processed and **address=Some Value**, the default value, is returned.

16. Press the Back button to return to the form.

17. Change the text and submit the form.

The form is processed and the result is now **address=**{*text you typed in*}.

Limiting the Length of Text

Databases usually have fixed-length fields. It is a good idea to keep the length of the incoming data within the size limits of the field in the database. This is accomplished with the MAXLENGTH attribute. An example of this is:

```
<INPUT TYPE="text" NAME="Question4" MAXLENGTH=8>
```

18. Load http://{*server*}/Chapter8/form6t.html.

This form appears to be the same as several previous forms.

19. View the HTML source with File->View Source.

Notice that the MAXLENGTH attribute has been set to 8, as in the example above.

20. Enter the word snowflake.

Since snowflake has nine characters, the last character cannot be entered here. Most browsers will beep to indicate a problem if the system has that capability. When setting short limits on fields, it is a good idea to add a comment saying that you can use only x number of characters.

Changing the Size of the Displayed Text Box

Keeping data to a specific length is one thing; visually laying out text boxes is another. You cannot control the absolute layout of the screen because the user is free to adjust the browser window. However, if the size of a text box is limited, two text boxes can usually be placed on the same line. Normally a text box is 20 characters wide. Changing the size of the displayed text box is accomplished with the SIZE attribute. An example of this is:

```
<INPUT TYPE="text" NAME="Question4" SIZE=8>
```

SIZE can also be used to create a text box more than one row in height, by passing both a line width value and a row height value. An example of this is:

```
<INPUT TYPE="text" NAME="address" SIZE="10,2">
```

21. Load http://{*server*}/Chapter8/form7t.html.
The text box is shorter than previous text boxes were.

22. View the HTML source with File->View Source.
Notice that the SIZE attribute has been set to 8, as in the first example in this section.

23. Load http://{*server*}/Chapter8/form8t.html.
The text box is now two rows high. A scrollbar is displayed on the right side of the text box.

24. Type some text into the text box and press Enter.
In this case, the cursor advances to the next line. Text boxes that are higher than one row cannot be used to submit forms by pressing Enter.

25. Type a second line of text and submit the form.
The results of this text box are all placed on the same line when returned. The results look like: **Question4=**{*text typed on line 1*}%0A{*text typed on line 2*}.

Where you pressed the Enter key the text shows %0A. When a form is submitted, the information is placed in a single string and returned to the server. This string cannot have spaces, tabs, carriage returns, and some other special characters in the string during transmission, so the special characters are converted to their ASCII equivalents. This is discussed in depth in Chapter 9, *Processing Data From Forms* in the section *Parsing Input*.

Text Areas

The text entry fields above provide basic multiline capabilities. However, default multiline text can't be placed in those text boxes. Another way of creating text entry fields is to use the tag <TEXTAREA>. This tag requires an end tag, </TEXTAREA>. The required attribute NAME labels the data. An example is:

```
<TEXTAREA NAME="Text1"> </TEXTAREA>
```

1. **Load** `http://{server}/Chapter8/form1a.html`.
   This form resembles the basic text boxes explored above. It is only one row in height and 20 characters wide. The difference here is that the field has scroll bars even in its most basic definition, as shown in Figure 8-8.

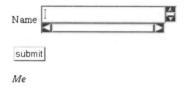

Me

Figure 8-8   Sample Text Area

2. **Type some text into the text area and press Enter.**
   The cursor advances to the next line. Text areas cannot be used to submit forms.

3. **Type a second line of text and submit the form.**
   The results resemble the output of the multiline text box in Step 25 above. Where the Enter key was pressed, the text again shows %0A.

Resizing a Text Area

The `<TEXTAREA>` tag uses the attributes ROWS and COLS to define the displayed size. An example of this is:

```
<TEXTAREA ROWS=3 COLS=25 NAME="Text2"> Default text </TEXTAREA>
```

4. **Load** `http://{server}/Chapter8/form2a.html`.
   The text area is now three rows in height.

5. **View the HTML source with File->View Source.**
   Notice that the ROWS and COLS attributes have been defined as in the example above.

Setting Default Text in a Text Area

Instead of using the VALUE attribute, the default text is placed between the start and end tags. All whitespace between the `<TEXTAREA>` tags is significant. The two examples below are not the same. In Example 1, there is a space before and after "Default Text." In Example 2, there is a carriage return before and after "Default Text." These definitions produce different form display and returned results.

HTMLExample 8-11 Defining the Default Text in a Text Area

Example 1
```
    <TEXTAREA NAME="Text2"> Default text </TEXTAREA>
```

Example 2
```
    <TEXTAREA NAME="Text2">
    Default text
    </TEXTAREA>
```

6. **Load** `http://{server}/Chapter8/form3a.html`.
   The text area has a default value of Start here. This value starts on the second line of the text area.

Figure 8-9   Sample Text Area with Default Text

7. **View the HTML source with File->View Source.**
   The text "Start here" begins on the line below the `<TEXTAREA>` tag. Carriage returns are significant characters within `<TEXTAREA>` tags.

8. **Submit the form.**
   Where the blank lines were in the text area, the text shows %0A. The results of submitting the form without any changes yields **Question5=%0AStart here %0A**.

9. **Load** `http://{server}/Chapter8/form4a.html`.
   The text area has two lines of default text. The second line has two spaces in front of the text "Text here."

10. View the HTML source with File->View Source.

The text "Text here" has two spaces at the beginning of the line. Spaces are also significant characters within <TEXTAREA> tags.

11. Submit the form.

Where the spaces were in the text area, the text shows spaces as well. The results of submitting the form without any changes yields **Question5=%0A Text here %0AMore Text %0A**.

Pull-Down Menus and Scrolling Lists

Although users shouldn't always have to type in the answers, displaying every option as a button consumes space. Pull-down menus and scrolling lists resolve both of these needs. A scrolling list resembles a regular list, as shown in Chapter 2, *The Basics*, in the section *Lists*, in that the tags <SELECT> and </SELECT> mark the start and end of the list and each list item is indicated by an <OPTION> tag. The required attribute NAME labels the data. The returned data is the text after the option. An example is:

HTML Example 8-12 Pull-Down Menu Tags

```
<SELECT NAME="Menu-Question6">
<OPTION> Option Text 1
<OPTION> Option Text 2
</SELECT>
```

A pull-down menu is actually a special case of a scrolling list. It can only be created when only one list item at a time is displayed or selectable.

1. Load http://{*server*}/Chapter8/form1o.html.

This form is a basic pull-down menu. Only one item is displayed. Clicking on the menu displays all of the items. Figure 8-10 illustrates a sample menu item.

Figure 8-10 Sample Menu Item As Displayed (on left) and Expanded (on right)

2. View the HTML source with File->View Source.
Compare this document with the next example. The <SELECT> definition in
this example resembles the example above.

3. Submit the form.
The text of the selected pull-down item becomes the returned value for this
list. If Option Text 2 is selected, the result is Menu-Question6=Option Text 2.

Displaying Two Items At Once

It isn't aesthetically pleasing to display all ten items on a list, thus filling up the
screen with one question or prompt, but there are times when more than one item
should be displayed. Displaying multiple items is accomplished by adding the
SIZE=*x* attribute to the <SELECT> definition. By displaying more than one item,
the pull-down menu becomes a scrolling list.

An example of adding the attribute is:

```
<SELECT NAME="Menu-Question6" SIZE="2">
```

4. Load http://{*server*}/Chapter8/form2o.html.
This form is now a scrolling list with two items displayed, as shown in
Figure 8-11.

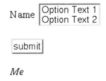

Figure 8-11   Sample Scrolling List

5. View the HTML source with File->View Source.
The only HTML change between the previous form and this one is the SIZE=2
attribute added to the <SELECT> tag. This one modification alone changed the
form from a pull-down menu to a scrolling list.

**6. Select a menu item. Hold down the Control key and select another menu
item.**
Only one item at a time can be selected.

Selecting Multiple Items

Only one item could be selected in the example above. As with check boxes, there are times when a question can have more than one answer. To enable multiple item selection, use the MULTIPLE attribute in the <SELECT> definition. The definition line looks like the following:

```
<SELECT NAME="Menu-Question6" MULTIPLE>
```

7. Load http://{server}/Chapter8/form3o.html.
This form is a scrolling list with several items displayed.

8. View the HTML source with File->View Source.
The <SELECT> line has been changed to resemble the example above. The attribute SIZE is not used here, but the scrolling list displays more than one item.

9. Select a menu item. Hold down the Control key and select another menu item.
More than one item can now be selected here.

10.Submit the form.
The result of this form is two values for the item Menu-Question6:

* Menu-Question6=Option Text 1 (or whatever was selected)
* Menu-Question6=Option Text 3 (or whatever was selected)

11.Load http://{server}/Chapter8/form4o.html.
This form is a scrolling list with two items displayed and three items total. When MULTIPLE was used alone, all items were displayed. The number of displayed items can be controlled by means of the SIZE attribute.

Default Item Selection

Specifying default values can be done with pull-down menus and scrolling lists by adding the SELECTED attribute to the <OPTION> tag. An example is:

```
<OPTION SELECTED> Option Text 3
```

12. Load `http://{server}/Chapter8/form5o.html`.

This scrolling list has the first and fifth items initially selected, as shown in Figure 8-12.

Me

Figure 8-12 Sample Scrolling List with Multiple Items Selected

13. View the HTML source with File->View Source.

The form is similar to the example below:

HTML Example 8-13 Scrolling List Example with Default Items Selected

```
<SELECT NAME="Menu-Question6" MULTIPLE>
<OPTION SELECTED> Option Text 1
<OPTION> Option Text 2
<OPTION> Option Text 3
<OPTION> Option Text 4
<OPTION SELECTED> Option Text 5
<OPTION> Option Text 6
<OPTION> Option Text 7
</SELECT>
```

The SIZE attribute isn't specified in this list, but only five items are displayed. All the preselected items are displayed if the SIZE attribute isn't specified but the MULTIPLE attribute is used.

14. Submit the form.

The result of this form is two values for the item **Menu-Question6**:

- Menu-Question6=Option Text 1 (or whatever was selected)
- Menu-Question6=Option Text 5 (or whatever was selected)

15. Load `http://{server}/Chapter8/form6o.html`.

The form contains a pull-down menu that has the second item initially selected.

16.View the HTML source with File->View Source.

The attributes SIZE and MULTIPLE are not specified; thus, the display is again a pull-down menu. However, more than one item has the SELECTED attribute.

17.Submit the form.

The result of this form is the first selected value for the item **Menu-Question6, Menu-Question6=Option Text 2**. As with radio buttons, only the first item is returned when multiple items are selected but the MULTIPLE attribute isn't used.

Clearing Entries and Resetting Defaults

Each type of input form can set default values. This capability can save the user some time, or in the case of text entries, give the user an idea of what format to use. Default values are also useful when the user isn't guaranteed to answer that question.

What about the case where the user has filled out part of the form and wants to start over? This capability is provided by the TYPE="reset" attribute for the <INPUT> tag. By adding a reset button to your form, you allow users to erase or clear their partially completed form. An example of the reset button definition is:

```
<INPUT TYPE="reset">
```

As with the submit button, the text on the reset button can be changed with the VALUE attribute. An example is:

```
<INPUT TYPE="reset" VALUE="Clear">
```

1. **Load** http://{server}/Chapter8/form1r.html.
   This form has buttons, text boxes, text areas, and scrolling lists. At the bottom of the page is a button labeled **clear**.

2. **View the HTML source with File->View Source.**
   The HTML code looks like the example below:

HTML Example 8-14 A Full-Fledged Form Example

```
<html> <head>
<title> Form Template </title>
</head> <body>

<FORM ACTION="/cgi-bin/query.pl" METHOD="GET">
Question 1:Do you use the Web at work or at home?<P>
```

HTML Example 8-14 A Full-Fledged Form Example (Continued)

```
<INPUT TYPE="radio" NAME="Question1" VALUE="work"> At Work <P>
<INPUT TYPE="radio" NAME="Question1" VALUE="home"> At Home <P>
Question 2:Do you use Mosaic? <P>
<INPUT TYPE="radio" NAME="Question2" VALUE="yes"> Of Course <P>
<INPUT TYPE="radio" NAME="Question2" VALUE="no"> No Way!! <P>
Question 3: What OS's do you use?<P>
<INPUT TYPE="checkbox" NAME="Question3" VALUE="UNIX"> UNIX <P>
<INPUT TYPE="checkbox" NAME="Question3" VALUE="DOS"> DOS <P>
<INPUT TYPE="checkbox" NAME="Question3" VALUE="WinNT"> WinNT <P>
Question 4: What is your email address?
<INPUT TYPE="text" NAME="Question4" MAXLENGTH=25 > <P>
Question 5: What is your real name and address?
<TEXTAREA NAME="Question5" ROWS=3 COLS=10 >
</TEXTAREA> <P>
Question 6: What do you use the Internet for?<P>
<SELECT NAME="Menu-Question6" MULTIPLE>
<OPTION> Surfing
<OPTION> Obtaining Programs
<OPTION> Reading Netnews
<OPTION> Teleconferencing
<OPTION> Sending and Receiving Email
<OPTION> Playing NetTrek
</SELECT> <P>
<INPUT TYPE="submit" VALUE="submit">
<INPUT TYPE="reset" VALUE="clear">
</FORM>

<address> Me </address>
</body> </html>
```

3. **Enter some information.**

4. **Press the clear button to reset the form to its initial condition.**
   Notice that all fields clear, the buttons become unchecked, and scrolling lists and pull-down menus return to the first item.

5. **Load** `http://{server}/Chapter8/form1r.html`.
   This form has the same buttons, text boxes, text areas and scrolling lists, but there are now default values in the form components.

6. **View the HTML source with File->View Source.**

The HTML code looks like the following example:

HTML Example 8-15 HTML Source with Default Entries Defined

```
<html> <head>
<title> Form Template </title>
</head> <body>
<FORM ACTION="/cgi-bin/query.pl" METHOD="GET">
Question 1:Do you use the Web at work or at home?<P>
<INPUT TYPE="radio" NAME="Question1" VALUE="work" CHECKED> At Work
<P>
<INPUT TYPE="radio" NAME="Question1" VALUE="home"> At Home <P>
Question 2:Do you use Mosaic? <P>
<INPUT TYPE="radio" NAME="Question2" VALUE="yes" CHECKED> Of Course
<P>
<INPUT TYPE="radio" NAME="Question2" VALUE="no"> No Way!! <P>
Question 3: What OS's do you use?<P>
<INPUT TYPE="checkbox" NAME="Question3" VALUE="UNIX" CHECKED> UNIX
<P>
<INPUT TYPE="checkbox" NAME="Question3" VALUE="DOS"> DOS <P>
<INPUT TYPE="checkbox" NAME="Question3" VALUE="WinNT"> WinNT <P>
Question 4: What is your email address?
<INPUT TYPE="text" NAME="Question4" MAXLENGTH=25
VALUE="me@mydomain.com"> <P>
Question 5: What is your real name and address?
<TEXTAREA NAME="Question5" ROWS=3 COLS=10 >
FirstName LastName
Street Address
City, State Zip Country
</TEXTAREA> <P>
Question 6: What do you use the Internet for?<P>
<SELECT NAME="Menu-Question6" MULTIPLE>
<OPTION SELECTED> Surfing
<OPTION> Obtaining Programs
<OPTION> Reading Netnews
<OPTION> Teleconferencing
<OPTION SELECTED> Sending and Receiving Email
<OPTION> Playing NetTrek
</SELECT> <P>
<INPUT TYPE="submit" VALUE="submit">
<INPUT TYPE="reset" VALUE="Reset Values">
</FORM>
```

Notice that default entries have been defined this time.

7. Enter some information.

8. Press the Reset Values button to reset the form to its initial condition.
Notice that all fields return to their original values.

Figure 8-13 illustrates the form in HTML Example 8-14 displayed on a UNIX Mosaic browser.

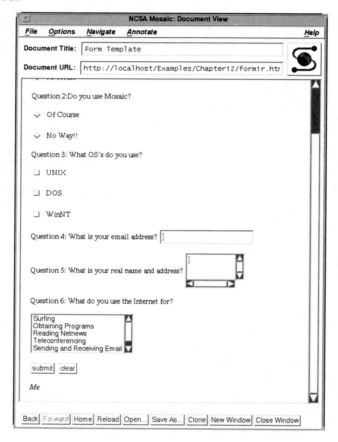

Figure 8-13   Full Form As Displayed on UNIX Mosaic Browser

Figure 8-14 illustrates the form in HTML Example 8-14 displayed on a Windows-based Mosaic browser.

Figure 8-14 Full Form As Displayed on Windows-based Mosaic Browser

Multiple Forms on the Same Page

It is possible to put more than one form on a web page. The only restriction is that forms cannot be nested within forms. The drawback here is that each form must have its own submit button or alternative submission method. That submission method returns only the data for the form for which it is defined. There is no way to request common information that is shared between forms. A workaround is to obtain the information in a previous page and carry it through as hidden information.

If you need users to fill out both forms, they must complete one form, submit the results, and then go back to the page with the forms and complete the second form. This sequence can cause confusion on the part of the user. Multiple forms on a page should be used only when only one form of several will be returned.

To reduce user confusion:

- Visually separate the forms with a horizontal rule or similar device.

- Give clear instructions on when to use each submit button.

Summary

In this chapter, you learned:

- **Submitting forms** — Forms can be returned to the server for processing by:
  - A clickable image, `TYPE="image"`
  - A submit button, `TYPE="submit"`
  - A single text box, `TYPE="text"`

- **Buttons** — There are four types of buttons:
  - Radio – used in sets for yes or no answers
  - Check box – used for one or more answers
  - Submit – used to submit a form
  - Reset – used to return a form to default values

- **Text** — Can be input via two methods
  - Text boxes – used for single line input and where the input string needs length control. Text boxes have limited use for multiline text
  - Text areas – used for multiline text input

- **Pull-down menus and scrollable lists** — Accomplished with the `<SELECT>` tag and various options

Tags Used in This Chapter

Table 8-1   Tags Used in Creating Forms

Tag	Attributes	Description and Comments
`<FORM>`		
	`ACTION`	Defines the cgi-bin script or program to execute with the incoming data.
	`METHOD`	Defines whether the incoming data will be stored in the environment variable `QUERY_STRING` or standard input.
`<INPUT>`		
	`TYPE`	Defines the type of input field. See Table 8-2.
`<TEXTAREA>`		
	`ROWS`	Defines the height of the text area.
	`COLS`	Defines the width of the text area.
	`NAME`	Defines the variable name.
`<SELECT>`		
	`NAME`	Defines the variable name.
	`SIZE`	Defines the number of items displayed.
	`MULTIPLE`	Indicates that more than one item can be selected.
`<OPTION>`		
	`SELECTED`	Makes the item selected by default.

Table 8-2   Input Values and Uses

Input Type	Attributes	Description and Notes
submit		
	`VALUE`	Alters the text on the submit button.
reset		
	`VALUE`	Alters the text on the submit button.
image		
	`SRC`	Defines the URL for the image.
	`NAME`	Defines a variable name to be prepended to x and y when returning coordinates.
hidden		
	`NAME`	Defines the variable name.
	`VALUE`	Defines the value of the variable listed in `NAME`.

Table 8-2   Input Values and Uses (Continued)

Input Type	Attributes	Description and Notes
radio		
	NAME	Defines the variable name.
	VALUE	Defines the value of the variable listed in NAME.
	CHECKED	Indicates selected by default
checkbox		
	NAME	Defines the variable name.
	VALUE	Defines the value of the variable listed in NAME.
	CHECKED	Indicates selected by default.
text		
	NAME	Defines the variable name.
	VALUE	Defines the value of the variable listed in NAME.
	SIZE	Defines the number of characters in the returned value.
	MAXLENGTH	Controls the display size of the text box.

Processing Data From Forms

In the previous chapter, you worked with the forms that gather data, and you were introduced to the script `query.pl` that lists the value(s) that each item in the form was set to. This chapter explains the scripts you have used thus far and introduces you to a sample script for processing the information that you received from the forms.

Basic CGI Input and Output

Moving data between the CGI and the script is an important part of how the script is written. Remember, the output of the CGI is the input for the script, and the output for the script is the input for the CGI.

Input

Originally, all information was passed from the CGI to the script or program via environment variables. People began to create forms that returned a large quantity of information that overflowed the QUERY_STRING variable. A method was developed to pass the information from the form to the executing routine via the *standard input*, or *stdin* in UNIX terminology, because standard input doesn't have size limitations on what it can transfer.

The script `test-cgi.pl` was used in Chapter 6, *Using the Common Gateway Interface (CGI)* to examine the variables that the executing routine received. The script lists all the information that it received, both from environment variables and from *stdin*.

Code Example 9-1 `test-cgi.pl` *Script*

```
#!/opt/internet/bin/perl
#
# test-cgi.pl
#
# test-cgi.pl,v 0.1 1994/06/30 Mary Morris
```

Code Example 9-1 `test-cgi.pl` *Script (Continued)*

```
#
# Example of test-cgi converted to perl
#

print "Content-type: text/html\n";
print "CGI/1.0 test script report<P>";

if ($ENV{'REQUEST_METHOD'} eq "POST") {
    $form = <STDIN>;
    print "$form \n";
} else {
print "argc is $#ARGV <P>argv is ";

while (@ARGV) {
    $ARGV=shift;
    print "$ARGV ";
}
}
print "<P>";
print "SERVER_NAME = $ENV{'SERVER_NAME'}<P>";
print "GATEWAY_INTERFACE = $ENV{'GATEWAY_INTERFACE'}<P>";
print "SERVER_ROOT = $ENV{'SERVER_ROOT'}<P>";
print "REQUEST_METHOD = $ENV{'REQUEST_METHOD'}<P>";
print "HTTP_ACCEPT = $ENV{'HTTP_ACCEPT'}<P>";
print "PATH_INFO = $ENV{'PATH_INFO'}<P>";
print "PATH = $ENV{'PATH'}<P>";
print "PATH_TRANSLATED = $ENV{'PATH_TRANSLATED'}<P>";
print "QUERY_STRING = $ENV{'QUERY_STRING'}<P>";
print "QUERY_STRING_UNESCAPED =
$ENV{'QUERY_STRING_UNESCAPED'}<P>";
print "REMOTE_HOST = $ENV{'REMOTE_HOST'}<P>";
print "REMOTE_IDENT = $ENV{'REMOTE_IDENT'}<P>";
print "AUTH_TYPE = $ENV{'AUTH_TYPE'}<P>";
print "CONTENT_TYPE = $ENV{'CONTENT_TYPE'}<P>";
print "CONTENT_LENGTH = $ENV{'CONTENT_LENGTH'}<P>";
print "DOCUMENT_ROOT = $ENV{'DOCUMENT_ROOT'}<P>";
print "DOCUMENT_URI = $ENV{'DOCUMENT_URI'}<P>";
print "DOCUMENT_NAME = $ENV{'DOCUMENT_NAME'}<P>";
print "DATE_LOCAL = $ENV{'DATE_LOCAL'}<P>";
```

Environment Variables

When the CGI started executing `test-cgi.pl`, the CGI set the variables that make up the environment in which the script runs. Perl accesses these variables by referencing them with $ENV{ *'env variable'* } or by setting a local variable in the script equal to the value of the environment variables, as in the line:

```
DOCUMENT_ROOT = $ENV{'DOCUMENT_ROOT'}
```

The information from a form submitted with the GET method has the item information stored in the variable QUERY_STRING. This information is stored in the format:

variable name=variable value

The information is referred to as *form variable information* to differentiate it from individual variables. This form variable information is also stored in the ARGV variable, which stores the string of incoming arguments. The following part of the script prints the variable information strings that were passed in to ARGV.

Code Example 9-2   ARGV Section of `test-cgi.pl` *– Used with the* GET *Method*

```
while (@ARGV) {
    $ARGV=shift;
    print "$ARGV ";
}
```

Perl code explanation – The @ sign at the start of a variable means that the variable is a list of items. The $ sign at the start of a variable means that the variable is an individual item. The example above says "While there is anything left in the ARGV (with an @) list, move (i.e., `shift`) the leftmost item into the single variable ARGV (with a $), print this item, and start over by fetching the next item."

Standard Input

When the POST method is used to submit data from a form, the input comes from the standard input, as discussed previously. The following part of the script reads this information and writes it out directly via the *$form* variable.

Code Example 9-3   Printing Form Variable Information with the POST Method

```
$form = <STDIN>;
print "$form \n";
```

Perl code explanation – The <> as used in Perl indicates a stream of information from a source outside the current script, such as receiving input from a specified source or sending output to a specific source. This is also referred to as a *file handle*, even if a disk file is not used. <STDIN> is the definition for receiving a stream of information from *stdin*. If input comes from another source such as a file, the source of the stream must be defined with an open statement, as in Table 9-1. It is important to differentiate between the <> used for file handles in Perl and for tags in HTML.

Parsing Input

The query.pl script returned information entered into forms in Chapter 8, *Creating Forms*. The actual script is shown below.

Table 9-1   query.pl Script

```
#!/opt/internet/bin/perl
#
# post-query.pl -- Conversion of post-query to Perl
#
# post-query.pl,v 0.1 1994/06/30 Mary Morris
#
# Example of post-query converted to perl
#

print "Content-type: text/html\n";
print "<HTML><BODY> <H1>Query Results</H1>\n";
print "You submitted the following name/value pairs:\n";
```

Table 9-1 `query.pl` *Script (Continued)*

```
if ($ENV{'REQUEST_METHOD'} eq "POST") {
    $form = <STDIN>;
} else {
    $form = $ENV{'QUERY_STRING'};
}
@pairs = split(/&/,$form);
print "<UL>";
while (@pairs) {
    $pair=shift @pairs;
    $pair =~ s/\+/ /g;
    print "<LI><CODE>$pair</CODE>\n ";
}
print "</UL>";
print "\n</BODY></HTML>";
```

In `query.pl`, the only difference between GET and POST data handling is the source of input to the *$form* variable. After the input is placed into the *$form* variable, the information is split into the individual variable information strings with:

```
@pairs = split(/&/,$form);
```

Perl code explanation – The `split` function divides a single item variable into a list of items, based on the character that is defined as the delimiter. In this case the & sign is a delimiter.

If the original input is:

```
name=Mary+Morris&email=marym&preference=UNIX
```

then the list now has three items that read:

```
name=Mary+Morris    email=marym        preference=UNIX
```

Each item of the list is then moved into the $pairs variable with:

```
$pair=shift @pairs;
```

≡ 9

Converting URL Encoding

Spaces make for difficult data transmission and variable differentiation while transmitting the data. However, spaces aren't the only character that is hard to deal with during data transmission and variable processing. In Chapter 8, *Creating Forms*, multiline text boxes returned a %0A instead of a carriage return. And since + marks a space, something else is needed to mark the occurrence of a +.

Actually, +, %, and & are the only nonalphabetic or non-numeric characters that are used in the form variable information strings. All other special characters, including tabs, carriage returns, parentheses, and even the real occurrences of +, &, and % are encoded with a % sign and their numeric ASCII value. This is called *URL encoding*.

Now that the form variable information strings have been split apart, the + can be changed back to a space. This is done with:

```
$pair =~ s/\+/ /g;
```

Note – =~ is a specific operator in Perl. It indicates that the translation rule following it will be performed on the designated variable and that the output will be placed back into the same variable. In this case, the translation rule is s for *substitute*. This substitute syntax came from the sed command in UNIX. For more information on this substitution method, refer to *Programming Perl* by Larry Wall and Randal L. Schwartz or see the man pages on a UNIX system.

All the encoded characters must be converted back into regular characters during the variable information string processing. Some lines that could be added to the current script are:

```
$pair =~ s/\%0A/\/n/g;
$pair =~ s/\%2B/\+/g;
$pair =~ s/\%28/\(/g;
$pair =~ s/\%29/\)/g;
$pair =~ s/\%26/\&/g;
```

Note – A few programs are available to split and unencode form variable information. Use them instead of reinventing the wheel. This information is here merely to explain what happens behind the scenes.

Output

Just as the CGI interface uses the standard input to pass information to a script or program, standard output is used to pass information from the program or script back to the CGI and on to the client's browser. Remember two key things when writing your output:

1. **Include meta-information** — The client browser needs to have information about the type of information that the browser is receiving.

2. **Include HTML formatting** — If the information you are returning to the client is to be used as HTML, it must include HTML formatting.

Meta-Information

The client must have information about the type of information it is receiving. This information should be a text string in the format:

```
Content-type: {A MIME type}
```

The two example scripts above used the statement:

```
print "Content-type: text/html\n";
```

If this information isn't passed back to the client, peculiar things occur. Some client browsers offer you the opportunity to save the returning data to a file. Other browsers receive the data and don't display it. This is a small part of a program, but it is by no means trivial. Some servers offer alternative methods for ensuring that a header is printed; however, for the present, include content headers in all programs.

HTML Formatting

When you have defined the returning information as HTML, you need to add HTML formatting to the information that you send back. In Perl, this is usually done with a `print` statement and the format needed. For example, where Perl would specify a new line with \n, the <P> or <BR> tags are used.

The \n is used in the meta-information listed above because it defines the type of information returning, but it is not displayed because it is meta-information.

Sample CGI Script

The most common form is one that collects feedback. This example shows how information from a form can be gathered and used.

Feedback Form

Two parts are involved: gathering information and using it.

The HTML page gathers the information. An example is `feedback.html`, shown below:

Code Example 9-4   Feedback Form Script: Part 1

```
<html> <head>
<title> Feedback Form </title>
</head> <body>

<H1> Feedback Form </H1>
<HR>
<FORM ACTION="/cgi-bin/contact.pl" METHOD="POST">

Name: <INPUT TYPE="text" NAME="name" MAXLENGTH=50 > <P>
Email Address: <INPUT TYPE="text" NAME="email" MAXLENGTH=50 > <P>
Comments:
<TEXTAREA NAME="comment" ROWS=3 COLS=50 > </TEXTAREA> <P>
</FORM>
<HR>
<address> Me </address>
</body> </html>
```

The second part of the form is the script that uses the information gathered by the web page. An example is `contact.pl`, shown below:

Code Example 9-5   Feedback Form Script: Part 2

```
#!/usr/local/sun4/perl
#
# Load environment variables
#
do '/WWW/cgi-bin/setenv.pl';
```

Code Example 9-5   Feedback Form Script: Part 2 (Continued)

```
#
# Return Meta-Information
#
print "Content-type: text/html\n\n";

#
# Parse the variables to be used
#
$NAME=`"$exeRoot/cgiparse" -value name`;
$EMAIL=`"$exeRoot/cgiparse" -value email`;
$COMMENT=`"$exeRoot/cgiparse" -value comment`;

#
# Setup templates for output to log and email and HTML output
#
format COMMENTFORM =
    =========================================================
    @<<<<<<<<<<<<<<<<<<<<<<<<<<<<<<<<<<<<<<<<<<<<<<<<<<<<<
    $NAME
    left this message about your web server
    @<<<<<<<<<<<<<<<<<<<<<<<<<<<<<<<<<<<<
    $EMAIL
    @*
    $COMMENT
    =========================================================
.

format STDOUT =
    <HR>
    Thank You,
    @<<<<<<<<<<<<<<<<<<<<<<<<<<<<<<<<<<<<<<<<<<<<<<<<<<<<<
    $NAME
    <P> We will contact you at:
    @<<<<<<<<<<<<<<<<<<<<<<<<<<<<<<<<<<<<
    $EMAIL
    <HR>
.

format MAILOMMENT =
    =========================================================
    @<<<<<<<<<<<<<<<<<<<<<<<<<<<<<<<<<<<<<<<<<<<<<<<<<<<<<
    $NAME
    left this message about your web server
```

9

Code Example 9-5   Feedback Form Script: Part 2 (Continued)

```
    @<<<<<<<<<<<<<<<<<<<<<<<<<<<<<<<<<<
    $EMAIL
    @*
    $COMMENT
    ========================================================

.

#
# Write the output to the appropriate places
#

open (COMMENTFORM,">> $logs/comments.log");
write (COMMENTFORM);
close (COMMENTFORM);

open (MAILCOMMENT,"|mail webmaster@finesse.com");
write (MAILCOMMENT);
close (MAILCOMMENT);

#
# Return a web page
#

select (STDOUT);
print "<html><head><title> Thanks for Your Comments
</title></head><body>";
write(STDOUT);
print "</body></html>";
```

Setting More Environment Variables

The first item of note in the script is the line:

```
do '/WWW/cgi-bin/setenv.pl';
```

This command executes the script setenv.pl. The results of setenv.pl are retained for use later in the script with the do statement. The setenv.pl script, shown in Code Example 9-6, sets environment variables beyond those known to the CGI. The CGI sets only the environment variables that it knows about from the httpd. Use setenv.pl to set all other variables that are needed for a script.

This method is also a handy way to make a set of scripts fairly portable by storing generic information in one place and referencing it from all scripts. Unfortunately, on a UNIX system, the `#!` line that defines where to look for the `perl` program still has to be coded into the individual script.

Code Example 9-6   Coding `perl` Program Location in `setenv.pl`

```
#!/usr/local/sun4/perl

$ServerRoot = "/WWW";
$DocRoot = "$ServerRoot/Docs";
$cgiRoot ="$ServerRoot/cgi-bin";
$logs = "$ServerRoot/logs";
```

Parsing the Form Variable Information

The second section parses each form variable and assigns the information to a perl variable. Another way to accomplish this task is with the program `cgiparse`, included in the CERN server utilities distribution. By means of `cgiparse`, the section can be reduced to Code Example 9-7, shown below.

Code Example 9-7   Using `cgiparse`

```
#
# Parse the variables to be used
#
$NAME=`"$exeRoot/cgiparse" -value name`;
$EMAIL=`"$exeRoot/cgiparse" -value email`;
$COMMENT=`"$exeRoot/cgiparse" -value comment`;
```

Using Perl Formats

Perl uses formats to lay out information in a pleasing and organized form. A format starts with the format definition and ends with a period. The period must be the only character on the line, and it must be in the first column. A format is composed of general text, such as the information line "left this message about your web server," variables, and variable pictures. Variable pictures are strings of characters that define how a field should be laid out. The following characters are used in this script for variable picture formatting:

- @ — indicates that a new field is starting
- < — indicates that the text should be left-justified
- @*— indicates that the data may be multiline or more than one line in size

The format shown below places the name variable on a line by itself and left-justifies it. Next, a text message is inserted. The email variable is placed on a left-justified line by itself, and the comment is displayed until all information is printed.

Code Example 9-8   Using Formats

```
============================================================
@<<<<<<<<<<<<<<<<<<<<<<<<<<<<<<<<<<<<<<<<<<<<<<<<<<<<
$NAME
left this message about your web server
@<<<<<<<<<<<<<<<<<<<<<<<<<<<<<<<<<<<<<
$EMAIL
@*
$COMMENT
============================================================
```

Writing to Various Output Locations

The format is given the same name as the output variable to which the data will be written. Thus, the data laid out in the format STDOUT will be written to stdout, and the data in format COMMENTFORM will be written to whatever output COMMENTFORM is written to.

Code Example 9-9   Defining Format Outputs

```
open (COMMENTFORM,">> $logs/comments.log");
write (COMMENTFORM);
close (COMMENTFORM);
```

In the example above, the output COMMENTFORM is set to append to the file comments.log in the defined logs directory. In the full example, there is an additional format output, MAILCOMMENT, which is currently usable only on UNIX systems.

Search For Data

When your server is large, it is a good idea to let users search for pages that meet their needs rather than load several pages to find what they are looking for. Several data location programs, each with its own methodology, are available for each platform. They fall into two categories, search tools and indexed databases.

Search tools define a directory tree or list of directories to search for the specific word that a user wants to look up. Many common tools, such as agrep and htgrep, are based on the UNIX grep tool.

Databases with indexes usually provide faster searching, and custom indexes, such as synonym indexes, make it easier to find a needle in a haystack. However, these databases require more maintenance. The indexes must be regenerated for new data, and they take up as much as 20% of the space of the data they are indexing. Most of the tools in this category are based on WAIS or the Z39.50 ISO standard. Refer to Appendix E, *More Information*, for pointers to these products.

The basic process of creating searchable information is as follows:

- Install the indexing or search software.
- Create the indexes if you are using indexing software.
- Create a web page to call the search tool.

You can create a regular web page that has a form with a text field for a simple search. However, this process has been automated. A single tag can now do the work of three. You can use the <ISINDEX> tag instead of a form with a text field. The <ISINDEX> tag has the ACTION attribute, just like a form. An example is:

```
<ISINDEX ACTION="/cgi-bin/newwais.pl/wwwserver">
```

This example in Figure 9-1 creates a search prompt.

Figure 9-1   Search Prompt Created with <ISINDEX> Tag

9

Summary

In this chapter, you learned:

- How to handle input from web forms.
- How to direct the output to the client via stdout, to a file, and, on UNIX systems, to email.
- How to create a feedback form.
- How to create a search prompt.

Tags Used in This Chapter

Tag	Attribute	Description
`<ISINDEX>`		Creates a prompt to gather a request for searching.
	ACTION	Defines the script or program called to complete the search.

Style Guide 10 ≡

Document Layout

The market is wide open for the companies that rent space on web servers. Costs can range from $10 to over $1000 per month. One of the key selling points touted for the more costly web servers is that they have better design skills. Unfortunately, cost isn't always related to design quality. This chapter discusses some standard style and design techniques.

Creating a Common Document Style with Templates

Users obtain more information if they know where to look for it. Documents should have a consistent look and feel. You should consistently put information in the same structural format. To begin with, you should create a template that includes the standard HTML formatting tags, a common titling methodology, and a set of navigation links.

Navigation

When documents form a set, there can be more than one way to step through the documents. They may have a linear progression. They may have a group of overview documents that can call task- or object-specific information. Whatever structure is implied in the documents should be reflected in the navigation tools offered to the user.

These tools are usually a set of links within each document and between related documents. There is a wealth of graphical images to use for these links. However, to accommodate the increasingly common use of browsers with Delay Image Loading, every navigational image should also have a word-based link in addition to the image link. The link can be created such that the anchor encompasses both the image and the text of the anchor as one link. An example of this is:

```
<a href=/> <img src="/images/home.gif"> Return to the Home Page </a>
```

In addition, all inline images should have the ALT attribute defined for the text-only browsers. An example is:

```
<a href="/">
<img src="/images/home.gif" alt="Return"> Return to the Home Page
</a>
```

All document sets should have some navigational control. Related documents should have even more control. The most commonly used controls are described below.

- **Go to Top** — When a document is more than two screen pages in length, a Go to Top link should return the user from the bottom to the top of a document. In documents that run more than ten screen pages in length, this control can be placed at the end of a main section or level-2 heading. To accomplish this, use a named anchor at the top of the document and a pointing anchor that starts with a # sign to avoid reloading the current document. For example, this identifier can be placed just after the <BODY> definition:

  ```
  <a name=top>
  ```

  This tag can be placed at the bottom of the document, and in cases of very large documents at the end of one section, just before starting the header for the next section.

  ```
  <a href=#top> Go to Top </a>
  <h2>
  ```

- **Previous Page/Document** — In document sets that follow a linear progression, for example, a book, usually only the Table of Contents and one previous chapter would point to the current document. In those case, a Previous Page or Previous Document link should point to the previous document in the linear progression. If access to a document can be described as random, such as man page references, this navigation tool is irrelevant, often confusing, and shouldn't be used.

- **Next Page/Document** —As with the Previous Page/Document navigation tool, a Next Page or Next Document link should point to the next document in the linear progression. If access to a document can be described as random, for example, man page references, this navigation tool is irrelevant, often confusing, and shouldn't be used.

- **Table of Contents** — If a document is three or more screen pages, a table of contents can be created at the top of the document listing the sections and allowing the user to jump forward to the sections. An example is:

HTML Example 10-1Sample TOC

```
{ Heading tags are above here}
<BODY><h1> Title of Document goes here </h1>
This chapter covers:
<ul>
<a href="#Section1"> First Section </a>
<a href="#Section2"> Second Section </a>
<a href="#Section3"> Third Section </a>
</ul>
<a name="Section1"> <h2> First Section</h2>
{ some text }
<a name="Section2"> <h2> Second Section</h2>
{ some text }
<a name="Section3"> <h2> Third Section</h2>
{ some text }
```

Even though the first section directly follows the Table of Contents, it should be included for consistency.

In sets of documents, it is also good to create a document that is a generic Table of Contents for all of the other related documents. In many cases, this page is also the home page.

- **Index** — Indexes can be placed on web pages with the Table of Contents or on the home page, or the indexes can be on a page by themselves. If you do have an index, the page with the index should be accessible from anywhere in the document structure.

- **Home** — Home can mean several things. Usually the home page is a web page at the top of the document set or even above the document set. The home page should be the starting point for a user browsing your web pages. Home, Index, and Table of Contents may all be the same page. Remember, people can enter a site at points other than the home page, for example, when they have been given a pointer from another person who has browsed the site.

A common convention is to place a horizontal rule at the bottom of the document and to put the standard navigational tools such as Home page, Index, and Comments page links below it.

10

Documenting for Universal Use

Just because you are creating a hypertext document in HTML doesn't mean that this information will never be needed in paper format. It is a good idea to create a document set that can be printed and read in bed as well as viewed on line. This means that each document that you create should be a standalone article.

Standardizing Between On-Line and Off-Line Documentation

When documents that will be used both as printed documents and on-line pages are created, each page can have links to a glossary or definition page. Since the printed document does show the link with an underline, the user can be informed on the first page that underlined items can be looked up in the glossary. This glossary can be printed separately and included at the end of the printed document set.

The other acceptable pointer within multiple-use documents are references to chapter or section headings when a Table of Contents is included. In this case the Table of Contents doesn't have to be at the top of each document. It can be a separate document itself that is included at the beginning of a printed document set. These references are usually noted with a "See Section {*Section name*}" to indicate that the reader should refer to the Table of Contents to locate the section.

User-Controlled Granularity

In addition to making each document into a standalone article, you should decide how much information should go into a single document. For example, you may have an employee handbook that is about 30 printed pages.

- *Should this become a single 30 page on-line document?*

  Not as the primary on-line copy. It might be nice to offer a version that is the entire document in a single file for the person who wants to print the whole thing. This is a nice add-on feature, but it should never be the primary method for managing the entire document.

- *Should this become six documents, with one for each chapter?*

  Maybe yes, and maybe no. It is debatable as to whether a document should be broken up at the chapter or section level. Ideally, no document meant for on-line use should be more than about eight to ten screen pages in length. (Screen pages vary from system to system, so your mileage may vary). As mentioned above, navigational controls such as Go To Top and an internal Table of Contents should be added to any document more than two screen pages in length.

- *Should this become thirty-six documents, with one for each topic section?*

Again, maybe yes and maybe no. The question here concerns how many of the sections an average user will access at a given time. If you expect users to read three or more sections in a row or if you expect users to want to print multiple sections, they will be using the document serially and it should be divided by chapters. However, if users will only refer to specific sections, making it reference material, splitting the document by sections is a better idea.

Audience Considerations

It is important to remember your audience when designing web pages. People will use different browsers and access methods.

Server Connection Speed

If you are serving only clients on a local area network, or LAN, the speed of the server-client connection should be a consideration only if the LAN is already fairly loaded. However, if you are serving documents to the Internet, the speed of the connection of both the client and the server to the Internet is an important consideration.

If the server's Internet connection is a dedicated T-1 or better, the server connection speed shouldn't be a design consideration. But if the server's connection is only a
56-Kbyte line and you expect to handle more than one client at a time, you should keep the data sent to the client small. This is primarily true in the case of images.
1-Kbyte images or 10-Kbyte images don't require significant transmission activity, but a 60-Kbyte or 100-Kbyte image will take significantly more time.

Servers generally have sufficient connection speed unless they are sharing their Internet connection with other traffic. If you notice overall performance degradation, upgrade your connection or make smaller building blocks.

Client Connection Speed

The connection speed of a client Internet connection is a significantly more important issue. Client connections can be generalized into two categories, home connections and work connections.

Home connections tend to be across a 14.4K modem and appear to be very sloooow. Many the home connection clients will use Delay Image Loading techniques for faster access to information and optionally load images only when they are interested. If your audience contains a significant number of home connections, you should:

- Limit your images to between one and three images per page and keep the total size of the images to less than 15 Kbytes.

- List the size of the image so that uses are prepared for what they are about to receive, especially if you are making pictures of your products available to a home-connection client.

- Make all of your links to other pages with text or a text/image combination. Users shouldn't have to download an image to decide if they want to follow the link.

- Avoid long, thin images such as specialty horizontal rules where the user is prone to use Delay Image Loading. That long, thin image becomes a square block that doesn't adequately separate sections of text.

Work connections are usually faster than home connections. If your audience are professionals viewing your work on higher-speed lines, then the sexy multimedia links such as images, sound, and movies can be used more frequently.

Even when most of your audience is in the high-speed, work-connection category, a low-impact text mode should be available. A common technique is to offer a link on the home page to an equivalent set of pages that are text-only.

Client Program Configuration and Use

HTML is not displayed the same way on various client browsers. Unless you expect to have a captive audience viewing your pages from the same browser, don't customize your pages to look perfect on one specific browser, as this usually makes them look lopsided on other browsers.

Don't assume that everyone uses the basic gray background. If someone has a black logo and the gray background, this will show up as a black square on a monochrome monitor. If someone sets the background to be white or purple instead of gray, a gray background will look ugly. Convert your images to use a transparent background, as described in *Creating Transparent Backgrounds* in Chapter 4, *Multimedia—Going Beyond Text.*

Don't base your color scheme on the gray background, either. A beautiful, multiple-shades-of-blue horizontal rule will stand out like a sore thumb for the user who prefers an orange background.

Use common MIME types when putting images and other multimedia data out for public consumption. Making Quicktime™ movies available is great for Macintosh clients, but Microsoft Windows and UNIX clients have a harder time finding a Quicktime player. Stick with the most common formats.

Tips

- **Test on multiple platforms** — Test your pages on multiple platforms before you release them to the world. What may look wonderful on the Macintosh may look horrible on a UNIX NCSA Xmosaic browser.

- **Use statistics and logs as course corrections** — Your logs are a gold mine of information. Look at what percentage of the users are loading the pages but not the images in the pages. Look at which pages have never or rarely been accessed.
  - Is the wording in the link unclear?
  - Is the link broken?

  Don't wait for people to tell you that there are problems. Most people find the problem and go away without saying a thing.

- **Avoid the aesthetic faux pas**
  - **Avoid *Click Here*** – The *only* exception to this rule is the home page of a WWW tutorial. If people are actively using a browser, they know what a link looks like and that they can click on it for more information. One alternative phrase is "More information is available on *link*."
  - **Don't use long titles** (such as ones that wrap around) – Remember that the title goes into the hotlist, where display space is limited.
  - **Always use text with images that are links** – This is one thing that can't be over-emphasized. There is nothing worse than encountering a home page that is a series of images without a single word on the entire page.

10

HTML for Fun and Profit

Work-Saving Tools

Because HTML is a structured formatting language, correct syntax is important. Unfortunately, it is the little things—such as forgetting to put the closing > on a tag, or forgetting the closing tag altogether—that can require debugging time. You may have documents from various word processing or desktop publishing programs that you want to put on line. Tools are available to save you the debugging and rekeying time. These tools fall into three categories: filters, templates, and editors or authoring tools.

Filters

Filters convert documents from one format to another and are useful when the documents already exist. Some documents use basic formatting instructions, such as *make the following text bold*. It is easy to convert an instruction like this into a pair of <B> and </B> tags. In other cases, the word processor may use logical words to define a block of text. For example, in the basic FrameMaker® documents there is a format definition called ScreenText. When you encounter this definition, you need to provide the word processor with a cross-referenced list of format instructions, such as ScreenText, and their HTML equivalents, such as <code>.

Dozens of filters are available for converting many types of documents to HTML. It would take an entire book to document how all the filters work. This chapter presents an example of how a filter might run. Refer to *Filters and Authoring Tools* in Appendix E, *More Information* to locate a current copy of the filters listed here.

Sample Filter Activity

To demonstrate how a filter works, we will convert backg.rtf to HTML with rtftohtml2.7.5 on a Macintosh.

1. **Start** rtftohtml2.7.5 **by double-clicking on it.**

2. **Select the Open option on the File menu.**

3. **From the list, select the file** `backg.rtf`.

4. **A message window opens and displays informational and error messages while the document is being converted. When the conversion is complete,** `backg.html` **and** `backg.err` **exist.**

`rtftohtml2.7.5` allows you to customize the cross-reference list of Rich Text Format (RTF) names to HTML markup. Formatting items that the program didn't recognize caused errors during the conversion process. We can customize the markup list by adding a definition for one of the items.

The file that lists the definitions is called `html-trans`. It has four sections: `.PTag`, `.TTag`, `.Pmatch`, and `.TMatch`. The `.PTag` and `.TTag` sections define paragraph and text HTML sequences, respectively. The `.PMatch` and `.TMatch` sections map the RTF formats to the HTML definitions in the `.PTag` and `.TTag` sections.

For this example, we will add a definition for the RTF format `Title.Title`. Since this is the title, it should be a heading-level one in HTML. By examining the `.PTag` section, we find that the name for heading-level one markup is called `h1`.

So, we will add an entry, which maps `Title.Title` to `h1`, in the `.PMatch` section, as in the following:

Code Example 11-1   Adding an Entry to `.PMatch` *Section*

```
# Starting with rtftohtml 2.7 all html-trans files have a version
number
{text deleted}

#  Format:
#  "Paragraph Style",NestLevel,"ParagraphStyleName"
#  First Entry is the default if no style match. Should be level 0
#  point to a Paragraph style with no markup
.PMatch
"heading 1",0,"h1"
"Title.Title",0,"h1"
```

Rerunning the conversion removes the error and properly formats the associated text.

Filters for Common Data

FrameMaker, Microsoft Word for Windows™ (for MS-Windows and Macintosh), and WordPerfect® are currently the most common word processors. Both Microsoft Word and WordPerfect can save their documents into RTF, Rich Text Format. FrameMaker saves its documents to MIF, Maker Interchange Format. RTF and MIF files can then be piped to a filter and output as HTML. Microsoft Word documents can also use templates, as discussed in the next section.

RTF Filters

You can find RTF-to-HTML filters from these sources.

- **rtftohtml**, at:

  `ftp://ftp.cray.com/src/WWWstuff/RTF/latest/binaries`

- **rtftoweb** by Christian Bolik — `rtftohtml` extensions for UNIX, at:

  `ftp://ftp.rrzn.uni-hannover.de/pub/unix-local/misc`

- **rtf2html** by Chuck Shotton, at:

  `ftp://oac.hsc.uth.tmc.edu/public/unix/WWW`

MIF Filters

You can find information about MIF or the MIF-to-HTML filters themselves from these sources.

- **WebMaker** by CERN Switzerland. Information is available at:

  `http://www.cern.ch/WebMaker`

- **fm2html** by Norwegian Telecom Research, available at:

  `ftp://bang.nta.no/pub/fm2html*.tar.Z`

- **Miftran** by Jim McBeath, available at:

  `ftp://ftp.alumni.caltech.edu/pub/mcbeath/web/miftran/miftran.tgz`

11

Templates

Templates are sets of formatting instructions that can be loaded into a familiar editor. The document created with this template is then saved directly as HTML. This document is usually used for creating new documents without forcing the user to learn a new tool. In most cases, the user must still learn about tags and how they are used.

BBEdit for Macintosh

BBEdit is a popular editor for the Macintosh. Since the creators of BBEdit offer an add-on package for creating extensions to the editor, BBEdit now has HTML extensions. HTML pages are created by typing in the text, then highlighting the text and selecting a specific extension.

Note – In BBEdit, the HTML templates are called extensions.

Word For Windows

The following templates can be used within Word for Windows.

- **ANT_HTML.DOT**— A template that works within Word for Windows 6.0 to facilitate the creation of hypertext documents. HTML code can be inserted into any new or previously prepared Word document or any ASCII document. New documents can be maintained entirely in Word with WYSIWYG-like editing and then exported to HTML. Version 2.0 is available for purchase.

- **CU_HTML.DOT**— Templates for both Word 2.0 and Word 6.0 that allow users to create HTML documents within WFW.

- **GT_HTML.DOT** — A set of macros in a template that help with HTML authoring.

- SGML Tag Wizard™ from NICE Technologies™ USA — A professional set of conversion tools for various formats, including Word for Windows, available at

    ```
    http://infolane.com/nice/nice.html
    ```

Authoring Tools

An authoring tool is an editor with a special role in life, editing HTML. Authoring tools provide an editing environment in which both text and formatting can be inserted correctly and completely. Some authoring tools offer syntax checking and correction as well.

Note – Several of these packages call themselves WYSIWYG or semi-WYSIWYG. It is important to remember that these packages can present the document with the format tags hidden and implemented, but that is no guarantee that the document will appear the same on various browsers. Take the WYSIWYG attribution with a grain of salt.

Authoring tools are available for all platforms: UNIX, Macintosh, and Microsoft Windows/Windows NT. Many of these products have a freeware or shareware version available on the Internet and a professional version that can be purchased. Sample sessions with two editors are shown below.

HTML Assistant

HTML Assistant™ is a shareware Microsoft Windows HTML editor. It has a companion professional version as well. Let's examine its operation by creating a web page. Figure 11-1 shows the main menu of HTML Assistant.

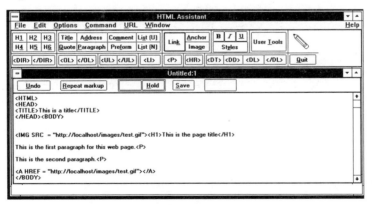

Figure 11-1   HTML Assistant

Here is a sample session with HTML Assistant.

1. Create a new document.
A new document is created just as with any other editor. Pull down the File menu and select New.

2. Do a general markup, that is, HTML and HEAD/BODY.
Either:
Pull down the Command menu and select Display Standard Document Wrapper;

Or:
Enter the document information first and then do the following:

   a. Highlight the entire document.

   b. Pull down the Command menu and select Mark Selected Text as HTML.

   c. Highlight the text in the head of the document.

   d. Pull down the Command menu and select Mark Selected Text as HTML.

   e. Highlight the rest of the document.

   f. Pull down the Command menu and select Mark Selected Text as BODY.

3. Add a title.
Either:
Type in a title for your document, highlight what you typed, and choose the Title button;

Or:
Choose the Title button and type between the tags that appear.

4. Add a heading (H1) for name.
Either:
Type in text, highlight it, and click on the H1 button to declare the tag;

Or:
Insert the tag first and then type the information between the start and end tags.

5. Add a picture.
A logo looks good next to the title, so do the following:

   a. Click to put the pointer before the <H1> tag.

   b. Click on the Image button.

c. Type in a URL in the URL text box.

Figure 11-2 illustrates the results of this step.

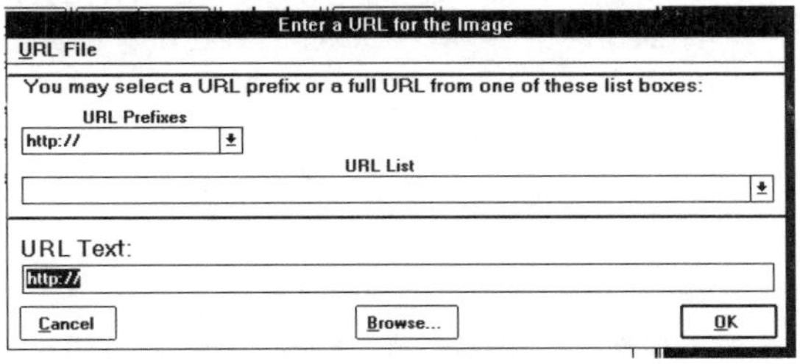

Figure 11-2   Adding a Picture via HTML Assistant

If you use the Browse button, the URL text box will have a local pathname that doesn't reflect the image's location on the Web.

After you have inserted an image into a document once, that URL is listed in the URL List. You can select the image again by clicking on it instead of typing it in several times. This is handy when you are using candy bullets or other repeating images.

6. Add a few paragraphs.

Either:

Type in the text and manually click on the <P> button at the end of each paragraph;

Or:

Follow these steps:

a. Type in all the text.

b. Highlight the text.

c. Pull down the Command menu and select Autoinsert Paragraph Markings.

7. Link to another web page.

Adding a link to another web page is done in the same way as adding an image, except that you click on the Link button instead of on the Image button.

≡ *11*

HoTMetaL and HoTMetaL Pro

SoftQuad of Toronto Canada has produced a product called HoTMetaL™; a shareware version of this product is included on the CD-ROM and is freely available on the Internet. An enhanced version called HoTMetaL Pro™ is available for purchase from SoftQuad.

HoTMetaL Pro offers spell checking, a thesaurus, syntax checking (validation), macro creation, and the capability to insert next-generation tags for tables. Figure 11-3 shows the main menu of HotMetaL Pro.

Figure 11-3   HoTMetaL Pro

Here is a sample session with HoTMetaL Pro.

1. Open a template.
You can start with a previously created template instead of starting from scratch. For example, you can open `homepage.html` and start with a page that already has the general markup (HTML, HEAD, and BODY), a title, an image, some text, and some links. We do that in this session.

Note – Tags are not directly editable in HoTMetaL Pro. They have a border around them to distinguish them from the actual text. To hide the tags (so you can see what the page looks like), pull down the View menu and select Hide Tags.

---

2. Add a title.
Because the template was loaded, just highlight the text between the title tags and type over it with your own text.

3. **Add a H1 for name.**
Because the template was loaded, just highlight the text between the H1 tags and type over it with your own text.

4. **Add a picture**
Since the image is already there, just change it to what you want for your image. To do this:

   a. **Place the cursor anywhere between the IMG tags.**

   b. **Pull down the Markup menu and select Edit URL.**

   c. **Modify the URL.**

   As in HTML Assistant, in HoTMetaL Pro you can browse to find the image that you want to use. Use this method here, because later in this exercise you will be able to modify the URL automatically.

5. **Add a few paragraphs.**
Because the template was loaded, just highlight the text around the <P> tags and type over it with your own text.

6. **Link to another server.**
Either:
Modify an existing link in the template by these steps:

   a. **Place the cursor anywhere between the Link tag.**

   b. **Pull down the Markup menu and select Edit URL.**

   c. **Modify the URL.**

   As in HTML Assistant, in HoTMetaL Pro you can browse to find the image that you want to use. Use this method here, because later in this exercise you will be able to modify the URL automatically.

Or:
Insert a new link by these steps:

   a. **Place the cursor where the link should be inserted.**

   b. **Pull down the Markup menu and select Insert Element.**

   c. **Select the Anchor element from the menu.**

   d. **Pull down the Markup menu again and select Edit URL**

   e. **Input the URL in the dialog box.**

7. **Check the spelling.**

   Pull down the Edit menu and select Check Spelling to verify the spelling on the web page.

   This is one of the features that makes HoTMetaL Pro resemble a full, word processing environment in the HTML world.

8. **Verify the syntax.**

   Pull down the Special menu and select Validate Selection to verify the syntax of your web page. If you left Rules Checking on, your web page should be correct to begin with. However, if you are importing a page from another source, Validate Selection is a handy method for isolating syntax errors.

9. **Publish.**

   Now that you have finished your document, you can change the URLs from `file://`— which they had when you used the browse feature on the Edit URL dialog— to true `http://` URL syntax. To do this, pull down the File menu and select Publish. A dialog box asks what to change the definitions to.

More Editors

HTML Assistant and HoTMetaL Pro are by no means the only editors available. The list is changing constantly. For the latest list of editors, refer to `http://www10.w3.org/hypertext/WWW/Tools/Overiew.html`.

Putting Data on the Internet   12 ≡

Not everyone will want to put their creations on the Internet, but most people will. This chapter covers what is involved when putting data on the Internet. If you have a large and complex server configuration, you may want to have your own server. However, having your own server means that you provide both system and WWW server administration, security maintenance, and Internet connectivity. That is a large task for many small organizations, and it is beyond this book. Appendix E, *More Information*, lists some books and other resources for researching this subject in depth.

Service Providers

Several Internet media service providers offer both the server on which to put your web pages and the maintenance of that server. They vary widely in services provided and cost, so it is important to shop around.

Different service providers charge for different things. The most common things to charge for are:

- **Disk Space** — Many service providers charge by how many megabytes of data you store on the WWW server. Some services are more granular than that and charge by the kilobyte instead of by the megabyte.

- **Traffic** — Every time someone requests your pages from the WWW server, the server must use a little CPU time and a little bit of its connectivity bandwidth. Each connection alone is very little overhead. However, it you have 1,000 people checking out your pages every day, the processing adds up.

- **Extra Services** — Processing forms, using clickable images, doing WAIS searches, and running other CGI scripts and Server Includes takes processing power. WAIS databases also take up disk space. Many service providers charge extra for these capabilities, and some don't even provide these services at all.

- **Server Index or Company Listing** — Some service providers offer an index or company listing to link your pages into. If you are expecting added value from this listing, it is a good idea to browse prospective service providers' web sites before making your decision. Some service providers may have a hundred, different web page listings. If your listing doesn't explain itself well enough to tempt people to look at the page, the additional listing isn't worth the cost. On the other hand, service providers may have a hundred listings or more, but have them grouped intelligently. In this case, your listing may stand out for the people who are looking for what you provide.

If you don't know of any places that are renting web space, look at the WWW Service Providers list. A copy of this frequently updated list is on the CD-ROM under `/docs/WWWProv.doc`. You can obtain the latest version via ftp from `ftp://ftp.einet.net/pub/INET-MARKETING/www-svc-providers`, or send email to `LISTPROC@EINet.net` with the message

```
GET INET-MARKETING WWW-SVC-PROVIDERS
```

in the body of the email.

Announcing a WWW Page

Once the web pages have been created, people need to use them. This will happen only if people know about them. There are a few things to consider when creating and posting an announcement.

Netiquette

On the Internet it is important to remember that everything is content-based. Hype is viewed as *very* poor taste. Your announcement should be a simple, matter-of-fact description of your server's URL, its contents, and the intended audience. Don't include any subjective descriptions such as *great* or *unique*. **Never** use exclamation marks. An example announcement is:

Announcing. the Webserver for the Clueless, an unusual look at those trapped on the Information Superhighway without a roadmap. On the server you can find some information about the latest Internet disease, Information Overload, some tips for travellers, and news about the development and construction of the Infobahn. Get snapshots, full reports, the latest news releases, and the current traffic reports of participating on-ramps. Our URL is:

http://www.noclue.com/

<a href="http://www.noclue.com/"> The Webserver for the Clueless </a>

Places to Tell the World About Your Web Pages

Blatant and intrusive advertising is also in poor taste, and *netizens*, or net citizens, will acquaint you with this fact if you overstep social propriety. They may acquaint you with this fact by *flaming* you, that is, by sending you a very heated note, or they may send you hundreds of copies of your announcement, a practice called mailbombing. Fortunately, there are some places that you can go to announce your addition to the web.

- **Net-Happenings Mail List** — An announcement area for all types of events on the Internet. The subject line usually starts with an all-capital letter word that describes the type of item. Web pages are usually announced with a **WWW>** at the start of the subject line. Send announcements to:

  `net-happenings@is.internic.net`

- **Directory of Directories** — An index of pointers to key resources on the Internet. The DofD is maintained by the Internic, a U.S. government-sponsored agency devoted to assisting with the Internet. The DofD offers two levels of entries. You can post a limited entry for free, or pay for an extensive entry. Send email to `admin@ds.internic.net` to obtain the template for submitting your entry.

- **Mother-of-all-BBS**— A hierarchical, subject-based list. Add an entry by completing the form found at:

  `http://www.cs.colorado.edu/home/mcbryan/public_html/bb/add.html`

- **Open Market's Commercial Sites Index** — A list of commercial web sites. Add an entry by completing the form found at:

  `http://www.directory.net/dir/submit.cgi`

- **New Internet Knowledge System** — A new list of web sites. Add a *noncommercial* entry by sending email to `javiani@rns.com`.

- **WWW Virtual Library** — A subject-oriented index of web sites. Various people maintain each subject area. To contact the person who manages the area to which you want to submit your entry, refer to:

`http://info.cern.ch/hypertext/DataSources/bySubject/Maintainers.html`

If you can't find an area that covers your entry, send email to `www-request@info.cern.ch`. If you send an announcement to `www-announce@info.cern.ch`, this directory will be automatically updated as well.

- **CERN's WWW Server List** — Fill out the form found at:

  ```
  http://info.cern.ch/hypertext/DataSources/WWW/Geographical
  _generation/new.html
  ```

- **What's New Announcements** — There are a few, different "What's New" lists on the Net.
  - **NCSA's What's New Page** - The publicly distributed copies of Xmosaic, WinMosaic, and MacMosaic all include an automatic pointer to NCSA's What's New page. To add an entry to this list, fill out the form found at:

    ```
    http://www.ncsa.uiuc.edu/SDG/Software/Mosaic/Docs/whats-new-
    form.html
    ```

  Or send email to whats-new@ncsa.uiuc.edu.

- **Registering with the Spiders** — Several organizations canvass the net and record new web sites. These programs are called *spiders*. When you register with these servers, it means that you want your server added to the list the next time the spider investigates the net. This investigation may occur the next day or two months later. This site is not for short-term announcements; instead, it is more of a long-term index where people can find you through indexes. Some of the indexes for probing that you can register with are:
  - **Lycos** – To register with the Lycos spider, complete the form found at:

    ```
    http://fuzine.mt.cs.cmu.edu/mlm/lycos-register.html
    ```

  - **ALIWEB** – To register with the ALIWEB spider, complete the form found at:

    ```
    http://web.nexor.co.uk/aliweb/doc/register-form.html
    ```

  - **World Wide Web Worm** – The World Wide Web Worm or WWWW is an index of web sites. Add an entry by completing the following link to a form:

    ```
    http://www.cs.colorado.edu/home/mcbryan/WWWW.html#new
    ```

- **www-announce** — Send the email announcement to www-announce@info.cern.ch.

- **Netnews group**s — It is important to limit your announcements to relevant groups. Following is a list of Netnews groups that would be interested in web servers related to their focus. Also, review *.announce groups and, if your web server has a local focus, consider posting to *{local area}*.announce, for example, ba.announce for San Francisco Bay Area announcements.

- **comp.newprod netnews group** – If you have new computer products on your web page, announce it here.
- **comp.infosystems.announce** – This is a fairly generic announcement area.
- **biz.*** – If your web site has a business focus, you may want to post to the appropriate group here.

≡ 12

___

HTML for Fun and Profit

Netscape 13 ≡

Netscape has produced a browser called Netscape Navigator or Mozilla. The informal Mozilla name is often used in conversations, and Mozilla is the name that the browser identifies itself as when communicating with servers. This browser implements a superset of HTML 2.0, including some HTML 3.0 specifications. In cases where Netscape developed features that were not in the HTML 3.0 specification, Netscape is actively working to add these features to the HTML 3.0 standards. Since the HTML 3.0 standards will not be finalized in 1995, it is not known if these enhancements will become official HTML 3.0 specifications.

Netscape enhancements initially can only be used on Netscape's browsers. Other browsers may choose to implement these features in the short term, they may implement whatever HTML 3.0 standards are firmed up, or they may wait until HTML 3.0 is officially standardized.

The use of these enhancements is the source of great debate. On the one hand, they add considerably to the layout control and visual communication aspects of the Web. On the other hand, since they are not implemented on many other browsers, the display of a Netscape-enhanced page on a non-Netscape browser may be poor. Keep your audience in mind when developing Netscape-enhanced web pages.

Netscape has added only a few new tags. The majority of their augmentation is in the addition of attributes to many current tags. These enhancements touch upon a wide range of areas, including document-wide color controls, image manipulation, and layout and sizing of many character, paragraph, and table items.

Document Enhancements

The most distinctive enhancements that Netscape has added are in the area of color. Until Netscape Navigator 1.1, text was always black, links were always blue, the background was always gray—unless, of course, the user chose to modify the color scheme. If you have access to a Netscape browser, you can view the HTML file by loading `http://{server}/Chapter13/bg.html` or `http://{server}/Chap13/bg.htm` on a Microsoft Windows system.

Colors

You can now add attributes to the <BODY> tag to control the colors displayed. The attributes are listed in Table 13-1.

Table 13-1   Body Attributes for Color Control

Attribute	Controls Display Item Color Of
TEXT	Plain text, headings, all basic text in a document.
LINK	Link text.
VLINK	Link text for a link that has already been visited.
ALINK	Active link text—the color a link is while it is being clicked on.
BGCOLOR	The color of the background.

All of these attributes are defined with an RGB color definition. RGB colors were introduced in Chapter 4, *Multimedia—Going Beyond Text*. An example is:

HTML Example 13-1   Setting Colors

```
<BODY BGCOLOR="FF33FF" LINK="FFFFFF" TEXT="000000" VLINK="CCFFFF">
```

Note – Many people have discovered that the use of multiple <BODY> tags with different BGCOLOR definitions can cause the background to cycle through the different colors specified while the document is being loaded. This is *not* a recommended action. The HTML specification only allows one <BODY> tag per document, and support for use of multiple <BODY> tags is not guaranteed in future releases.

Background Images

Instead of displaying a different color for a background, you can display an image. This is implemented with the BACKGROUND=*url* attribute. An example of this is:

HTML Example 13-2   Setting a Background Image

```
<BODY BACKGROUND="./something.gif" LINK="FFFFFF" TEXT="000000"
VLINK="CCFFFF">
```

Background images should be made fairly small. The image will be tiled across the background of the page. If a large background image is used, the user must load the image before the page can be seen, and this requirement can cause frustration.

Note – It is important to always set the text and link colors when modifying the background. Systems display color slightly differently depending on the gamma of the monitor. Blue text on a blue background may not be readable for everyone, even if it is readable to you. Make sure that your color scheme offers enough contrast to guide the user.

Image Enhancements

Images are the bane and blessing of the Web. The average person is attracted to images, primarily because of the visual stimulation. Unfortunately, downloading images can be a tedious process on a slow bandwidth line. The wide variety of screen display characteristics can also make for some interesting viewing. If you have access to a Netscape browser, you can view the HTML file by loading http://*{server}*/Chapter13/image.html or http://*{server}*/Chap13/image.htm on a Microsoft Windows system.

Image Loading

Netscape has introduced multiple methods for reducing image loading impact on a browser. These include displaying interlaced images as they are loaded and offering the ability to load a low-resolution image initially and then loading a high-resolution image later.

Interlaced Images

GIF images are loaded line by line. Netscape has added the option of displaying the image as it is loading. The fact that an image is appearing tends to make the wait seem shorter. One effect that *speeds up* this process even further is interlacing an image. Interlacing is writing the image out to its file out of sequence. For example, the first line can be written out, then the third, then the fifth line. When the end of the image is reached, the second, fourth, sixth lines and so on, can be displayed. Seeing part of an image, the human eye tends to fill in the missing pieces, and an image can be presented, albeit a lesser-quality image, in half the time. Many graphics tools offer the option of interlacing images. Check your tools for this capability. No HTML coding is required to implement this feature.

Managing Image Impact

For those people who want to present a really high-resolution image (that will take considerable time to load, even interlaced), there is an additional option for easing the user wait. This is to load a quick version of the image immediately, and then start loading the large image. The quick version of an image is usually created in JPG format, since JPG usually creates a smaller image for photographic quality images. The initial image to load is specified by the LOWRES attribute to the <IMG> tag. An example of this is:

HTML Example 13-3   Loading a Low-Resolution Image

```
<img src="url.gif" lowsrc="lowres.jpg">
```

Aligning Images

In HTML 2.0, everything is left-justified. Netscape offers several alternatives for image placement. An image can now be placed along the left margin with ALIGN=LEFT, the right margin with ALIGN=RIGHT, or in the center of the page with ALIGN=CENTER. An example of this is:

HTML Example 13-4   Aligning Images

```
<IMG SRC="ensmall.gif" ALIGN=LEFT>
<IMG SRC="ensmall.gif" ALIGN=RIGHT>
Images can be aligned on the left or on the right. In fact, you can
put text between two images.<P>
```

Figure 13-1 shows how this alignment appears on a screen.

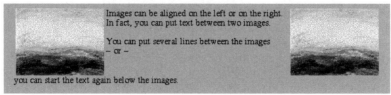

Figure 13-1   Aligning Images

Wrapping Text Around an Image

Multiple lines of text surrounding an image can now be made to flow
appropriately. The ALIGN=TOP, MIDDLE, or BOTTOM attribute performs this
function.

Managing Text Flow

There are times when you may want to start text after the image. The standard

 or <P> tags won't accomplish this function. A new attribute, CLEAR, resets
text flow patterns. CLEAR can be used with RIGHT, LEFT or ALL variable options.
An example of this is:

HTML Example 13-5   Managing Text Flow Around Images

```
You can put several lines between the images
<BR> - or -
<BR CLEAR=ALL>
you can start the text again below the images.<P><HR>
```

Figure 13-1 also shows this example.

LEFT will start the text flow after clearing all image constraints on the left side,
and RIGHT will clear image constraints only on the right. This can be used in the
case where you may have a long image on the left and three small images on the
right, each with associated text. By using CLEAR=RIGHT, the text associated with
each image can be properly formatted while a common image on the left is
maintained. The ALL option is used to start the text flow at the end of all images.

Creating Gutters Around an Image

By default, text starts immediately to the left of an image. Text is more readable when there is a margin or gutter of blank space between the image and the text. The VSPACE and HSPACE attributes control the amount of vertical and horizontal space around an image, respectively. An example of this is:

HTML Example 13-6   Adding a Gutter Around an Image

```
<IMG SRC="ensmall.gif" ALIGN=LEFT VSPACE=10 HSPACE=20>
<IMG SRC="ensmall.gif" ALIGN=RIGHT VSPACE=10 HSPACE=20>
The spacing between images and text can also be controlled. For
example, if I want a large blank space around and image I can
specify the <code>vspace</code> and <code>hspace</code> attributes.
<BR CLEAR=ALL>
This gives a wide berth to text, images, and horizontal rules.
```

Figure 13-2 shows an example of adding gutters.

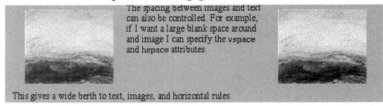

Figure 13-2   Adding a Gutter Around an Image

Scaling Images

By default, images are rendered in the size that they were created. However, browsers display differently. It is a good practice to create images no wider than about 550–580 pixels, to accommodate the users with a 640 x 480 display. The image can then be scaled with the WIDTH attribute to 100%. This eliminates the need for any user to scroll horizontally. Images can also be scaled with the HEIGHT attribute. One benefit of scaling is that one image can be used as both the corporate logo and a bullet image marker, thus saving transfer time of a second image. An example of this is:

HTML Example 13-7   Scaling Images

```
Images can be made larger or smaller,
<IMG SRC="ensmall.gif" WIDTH=80%>
<IMG SRC="ensmall.gif" HEIGHT=5%>
```

Figure 13-3 shows an example of scaling.

Figure 13-3   Scaling Images

By only specifying either the WIDTH or HEIGHT attribute, the proportions of the image are retained. An image can be stretched by specifying both the WIDTH and HEIGHT attributes at the same time. Another variation is to specify the WIDTH and HEIGHT attributes as numbers instead of percentages. An example of this is:

HTML Example 13-8   Stretching an Image

```
or stretched in funny ways.<P>
<IMG SRC="ensmall.gif" HEIGHT=50% WIDTH=25>
```

Figure 13-4 shows an example of stretching.

Figure 13-4   Stretching an Image

Paragraph Enhancements

Netscape has added alignment enhancements to many of their paragraph tags. They have also created some custom visual enhancements for horizontal rules and lists.

Horizontal Rules

Horizontal rules are used to place visual breaks in page. The default rule is a black line with a white line underneath it to make the line appear to have a shadow. The height, width, and alignment can be modified with Netscape enhancements. If you have access to a Netscape browser, you can view the HTML file by loading `http://{server}/Chapter13/hr.html` or `http://{server}/Chap13/hr.htm` on a Microsoft Windows system.

Adding Thickness

Netscape has added the `size` attribute to control the height of a horizontal rule. A numerical value is required for the `size` attribute. The default size is 1. An `<HR>` tag with size defined looks like:

HTML Example 13-9   Changing the Height of a Horizontal Rule

```
<hr size=5>
```

Figure 13-5 shows horizontal rules of size 1 and 10.

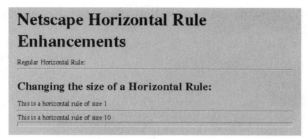

Figure 13-5   Changing the Height of a Horizontal Rule

Modifying the Width

By default, a horizontal rule stretches across the screen. Netscape has added the width attribute to control the width of a horizontal rule. A numerical value for pixels or percentage is required for the size attribute. The default size is 100%. An <HR> tag with width defined by percentage looks like:

HTML Example 13-10 Changing the Width of a Horizontal Rule

```
<hr width=50%>
```

An <HR> tag with width defined by pixels, looks like:

HTML Example 13-11 Changing the Width of a Horizontal Rule

```
<hr width=200>
```

Figure 13-6 shows horizontal rules where the pixel width is 10 and 100 and the width in percent is 10% and 100%.

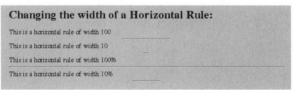

Figure 13-6   Changing the Width of a Horizontal Rule

Note – Widths should be specified in percentages in most cases. Doing so will accommodate varying screen sizes.

Modifying the Alignment of a Horizontal Rule

By default, a horizontal rule stretches across the screen. In cases where the width has been reduced from 100%, the horizontal rule will be centered. The rule can be aligned differently with the `align` attribute. The `align` attribute can take *left*, *center*, or *right* as variable definitions. An <HR> tag with alignment defined looks like:

HTML Example 13-12 Changing the Alignment of a Horizontal Rule

```
<hr align=left>
```

Figure 13-7 shows horizontal rules where the alignment is left, right, and centered.

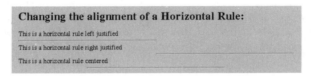

Figure 13-7   Changing the Alignment of a Horizontal Rule

Removing Shading

Normally, Netscape's horizontal rules appear shaded. Netscape has added the `noshade` attribute to remove the shading of a horizontal rule. No value is required for the `noshade` attribute. An <HR> tag with shading turned off looks like:

HTML Example 13-13 Removing the Shading of a Horizontal Rule

```
<hr noshade>
```

Figure 13-8 shows a horizontal rule without shading.

Removing shading from a Horizontal Rule:

This is a horizontal rule centered

Figure 13-8   Removing the Shading of a Horizontal Rule

Alignment Enhancements

The HTML 3.0 specification declares that headings and paragraphs can be aligned by use of the `align=value` attribute. To implement this, the `<P>` tag needed to change from being an empty element to being a container. When left alignment (the default) is used, the `<P>` tag can still be used by itself. However, for all alignment changes, the `<P>` tag must be accompanied by a closing `</P>` tag. If you have access to a Netscape browser, you can view the HTML file by loading `http://{server}/Chapter13/alignment.html` or `http://{server}/Chap13/align.htm` on a Microsoft Windows system.

Note – It is good practice to use the `<P>` and `</P>` tags together in all cases.

An example of text alignment looks like:

HTML Example 13-14 Aligning with the ALIGN=center Attribute

```
<P ALIGN=CENTER> In HTML 3.0, all text alignment can be <br>changed
with the <code> align=<em>description</em></code> attribute.
<br>. This goes for the P, and H1-H6 tags too. </P>
```

Figure 13-9 shows the alignment.

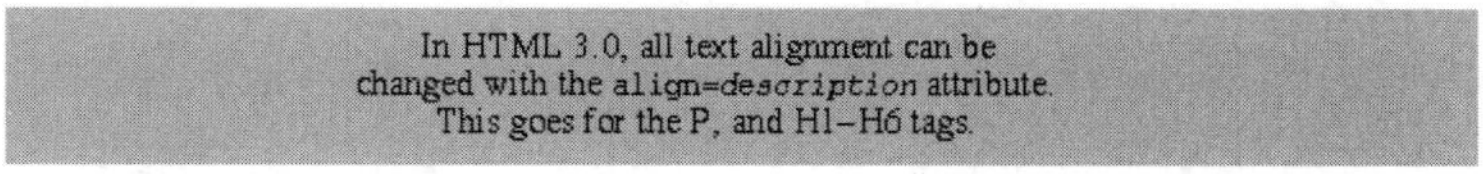

> In HTML 3.0, all text alignment can be
> changed with the `align=description` attribute.
> This goes for the P, and H1–H6 tags.

Figure 13-9   Aligning with the ALIGN=center Attribute

Netscape initially found problems with implementing a `<P ALIGN=center>` configuration and created a `<CENTER>` tag to take the place of `<P ALIGN=center>`.

An example of this looks like:

HTML Example 13-15 Aligning with the <CENTER> Tag

```
<CENTER> Netscape has chosen to <br> use a different tag for the
aligning of paragraphs,<br> namely the CENTER tag.</CENTER>
```

Figure 13-10 shows the alignment.

> Netscape has chosen to
> use a different tag for the aligning of paragraphs,
> namely the CENTER tag.

Figure 13-10 Aligning with the <CENTER> Tag

As of Netscape 1.1N, Netscape now supports both <CENTER> and <P ALIGN=center>. Netscape has also implemented HTML 3.0 standard centered alignment on headings. However, as of Netscape 1.1N, the ALIGN=*right* attribute has not been implemented for either the heading or paragraph tags.

An example of aligning text on the right looks like:

HTML Example 13-16 Aligning with the ALIGN=right Attribute

```
<P ALIGN=RIGHT> Netscape 1.1N does not implement the HTML 3.0
ALIGN=right option.</P>
```

Figure 13-11 shows the alignment.

> Netscape 1.1N does not implement the HTML 3.0 ALIGN=right option.

Figure 13-11 Aligning with the ALIGN=right Attribute

The alignment of headings can also be controlled with the ALIGN option.

An example of aligning headings looks like:

HTML Example 13-17 Aligning Headings with the ALIGN Attribute

```
<H3 ALIGN=CENTER> Netscape implements both<br> CENTER and
P ALIGN=CENTER standards, for centering only, while previous
versions of Netscape<br> only support the CENTER method. </H3>
```

Figure 13-12 shows the alignment.

> Netscape 1.1N does not implement the HTML 3.0 ALIGN=right option.

Figure 13-12 Aligning Headings with the ALIGN Attribute

List Enhancements

There are quite a few enhancements for lists suggested by the proposed HTML 3.0 standard. Netscape's current implementation of lists differs noticeably from the proposed HTML 3.0 standard drafted on March 28, 1995. The HTML 3.0 specification does evolve as time goes on, and the specification won't be accepted as a standard until late 1996 or 1997, so the differences may be reconciled before the standard is formally accepted. In the meantime, it is important to note the differences.

Netscape has implemented the TYPE attribute. The TYPE attribute allows the HTML author to control the type of bullet or other mark that starts off each list item.

If you have a Netscape browser, you can follow along by loading `http://{server}/Chapter13/list1.html` or `http://{server}/Chap13/list1.html` if you have a Microsoft Windows system.

Unordered Lists

For unordered lists, a filled-in circle, a hollow circle and a hollow square can be defined as follows:

HTML Example 13-18 Defining Unordered List Item Markers

```
<ul type=disc>
<li> One item for a filled in circle
<li> Another item for a filled in circle
</ul>

<ul type=circle>
<li> One different item for a filled in circle
<li> Another different item for a filled in circle
</ul>

<ul type=round>
<li> One item for a circle - not filled in
<li> Another item for a circle - not filled in
</ul>

<ul type=square>
<li> One item for a square
<li> Another item for a square
</ul>
```

Figure 13-13 shows what each entity looks like:

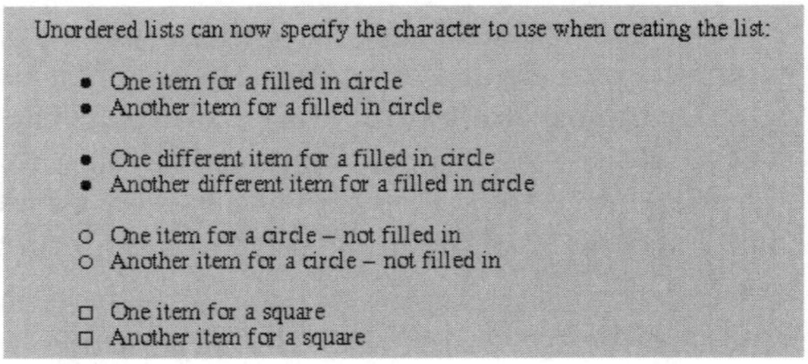

Unordered lists can now specify the character to use when creating the list:

- One item for a filled in circle
- Another item for a filled in circle

- One different item for a filled in circle
- Another different item for a filled in circle

○ One item for a circle – not filled in
○ Another item for a circle – not filled in

□ One item for a square
□ Another item for a square

Figure 13-13 Unordered List Item Markers

Ordered Lists

Ordered lists can now use capital or small letters, capital or small Roman numerals, or regular numbers, as in the example below:

HTML Example 13-19 Defining Ordered List Item Markers

```
Ordered lists can also be changed. Their options include:

<ol type=A>
<li> Capital Letters
<li> Capital Letters
</ol>

<ol type=a>
<li> Small Letters
<li> Small Letters
</ol>

<ol type=I>
<li> Capital Roman Numerals
<li> Capital Roman Numerals
</ol>

<ol type=i>
<li> Small Roman Numerals
<li> Small Roman Numerals
</ol>

<ol type=1>
<li>  Numbers
<li>  Numbers
</ol>
```

Figure 13-14 shows what each ordered list item marker looks like:

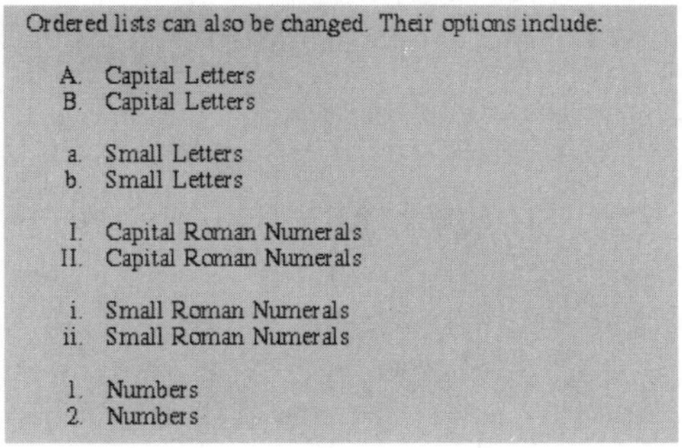

Ordered lists can also be changed. Their options include:

A. Capital Letters
B. Capital Letters

a. Small Letters
b. Small Letters

I. Capital Roman Numerals
II. Capital Roman Numerals

i. Small Roman Numerals
ii. Small Roman Numerals

1. Numbers
2. Numbers

Figure 13-14 Ordered List Item Markers

By default, ordered lists start at A, a, I, i, or just plain 1. By using the START attribute, an ordered list can be started somewhere other than the beginning. START takes a numeric value, regardless of the type specified. Therefore, START=5 can be E, e, V, v, or 5. An example of this is:

HTML Example 13-20 Starting an Ordered List at Something Other Than 1

```
Ordered lists can also be started from anywhere. You don't have
to start at 1.
<ol Start=2 type=A>
<li> The start attribute is always a number regardless of the list
system.
</ol>
```

Figure 13-15 shows what this would look like:

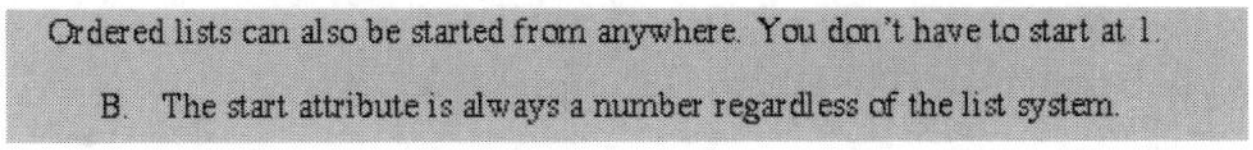

Ordered lists can also be started from anywhere. You don't have to start at 1.

B. The start attribute is always a number regardless of the list system.

Figure 13-15 Ordered List Starting at Something Other Than 1

With Netscape, the TYPE definition can be taken to yet another level of
granularity. The TYPE definition can be applied to the <LI> tag so that each list
item can have a different marker. This can be seen in the following example:

HTML Example 13-21 Using Different List Item Markers for Each Item

```
Then again, there is also the feature of making each list item a
different type.

<ul>
<li type=disc> One item for a filled in circle
<li type=circle> Another item for a filled in circle
<li type=round> Yet another item for a circle - not filled in
<li type=square> One item for a square
</ul>

Ditto for ordered lists:

<ol>
<li type=A> Capital Letters
<li type=a> Small Letters
<li type=I> Capital Roman Numerals
<li type=i> Small Roman Numerals
<li type=1> Regular Numbers
</ol>
```

Figure 13-16 shows what the HTML above looks like.

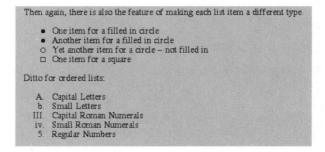

Figure 13-16 Different List Item Markers for Each Item

List Differences Between HTML 3.0 and Netscape

The proposed HTML 3.0 standard handles lists in a significantly different manner. Be prepared for additional Netscape enhancements and proposed standard changes to bring the two methods of implementing lists into accord. Some of the most notable changes are

- List item typing, such as Netscape's ordered list implementation, is proposed to be included in the stylesheet, not within the list declaration itself. This allows for a wider range of listings including nesting list item numbering such as 5a, 5b....
- The proposed standard uses the attribute SEQNUM instead of START.
- List sequences can be continued over multiple list declarations with the CONTINUE attribute instead of manual declaration of a start point. This is a good idea for reducing the maintenance of changing lists.
- Unordered list marks are taken from a DINGBAT icon definition.
- Lists can have headings declared for them.
- Unordered lists can be declared as PLAIN, eliminating the need for a MENU or DIR list type.

Character Enhancements

In order to capture the user's attention, important text needs to be set apart in some way. By character modification, text can be brought to the user's attention much faster. Netscape has added two features to enhance characters and bring them to awareness faster. If you have access to a Netscape browser, you can view the HTML file by loading http://{server}/Chapter13/font.html or http://{server}/Chap13/font.htm on a Microsoft Windows system.

Font Size Control

Changing the font size on a line has always been a good attention getter. In standard HTML 2.0, the only way to affect the size of the fonts was to make a heading. Adding strong or bold effects changed only the weight of the font, not the size. One of the big problems with changing font size by creating a heading was that the new font always started on a new line. There was no way to put different-sized fonts on the same line.

Font sizes can now be controlled by the <FONT> tag as well as by the <H1>...<H6> tags. Font sizes range from 1 to 7, with 3 being default text font size. An example of font size changes is:

HTML Example 13-22 Font Size Changes

```
Netscape now offers the ability to change font sizes independent
of defining specific paragraph formatting such as headings.<P>

<FONT SIZE=1> This is a size 1 font line. </FONT><P>
<FONT SIZE=2> This is a size 2 font line. </FONT><P>
<FONT SIZE=3> This is a size 3 font line. Paragraph text is
implemented
at this size by default.</FONT><P>
<FONT SIZE=4> This is a size 4 font line. </FONT><P>
<FONT SIZE=5> This is a size 5 font line. </FONT><P>
<FONT SIZE=6> This is a size 6 font line. </FONT><P>
<FONT SIZE=7> This is a size 7 font line. </FONT><P>
```

Figure 13-17 demonstrates these changes.

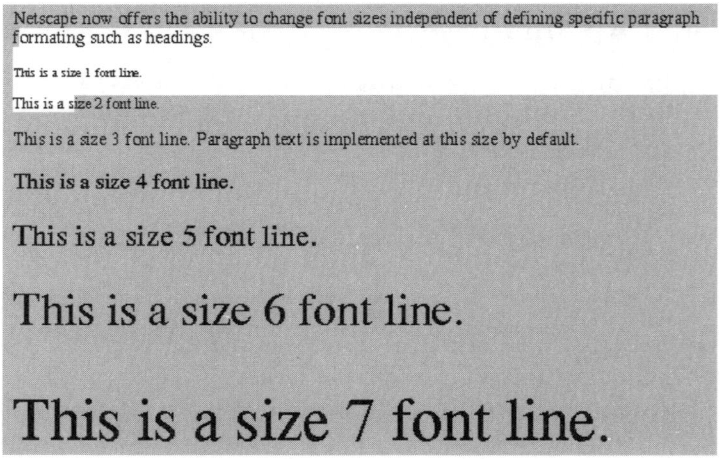

Netscape now offers the ability to change font sizes independent of defining specific paragraph formating such as headings.

This is a size 1 font line.

This is a size 2 font line.

This is a size 3 font line. Paragraph text is implemented at this size by default.

This is a size 4 font line.

This is a size 5 font line.

This is a size 6 font line.

This is a size 7 font line.

Figure 13-17 Font Size Changes

Blinking Text

Changing the size of the font on a line draws the user's eye to that area. Netscape has also included the ultimate attention-getting device, the <BLINK> tag. This tag is implemented as follows:

HTML Example 13-23 Blinking Text

```
<BLINK> Blinking text </BLINK>
```

Unfortunately, blinking text cannot be reproduced on this archaic medium.

Note – Blinking text is the ultimate attention getter. To avoid cognitive overload, the HTML author should make *only one* blinking text item per web page. It is recommended that <BLINK> be used only in very important situations—not just to highlight the webmaster's address, for example.

Table Enhancements

Netscape has implemented tables quite effectively and has added some layout features. If you have access to a Netscape browser, you can view the HTML file by loading `http://{server}/Chapter13/table.html` or `http://{server}/Chap13/table.htm` on a Microsoft Windows system.

Modifying Table Borders

With standard HTML 3.0, the BORDER attribute is used if a table should display a border. Netscape uses the BORDER attribute to define the size of the border. Thus, BORDER=0 means don't display a border to a Netscape browser. Unfortunately, many other browsers that do handle tables follow the HTML 3.0 standard. When they encounter the BORDER=0 attribute, some do display a border.

With Netscape, the border can be sized by using a number larger than 1 for the BORDER attribute. An example of this is:

HTML Example 13-24 Changing Border Size

```
With Netscape, the BORDER command can be set to larger numbers
(default of 1) to make thicker borders.<P>
<table border=4>
<th rowspan=2 colspan=2> Corner Headings  </th>
```

HTML Example 13-24 Changing Border Size (Continued)

```
<th colspan=3> This is the top line explaining the headings - Food
</th>
<tr>
<th> Meat </th>
<th> Fruit </th>
<th> Breads </th>
<tr>
<td rowspan=2> This is a sidebar explaining the side heads - required
</td>
<td> Yes </td>
<td> X </td>
<td> X </td>
<td> X </td>
<tr>
<td> No </td>
<td> - </td>
<td> X </td>
<td> - </td>
</table><P>
```

Figure 13-18 shows the different border.

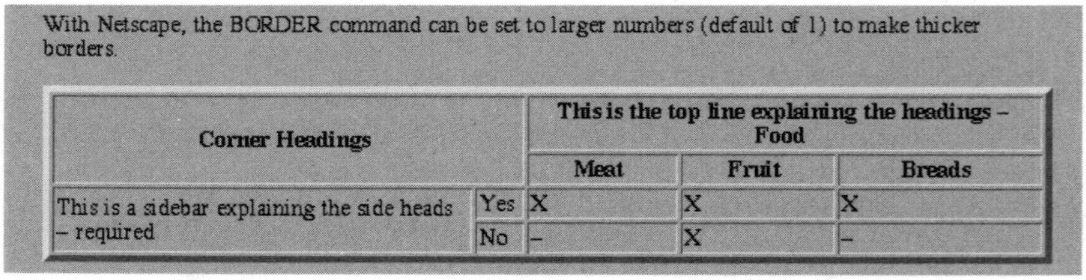

Figure 13-18 Changing Border Size

Modifying Data Alignment

In *Formatting Data in Cells* on page 86 of Chapter 5, *Tables*, basic alignment of data was covered. Netscape has effectively implemented this by using ALIGN=LEFT, RIGHT or CENTER for horizontal formatting, and VALIGN=TOP, MIDDLE or BOTTOM for vertical formatting.

An example of this is:

HTML Example 13-25 Controlling Data Alignment

```
The alignment of each cell (both horizontal and vertical) can be
adjusted with the ALIGN and VALIGN attributes<P>

<table border=2>
<th rowspan=2 colspan=2> Corner Headings  </th>
<th colspan=3> This is the top line explaining the headings - Food
</th>
<tr>
<th> Meat </th>
<th> Fruit </th>
<th> Breads </th>
<tr>
<td rowspan=2> This is a sidebar explaining the side heads - required
</td>
<td> Yes </td>
<td> X <br>X</td>
<td valign=bottom> X </td>
<td valign=middle> X </td>
<tr>
<td> No way at all</td>
<td align=middle> Middle </td>
<td align=right> Right </td>
<td> - </td>
</table><P>
```

Data alignment is shown in Figure 13-19.

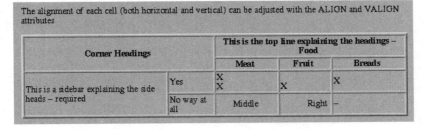

Figure 13-19 Controlling Data Alignment

Adding Space and Definition

When the alignment is defined as left or right, text is started right next to the cell wall. Visually, the text line can be made more effective by adding some space around the text. This is accomplished by the CELLSPACING attribute.

In the example above where the BORDER attribute was given a larger size, this size applied only to the external border of the table. The internal lines can also be resized with the CELLPADDING attribute. It is important to note here that it doesn't matter how large the CELLPADDING attribute is, it will never be displayed larger than the BORDER attribute value.

An example is:

HTML Example 13-26 Adding Space Around Text

```
Instead of creating a row with extra spaces and positioning
the text in the middle, the CELLPADDING will add space around
the data<P>
The CELLSPACING attribute changes the internal borders of a
table. If the external border is set to be smaller than the
internal borders, the external border will be made to equal
the size of the internal borders.<P>

<table border=2 CELLPADDING=8 CELLSPACING=8>
<th rowspan=2 colspan=2> Corner Headings  </th>
<th colspan=3> This is the top line explaining the headings - Food
</th>
<tr>
<th> Meat </th>
<th> Fruit </th>
<th> Breads </th>
<tr>
<td rowspan=2> This is a sidebar explaining the side heads - required
</td>
<td> Yes </td>
<td> X </td>
<td> X </td>
<td> X </td>
<tr>
<td> No </td>
<td> - </td>
<td> X </td>
<td> - </td>
</table><P>
```

Figure 13-20 shows an example of defining data by padding cell walls and spacing the data.

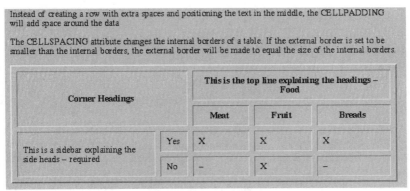

Figure 13-20 Adding Space Around Text

Summary

In this chapter, you learned how to enhance web pages with the following Netscape features:

- Background images and color changes
- Image customization
- Lists
- Horizontal rules
- Fonts
- Text alignment
- Tables

Tags Used in This Chapter

Tag	Attributes	Description and Comments
<BODY>	BACKGROUND	Defines an image to be used for a background.
	BGCOLOR	Defines a background color.
	TEXT	Defines text color.
	ALINK	Defines active link color.
	LINK	Defines link color.

Tag	Attributes	Description and Comments
	VLINK	Defines visited link color.
<IMG>	LOWSRC	Defines a low-resolution image to be loaded initially.
	VSPACE	Defines space on the side of an image.
	HSPACE	Defines space on the top and bottom of an image.
	ALIGN	Defines the alignment of images and the text around them.
	WIDTH	Defines the width of an image.
	HEIGHT	Defines the height of an image.
<HR>	ALIGN	Defines the alignment of a horizontal rule.
	WIDTH	Defines the width of a horizontal rule.
	SIZE	Defines the height of a horizontal rule.
	NOSHADE	Removes shading from a horizontal rule.
<CENTER>		Centers paragraph text.
<P>	ALIGN	Aligns paragraph text.
	CLEAR	Starts text in the next clear area.
 	CLEAR	Starts text in the next clear area.
<H1>...<H6>	ALIGN	Aligns heading text.
<UL>	TYPE	Defines the bullet marker.
<OL>	TYPE	Defines the list marker type.
	START	Defines the starting value for list markers.
<LI>	TYPE	Defines the list marker type.
<FONT>		Modifies text font size.

Tag	Attributes	Description and Comments
	SIZE	Defines the size of the font.
<TABLE>	BORDER	Defines the size of the border.
	CELLSPACING	Defines the space between cells.
	CELLPADDING	Defines the space at which text starts from a cell wall.
	ALIGN	Defines horizontal alignment of cell contents.
	VALIGN	Defines vertical alignment of cell contents.

13

HTML for Fun and Profit

Future Directions 14 ≡

The Web is far more than just its display language, HTML. However, enhancements to other parts of the web infrastructure can make a difference in the creation and design of a web page.

An organization called W3C (World Wide Web Consortium) has been formed to direct the development of new WWW technology; it includes some of the original WWW creators and many current web product developers. Many of the current WWW projects were started before the formation of W3C, so some integration work to manage and point these projects in a common direction will be needed.

Future Generations of HTML

HTML was created by refining SGML to a small set of simple tags. HTML 1.0 can best be described as a pidgin language. HTML 2.0 can be described as adding interactivity tools to the HTML standard. The use of forms is the primary addition in HTML 2.0. The HTML 2.0 standard should be formalized sometime around March of 1995.

The nuances that are found in a fully developed display language are still evolving in the next generation of HTML, 3.0. Even farther down the road, the sexiest part of WWW capabilities, namely, multimedia, is being integrated, creating not just an application, but an entire environment.

HTML 3.0 or HTML+

HTML 3.0 or HTML+ is evolving the components needed to raise HTML from pidgin status to a full-fledged display language. Its wide range of new enhancements includes:

- Implementation of complex elements such as tables and mathematical equations
- Hidden information enhancements, called meta-tags, and enhanced uses for the `<BASE>` tag.

211

- Display control enhancements
  - modifying the size and justification of text
  - adding whitespace control attributes
  - enhancing list bullets and markings
  - creating the note item, which is meant to be a graphic and text combination that draws the user's attention to something.

- Changes to the grammar for some tags, from empty elements to containers to add text formatting enhancements, such as modifying justification

VRML (Virtual Reality Markup Language)

The sexiest part of the WWW is the use of graphics and other multimedia data. The next sexiest use of the WWW may well be adding 3-D environment enhancements. The most notable next-generation markup language is Virtual Reality Markup Language, or VRML. VRML departs from the primarily textual basis of HTML, SGML, and other predecessors and relies first and foremost on creating an environment for intuitive interaction rather than relying on the studied reaction of clicking on a page of text.

Conceptual examples: You start up a browser that shows a room. If you click on a picture on the wall, a viewer downloads and displays a large version of the picture seen there. Open a book, and a document is loaded for reading. Click on a TV set, and an MPEG movie is downloaded and displayed. Open a door and step across a link to another reality room.

VRML is still in its infancy. It has only recently passed its proof-of-concept stage with a demonstration in Washington DC. The reviews were positive, with one Internet-savvy youth declaring it *cool*. Look for this to be a hot new area in two years.

Security Issues

With the growth of WWW use for electronic storefronts. security is becoming a big issue. Currently, WWW servers can provide basic authentication, as follows. The server maintains a database of authorized users. When users want to access restricted pages, they must go through a form that asks them for their user name and password. These items are then compared with the database of authorized users, and, if correct, the user name is compared with the access control list for that file, directory, or directory tree. If the user exists in the *allow* portion of the access control list, then access is granted.

Note – The term *allow* refers specifically to the UNIX servers. Other servers may use alternative methods for controlling access control lists. When discussing access, the term *allow* defines the process for granting access for all servers.

There are some significant problems with this method. First, the password is sent in clear-text mode. This means that anyone who has the capability to listen to the physical network can see the password. Admittedly, in order to get this type of access, the person attempting to gain unauthorized access, aka *cracker*, would need either *root* privileges on a system located directly on the physical network cable or would need access to attach another piece of equipment onto that network cable. Most businesses do maintain this level of security.

The problem isn't isolated to the network connection at the business end. It comes about on all of the pieces of cabling that lie between the client and the server. There is concern about access to the Internet by cable TV equipment, as well as about the infrastructure required by the U.S. digital wiretap law.

- Cable TV wires are shared by houses or apartments in a one- or two-block area. This situation makes a client vulnerable to anyone who can access the physical cable for that neighborhood.

- The digital wiretap requirements specify that the core components needed to listen to the vast ocean of data be installed in a common carrier's site. Although this makes the U.S. government agencies more effective in their jobs, it opens a large hole for the hacker to gain access and use this same wiretap equipment.

Some of the proposals for providing security on insecure network cabling are: Scramble the messages returning from the client, provide private lines for messages returning to the server, use encryption between the server and the client, or use a more robust authentication system that relies on encrypting passwords. The first two methods rely on security provided by the network cable vendor and require extreme measures to circumvent the common-carrier sites. The last two methods will be implemented in future versions of WWW software.

The encryption algorithm that is gaining support currently is RSA. Secure HTTP or SHTTP, developed by Commercenet is based on RSA. Netscape Communications has also developed an RSA-encryption-based product. Unfortunately, the two products use different methods for trading the encryption information. Interoperability between these methods is unknown at this point.

Interoperability is the second problem with the current state of security. The only method currently available for encrypting things like credit card numbers requires special browsers and servers. A common, encryption-method standard is needed to allow all browsers and servers to speak the same language. Without this, Netscape browsers may not be able to send encrypted messages to SHTTP servers, and Enhanced Mosaic browsers may not be able to communicate with Netsite servers.

Other Enhancements

All the components of the Web—browser, server, http protocol, and HTML language—are being improved. The enhancements not only expand the capabilities of the Web, the enhancements also create custom uses.

Additional Uses

Browsers and client applications are being developed to cover a wider range of functions, and several additional uses for WWW software are being developed. It is foreseeable that the WWW browser will be used as the front-end for many applications in the near future. Having a common interface would facilitate learning.

- HyperMail — One problem with email is that of missed messages. If you're not on the mailing list when email is sent, you miss the messages and the senders must resend them. To solve the problem, email is archived more and more often. HyperMail offers a method of maintaining and presenting these archives with WWW.

- MultiUser Dungeons (MUDs) — Many years ago a program called Adventure captured the hearts of many people. It was a game about searching through a dungeon to get items, kill monsters, and rack up points. This game has evolved into MUDs, where people create rooms and entire dungeons for other people to wander around in. Dungeons are an interactive place where each person can leave a unique mark on a room for future visitors. MUDs are being integrated with WWW to create exploration environments.

- Kiosk systems — The newer versions of NCSA Mosaic have a kiosk mode in which users can browse only the pointers provided by the server. Kiosk mode was developed for use in trade shows and kiosks, when vendors want to show only their products.

Common Client Interface — CCI

Most browsers do more than just display HTML. They communicate with gopher, WAIS, and Netnews to provide an interface to those types of servers. They spawn applications to display data that they can't display internally. Commentary on web pages can be stored in annotations, readable by only selected people or by a wide audience. Some browsers offer a basic editor to modify web pages without invoking another application.

Until now, the external applications that were spawned received data from the browser, but did not pass information back to the browser. Because of this, interactivity was primarily limited to server-side processing with the CGI interface. NCSA has proposed a Common Client Interface to allow clients to pass information and requests back and forth between the browser and an external viewer.

For example: Adobe Acrobat 2.0 allows linking between documents. A document is downloaded and displayed with an external viewer. The user then selects a link in the document that points to another document. The viewer then passes this request back to the browser, which requests the other document from the server.

Server Improvements

Several improvements have been proposed for servers, including:

- Additional meta-information, such as rating web pages.

- Performance enhancements, such as sending a page and all graphics for that page in one connection. Currently, each time a browser makes a request, it must contact the server, identify itself, and request a single file. If a web page has four images, five connections (one for the page and four for the images) will be made.

- Charge mechanisms, such as charging for pages to facilitate distribution of information that may not be free.

- Security, as noted earlier in this chapter.

Conclusion

There are people years, and there are dog years, which are supposedly seven times as fast as people years. And then there are Internet years. Internet years don't seem to pass at a constant rate, but they are definitely faster than dog years.

≡ *14*

Things that are created on the Internet experience a very fast evolutionary rate, and WWW is not the exception. The topics listed here should be passé by 1996, and a new future as yet undreamed will be evolving.

Xmosaic

To see and test the web pages that you create, you must use a browser. There are dozens of browsers for all different platforms. Xmosaic, the UNIX implementation of Mosaic, was the first GUI-based browser. It has maintained its popularity, and it continues to implement new features such as tables. This appendix describes installation and basic use of Xmosaic.

Installing Xmosaic

The UNIX version of the Mosaic application is called Xmosaic because it runs under
X-Windows. However, the file itself is usually just called Mosaic. There are cases when this nomenclature can cause confusion. When we discuss the UNIX implementation of Mosaic in this appendix, we use the term Xmosaic.

Obtaining Xmosaic

The latest version of Xmosaic can be obtained from NCSA via anonymous ftp at `ftp://ftp.ncsa.uiuc.edu/` or one of their mirror sites. If you try NCSA and it is busy, the current mirror sites are listed. Xmosaic comes as a compressed file (i.e., it ends in `.Z`).

1. **Download Xmosaic via anonymous ftp.**
   Use the `bin` command to receive the file as binary information, not text. Use the `hash` command to print pound (#) signs to monitor the progress of the download.

Code Example A-1   Downloading Xmosaic via Anonymous ftp

```
% ftp ftp.ncsa.uiuc.edu
Connected to ftp.ncsa.uiuc.edu.
220 curley FTP (Version wu-2.4(25) Thu Aug 25 13:14:21 CDT 1994)
ready.
Name (ftp.ncsa.uiuc.edu:marym): anonymous
```

A

Code Example A-1   Downloading Xmosaic via Anonymous ftp (Continued)

```
331 Guest login ok, send your complete e-mail address as password.
Password: {Type your email address here}
ftp> bin
200 Type set to I.
ftp> hash
Hash mark printing on (8192 bytes/hash mark).
ftp> get Mosaic-2.5b2-solaris.Z
200 PORT command successful.
150 Opening BINARY mode data connection for readme.txt (683 bytes).
#
226 Transfer complete.
local: Mosaic-2.5b2-solaris.Z remote: Mosaic-2.5b2-solaris.Z
683 bytes received in 0.51 seconds (1.3 Kbytes/s)
ftp> quit
221 Goodbye.
```

2. Uncompress Xmosaic.

```
uncompress Mosaic-2.5b2-solaris.Z
```

3. Place Xmosaic in the appropriate directory and change name to Mosaic,
mosaic, **or the name of your choice.**
After the file is uncompressed, move it to the directory where it should reside
permanently. You can also change the name to something simpler, like Mosaic.

```
mv Mosaic-2.5b2-solaris /usr/local/bin/Mosaic
```

4. Change owner and permissions.
Set permissions on the file.

```
chmod 0555 /usr/local/bin/Mosaic
```

Configuring Xmosaic

After installing the program, customize Xmosaic. Xmosaic can be configured in
different ways:

- In the user's .Xdefaults file.

- With environment variables and command-line flags. Use this method when
  configuration needs to be manually generated each time, for example, when a
  central file server supports a large number of user machines with individual
  configurations.

Setting Home Page

The home page is the page that is loaded when Xmosaic is started and when the Home button is used. If this page is left with the default value, Xmosaic attempts to load the Xmosaic home page at NCSA. We recommend that you point this to a local page. The home page can be changed via `.Xdefaults` file, a command-line flag, or an environment variable. If more than one method is used, the environment variable takes precedence, followed by the command-line flag. The `.Xdefaults` value is used only if neither other method is used.

Command-line flag:	`-home` *URL*
Example:	**`Mosaic -home http://www.mydomain.com/`**
.Xdefaults entry:	`Mosaic*homeDocument:` *URL*
Example:	`Mosaic*homeDocument:`
`http://www.mydomain.com/`	
Environment Variable:	`WWW_HOME`
Example:	`setenv WWW_HOME http://www.mydomain.com/`

Setting Proxy Server

Proxy servers are primarily used as firewalls to protect clients. Some proxy servers also function as caching servers to store retrieved web pages and to minimize bandwidth impact.

.Xdefaults entry:

```
Mosaic*ftpProxy:     Servername
Mosaic*gopherProxy:  Servername
Mosaic*httpProxy:    Servername
Mosaic*waisProxy:    Servername
Mosaic*ProxyGateway: Servername
```
Example: `Mosaic*ProxyGateway: proxy.mydomain.com`

Setting Delay Image Loading

Image loading can be configured as on-demand only. This configuration is effective when network speed is slow.

Command-line flag:	`-dil`
Example:	**`Mosaic -dil`**
.Xdefaults entry:	`Mosaic*delayImageLoads:`
Example:	`Mosaic*delayImageLoads: true`

A

Setting Image Cache Size

When images are loaded, they are stored in an image cache on the user's system for the duration of the session. The image cache is set to 2 Mbytes or 2048 Kbytes by default. Values are always given in Kbytes.

Command-line flag:	`-ics ####`
Example:	**Mosaic -ics 4096**
.Xdefaults entry:	`Mosaic*imageCacheSize: ####`
Example:	`Mosaic*imageCacheSize: 4096`

Mailcap

The MIME type-to-viewer mapping is performed in the `mailcap` file. By default, Xmosaic looks in `/usr/local/lib/mosaic/mailcap` for this information. The `.Xdefaults` file can be used to change this file and pathname.

.Xdefaults entry:	`Mosaic*globalTypeMap: path`
Example:	`Mosaic*globalTypeMap:`
`/opt/local/mosaic/mailcap`	

In addition, users can override the system-wide `mailcap` configurations with the `.mailcap` file in their home directory. This location can be redirected with another `.Xdefaults` entry.

.Xdefaults entry:	`Mosaic*personalTypeMap: path`
Example:	`Mosaic*personalTypeMap: ~/confs/.mailcap`

MIME Types

The filename extension to MIME type mapping is performed in the `mime.types` file. By default, Xmosaic looks in `/usr/local/lib/mosaic/mime.types` for this information. The `.Xdefaults` file can be used to change this file and pathname.

.Xdefaults entry:	`Mosaic*globalExtensionMap: path`
Example:	`Mosaic*globalExtensionMap:`
`/opt/local/mosaic/mime.types`	

In addition, users can override the system-wide `mime.types` configurations with the `.mime.types` file in their home directory. This location can be redirected with another `.Xdefaults` entry.

.Xdefaults entry:	`Mosaic*ExtensionMap: path`
Example:	`Mosaic*personalExtnsionMap:`
`~/confs/mime.types`	

Loading Configuration

If you have made changes to your `.Xdefaults` file, reload the modified file with:

```
xrdb ~/.Xdefaults
```

Installing Viewers

When Xmosaic receives a file of a type that it can't render internally, it checks its list of MIME type mappings to see if a viewer is configured to render the file. Viewers are primarily used to output sound, pictures, and movies.

Many vendors are making viewer programs to integrate the output from their products with the Web. For example, the Adobe product, Acrobat, uses a file type of PDF. Adobe has released read-only versions of Acrobat, called Acroread, to display PDF files on the Web.

Since there are several different types of data and, in some cases, more than one viewer can render a specific type of data, make a list of the viewers that you want to use for each type of data. That way, you won't miss covering a specific data type. Table A-1 lists viewer programs.

Table A-1   Viewer Programs for Various MIME Types

MIME Type	Viewer Programs for Xmosaic
PostScript	`ghostview/ghostscript`
Sound/Au (Basic)	`soundtool (Sun)` `xplaygizmo`
Sound/Wave	`xplaygizmo`
Image/Gif	`xv`
Image/Jpeg	`xv`
Image/Tiff	`xv`
Video/Mpeg	`mpeg_play` `xmpeg_play` `xplaygizmo`

Obtaining Viewers

The source code for many viewers can be downloaded from NCSA at the same time Xmosaic is downloaded. Unfortunately, this means that you must compile the programs before using them. If you don't care to compile the programs, use `archie`, an Internet tool for searching anonymous ftp sites, to find compiled versions of browsers. Then, use the ftp method shown previously to download the viewer programs.

A

Installing a Viewer

Each viewer is installed differently. Read the README file that comes with the viewer to obtain installation instructions.

Configuring a Viewer

After you have installed the viewer and verified that it works, update the mailcap entry to reflect this installation. Both the global and personal mailcap files have the same format. A mailcap file looks like Code Example A-2, where the MIME type definition is the leftmost item, the command to execute is next, and the items are delimited by a semicolon.

Code Example A-2   Configured mailcap *File*

```
# This is a simple example mailcap file.
# Lines starting with '#' are comments.

audio/*; soundtool %s

# This maps all types of images (image/gif, image/jpeg, etc.)
# to the viewer 'xv'.
image/*; xv %s

# This maps MPEG video data to the viewer 'mpeg_play'.
video/mpeg; mpeg_play %s
```

If you are adding a viewer for a new MIME type, you must also add the new entry to the mime.types file. As with the mailcap file, both mime.types files have the same format. A mime.types file looks like Code Example A-3, where the MIME definition is in the left-hand column and the file extension is in the right-hand column.

Code Example A-3   Configured mime.types *File*

```
application/postscript          ai eps ps
audio/basic                     au snd
audio/x-aiff                    aif aiff aifc
image/gif                       gif
image/jpeg                      jpeg jpg jpe
image/tiff                      tiff tif
text/html                       html
```

Code Example A-3   Configured `mime.types` *File (Continued)*

```
text/plain                     txt
video/mpeg                     mpeg mpg mpe
```

Using Xmosaic

When Xmosaic is started, a window resembling that in Figure A-1 is displayed.

Figure A-1   Example of Xmosaic Home Page

A

Menu Tour

Along the top of the screen is a menu bar with these menus:

- **File** — Contains assorted items relating to the loading of a new page (file) and manipulating the current one, such as locating specific text, saving, mailing, and viewing the source of the page/file.

- **Options** — Deals with the configuration items. Since Delay Image Loading is included here, the other image items such as Load Images in Current and Flush Image Cache are also located here.

- **Navigate** — Offers several options for navigation, including hotlist maintenance.

- **Annotate** — Creates, deletes, and manipulates annotations. Refer to another book on Mosaic for more information on annotations.

- **Help** — Offers help on various facets of the browser and the Web in general.

Button Tour

The World Button, in the upper right hand corner of the screen, is a picture of the earth. When Mosaic is actively collecting information, the world spins, indicating that the application is doing something. However, the primary purpose of the world button is to allow you to interrupt the process of information gathering. To stop a download, click on the world button.

Along the bottom of the screen are these buttons:

- **Back** — Redisplays the page previous to the current one.

- **Forward** — If the Back button was used, the Forward button moves to the next page that you had already loaded.

- **Home** — Loads the home page.

- **Reload** — Reloads the current page. This button is useful when you have changed a document and want to redisplay the page.

- **Open** — Opens a pop-up window. Type in the URL to load and press Return, or click on Open on the pop-up to load a new page.

- **Save As** — Saves the text of the current page to a file on disk.

- **Clone** — Creates a second browser window with the same page loaded as in the original browser. This button is useful when documentation is online. You can use one browser to read the documentation and use the second browser to execute the steps or do some research.

- **New Window** — Creates a second browser window, but, unlike the Clone button, loads the home page.

- **Close Window** — Closes the current browser window. If this is the last browser window, then the application closes.

Other Items on the Browser

There are a few other key areas on the screen:

- **Document Title** — Displays the title of the currently loaded web page.

- **Document URL** — Displays the URL of the currently loaded web page.

- **Status Line** - An area at the bottom of the screen that displays messages when pages are loading or when errors occur.

Navigating

There are several ways to navigate on the Web.

- **Clicking on links** — Links are displayed as underlined and colored text. Click on a link to load the page that the link points to. This is the method used to create kiosk display systems using the Web.

- **Using the preconfigured items in the Navigate menu** — Under the Navigate menu are two pointers, *Internet Starting Points* and *Internet Resources Meta-Index*, to be used as starting points when surfing the Internet. These two places contain links to many other sites on the Internet.

- **Moving back and forth from page to page by using the Back and Forward buttons** — Use these buttons to move between pages that you have already loaded. They won't take you any place new, but they will help you navigate among pages loaded during the current session.

- **Selecting items from a hotlist** — If you visit a site that is interesting or that you want to go back to, place it in your hotlist by selecting *Add Current to Hotlist* from the Navigate menu. To return, invoke the hotlist by selecting *Hotlist* from the Navigate menu and select the site that you want to revisit.

A

- **Entering URLs** — You can reach most places eventually by clicking on or following links that others have created. However, many new sites don't have links to them yet, and some older sites may require several hops to reach. In these cases, you can specify the URL that you want to load to go directly there. To do so, click on the Open button at the bottom of the screen and enter the URL in the pop-up window that is now displayed.

WinMosaic   B

To see and test the web pages that you create, you must use a browser. There are dozens of browsers for all different platforms. This appendix covers installation and basic use of WinMosaic for Microsoft Windows and Windows NT platforms.

Installing WinMosaic

WinMosaic is the version of Mosaic for Microsoft Windows and Windows NT clients. Each version of NCSA Mosaic is slightly different. This version offers a wealth of starting points when navigating the Web. Otherwise, it functions about the same as its UNIX and Macintosh counterparts.

Obtaining WinMosaic

The latest version of WinMosaic can be obtained from NCSA via anonymous ftp at `ftp://ftp.ncsa.uiuc.edu/` or one of their mirror sites. If you try NCSA and it is too busy, the current mirror sites are listed. WinMosaic comes as a compressed file (i.e., it ends in `.zip`).

Microsoft Windows for Workgroups and Windows NT have the win32s subsystem built in. If you are running any other version of Microsoft Windows, you will also need to download and install `win32s.zip` before executing WinMosaic. It is important to verify that you have the correct version of the win32s subsystem to go with the specific version of Mosaic. For example, WinMosaic version 2.07a required win32s version 1.15, whereas WinMosaic version 2.08a required win32s version 1.2.

To use WinMosaic across a network, you also need a `winsock.dll`. This dynamically linked library is usually distributed with the networking software. Refer to the NCSA WinMosaic home page if you don't have a `winsock.dll`.

B

1. Download WinMosiac via anonymous ftp.

Use the `bin` command to receive the file as binary information, not text. Use the `hash` command to print pound (#) signs to monitor the progress of the download.

Code Example B-1   Downloading WinMosaic via Anonymous ftp

```
% ftp ftp.ncsa.uiuc.edu
Connected to ftp.ncsa.uiuc.edu.
220 curley FTP (Version wu-2.4(25) Thu Aug 25 13:14:21 CDT 1994)
ready.
Name (ftp.ncsa.uiuc.edu:marym): anonymous
331 Guest login ok, send your complete e-mail address as password.
Password:{Type your email address here}
ftp> bin
200 Type set to I.
ftp> hash
Hash mark printing on (8192 bytes/hash mark).
ftp> get wmos20a8.zip
200 PORT command successful.
150 Opening BINARY mode data connection for readme.txt (683 bytes).
#
226 Transfer complete.
local: wmos20a8.zip remote: wmos20a8.zip
683 bytes received in 0.51 seconds (1.3 Kbytes/s)
ftp> get win32s.zip
200 PORT command successful.
150 Opening BINARY mode data connection for readme.txt (683 bytes).
#
226 Transfer complete.
local: win32s.zip remote: win32s.zip
683 bytes received in 0.51 seconds (1.3 Kbytes/s)
ftp> quit
221 Goodbye.
```

Unpacking and Placing the Files

1. The files are compressed in zip format. Use `pkunzip` to unpack the files.

```
pkunzip wmos20a8.zip
```

2. Win32s contains directories of information. Use the `-d` option when uncompressing it.

```
pkunzip -d win32s.zip
```

3. **Move** `mosaic.ini` **to your** `\windows` **directory.**

4. **Move** `mosaic.exe` **to its long-term location.**

5. **Add a Program Item for WinMosaic by doing the following:**

   a. **Select the window in which you want the Mosaic icon to reside.**

   b. **Pull down the File menu on the Program Manager window and select New.**

   c. **Select Program Item and click on OK.**

   d. **Type in the name and path to** `mosaic.exe` **or click on the browse function and select** `mosaic.exe`.

   e. **Click on OK to complete.**

Installing Win32s

The win32s subsystem uses the standard Microsoft Windows installation program setup. To install win32s, do the following:

1. **Pull down the File menu and select Run.**

2. **Enter the path to the directory and file** `\disk1\setup.exe` **of the unzipped win32s package.**

3. **Click on OK to start.**

4. **The installation prompts you to confirm the location of the** `\windows` **directory and installation of a game called Freehand. Confirm both prompts by clicking on OK.**

5. **After the installation, restart the windows system. Click on OK to confirm this prompt.**

6. **After booting, start Microsoft Windows and start the game Freehand.**

7. **Once it has loaded successfully, exit from it.**
   If you are able to successfully load and exit Freehand, then the win32s subsystem was successfully installed.

Configuring WinMosaic

The next step is to edit the `mosiac.ini` file in your `\windows` directory. Load the file into an editor to modify it.

B

Defining the Home Page and Loading Procedures

The home page is the page that is loaded when WinMosaic is started and when the Home button is used. If this page is left with the default value, WinMosaic attempts to load the WinMosaic home page at NCSA. We recommend that you point this to a local page.

Modify the Home Page variable to point to a local page:

```
Home Page=http://www.server.com/Index.html
```

Or, turn off home page loading entirely, by setting Autoload Home Page to no.

```
Autoload Home Page=no
```

Managing Image Loading

Image loading can be configured as on-demand only. This configuration is effective when network speed is slow. This is accomplished by setting Display Inline Images to no.

```
Display Inline Images=no
```

Installing Viewers

When WinMosaic receives a file of a type that it can't render internally, it checks its list of MIME type mappings to see if a viewer is configured to render the file. Viewers are primarily used to output sound, pictures, and movies.

Many vendors are making viewer programs to integrate the output from their products with the Web. For example, the Adobe product, Acrobat, uses a file type of PDF. Adobe has released read-only versions of Acrobat, called Acroread, to display PDF files on the Web.

Since there are several different types of data, and, in some cases, more than one viewer can render a specific type of data, make a list of the viewers that you want to use for each type of data. That way, you won't miss covering a specific data type.

Table B-1   Viewer Programs for Various MIME Types

MIME Type	Viewer Programs for WinMosaic
Postscript	`ghostview/ghostscript`
Sound/Au (Basic)	`wham` `wplayany`
Sound/Aiff	`wham` `wplayany`
Sound/Wave	`mplayer`
Image/Gif	`lview`
Image/Jpeg	`.lview`
Video/Mpeg	`mpegplay`
Video/Quicktime	`qtw11`

Obtaining Viewers

The source code for many viewers can be downloaded from NCSA at the same time WinMosaic is downloaded. Unfortunately, this means that you must compile the programs before using them. Use `archie`, an Internet tool for searching anonymous ftp sites, to find compiled versions of browsers. Use the ftp method shown previously to download the viewer programs.

Installing a Viewer

Each viewer is installed differently. Read the README file that comes with the viewer to obtain installation instructions.

B

Configuring a Viewer

After you have installed the viewer and verified that it works by itself, update the `mosaic.ini` file to reflect the new MIME type. The MIME type definition area of the `mosaic.ini` looks like:

Code Example B-2   Updated `mosaic.ini` File

```
application/postscript="ghostview %ls"
application/x-rtf="write %ls"
image/gif="c:\windows\apps\lview\lview31 %ls"
image/jpeg="c:\windows\apps\lview\lview31 %ls"
video/mpeg="c:\winapps\mpegplay\mpegplay %ls"
video/quicktime="C:\WINAPPS\QTW\bin\player.exe %ls"
video/msvideo="mplayer %ls"
audio/wav="mplayer %ls"
audio/x-midi="mplayer %ls"
telnet="c:\trumpet\telw.exe"
```

Replace the path listed for each MIME type with the path to the viewer that you have selected and installed.

If you are adding a viewer for a new MIME type, you must also add the new entry to the Suffixes and Viewers sections of `mosaic.ini`. The Suffixes section is used to map filename suffixes to the appropriate MIME type definition. It looks like:

Code Example B-3   Suffixes Section of `mosaic.ini`

```
[Suffixes]
application/postscript=.ps,.eps,.ai,.ps
application/x-rtf=.rtf,.wri
audio/wav=.wave,.wav,.WAV
audio/x-midi=.mid
image/gif=.gif
image/jpeg=.jpeg,.jpe,.jpg
image/x-tiff=.tiff,.tif
video/mpeg=.mpeg,.mpe,.mpg
video/quicktime=.mov
video/msvideo=.avi
```

The Viewers section contains the TYPE definitions. Only ten MIME types can be defined (TYPE0-TYPE9). The Viewers section looks like:

Code Example B-4   Viewers Section of `mosaic.ini`

```
[Viewers]
TYPE0="audio/wav"
TYPE1="application/postscript"
TYPE2="image/gif"
TYPE3="image/jpeg"
TYPE4="video/mpeg"
TYPE5="video/quicktime"
TYPE6="video/msvideo"
```

B

Using WinMosaic

When WinMosaic is started, a window resembling the home page shown in Figure B-1 is displayed.

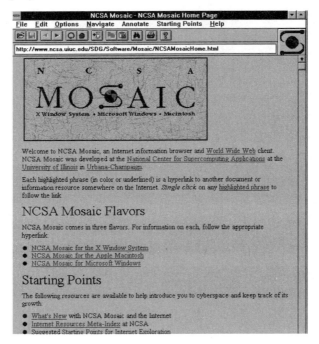

Figure B-1   WinMosaic Screen

Menu Tour

Along the top of the screen is a row of these menus:

- **File** — Contains assorted items relating to the loading of a new page (file) and manipulating the current one, such as locating specific text, saving, mailing, and viewing the source of the page or file.

- **Edit** — Contains standard clipboard operations, such as cut and paste.

- **Options** — Deals with the configuration items. Since Auto-Loading is included here, other image items, such as Flush Cache, are also located here.

- **Navigate** — Offers several options for navigation, including hotlist maintenance.

- **Annotate** — Creates, deletes, and manipulates annotations. Refer to another book on Mosaic for more information on annotations.

- **Starting Points** — Offers a menu of many additional places from which to start a search.

Button Tour

At the top of the screen are these buttons:

- **The World** — A picture of the earth. When Mosaic is actively collecting information, the world spins, indicating that the application is doing something. However, the primary purpose of the world button is to allow the user to interrupt the process of information gathering. To stop a download, click on the world button.

- **Open Local (open folder)** — Loads a file from a local disk.

- **Save As (disk)** — Saves the text of the current page to a file on disk.

- **Back (arrow pointing left)** — Redisplays the page previous to the current one.

- **Forward (arrow pointing right)** — If the Back button was used, the Forward button moves to the next page that you had already loaded.

- **Home (house)** — Loads the home page.

- **Reload (arrow in a circle)** — Reloads the current page. This button is useful when you have changed a document and want to redisplay the page.

- **Add to Hotlist (page on fire)** — Adds the current page to the hotlist.

- **Find (goggles)** — Searches the current page for a specified word.

Other Items on the Browser

There are a few other key areas on the screen:

- **URL** — Displays the URL of the currently loaded web page.

- **Status Line** — An area at the bottom of the screen that displays messages when pages are loading or when errors occur.

B

Navigating

There are several ways to navigate around the Web.

- **Clicking on links** — Links are displayed as underlined and colored text. Click on a link to load the page that the link points to. This is the method used to create kiosk display systems using the Web.

- **Using the preconfigured items in the Navigate and Starting Points menus** — Use these pointers as starting points when surfing the Internet; they contain links to many other sites on the Internet.

- **Moving back and forth from page to page by using the** Back **and** Forward **buttons** — You can move between pages that you have already loaded with these buttons. The Back and Forward buttons won't take you any place new, but they will help you navigate among pages loaded during the current session.

- **Selecting items from a hotlist** — If you visit a site that is interesting or that you want to go back to, place it in your hotlist by selecting *Add Current to Hotlist* from the Navigate menu. To return, invoke the hotlist by selecting *Hotlist* from the Navigate menu and select the site that you want to revisit.

- **Entering URLs** — You can reach most places eventually by clicking on or following links that others have created. However, many new sites don't have links to them yet, and some older sites may require several hops to reach. In these cases, you can specify the URL that you want to load to go directly there. To do so, enter the URL in the URL field at the top of the page and press Return.

MacMosaic

To see and test the web pages that you create, you must use a browser. There are dozens of browsers for all different platforms. In addition to the UNIX and Microsoft Windows Mosaic browsers, NCSA offers a version for the Macintosh. The Mac version has many fine features, and the final 2.0.0 release is expected to handle tables. This appendix describes installation and basic use of MacMosaic.

Installing MacMosaic

As of this writing, MacMosaic 2.0.0 is still in development. However, the features that the product offers make it worth using. A version 1.0.3, with fewer features, is available for people who feel uncomfortable using an unfinished product.

Obtaining MacMosaic

The latest version of MacMosaic can be obtained from NCSA via anonymous ftp at `ftp://ftp.ncsa.uiuc.edu/` or one of their mirror sites. If you try NCSA and it is too busy, the current mirror sites will be listed. The Mac version of Mosaic comes in two versions: one for the Motorola 68000 systems, identified with the 68K extension; one for the PowerMac systems, identified with a `.ppc` extension. If you are unsure about which system you have, download the 68K version.

1. **Download MacMosaic via anonymous ftp.**
   Use the `bin` command to receive the file as binary information, not text. Use the `hash` command to print pound (#) signs to monitor the progress of the download.

Code Example C-1   Downloading MacMosaic

```
% ftp ftp.ncsa.uiuc.edu
Connected to ftp.ncsa.uiuc.edu.
220 curley FTP (Version wu-2.4(25) Thu Aug 25 13:14:21 CDT 1994)
ready.
```

237

C

```
Name (ftp.ncsa.uiuc.edu:marym): anonymous
331 Guest login ok, send your complete e-mail address as password.
Password:{Type your email address here}
ftp> bin
200 Type set to I.
ftp> hash
Hash mark printing on (8192 bytes/hash mark).
ftp> get NCSAMosaic200A17.68k.hqx
200 PORT command successful.
150 Opening BINARY mode data connection for readme.txt (683 bytes).
#
226 Transfer complete.
local: NCSAMosaic200A17.68k.hqx remote: NCSAMosaic200A17.68k.hqx
xxx bytes received in xxxseconds (xxx Kbytes/s)
ftp> quit
221 Goodbye.
```

Unpacking and Placing the Files

1. If the ftp program that you used did not make the filename
   `NCSAMosaic200A.sea`, use Stuffit-Expander to unencode the data file.

2. Otherwise, double-click on the `.sea` file. This is a self-extracting archive
   that uncompresses itself.

3. Select a directory when prompted.

Configuring MacMosaic

1. Start MacMosaic by double-clicking on the world icon.

2. Pull down the Options menu and select Preferences.

A window like that in Figure C-1 is displayed.

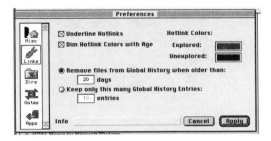

Figure C-1   MacMosaic Preferences Window

Setting the Home Page

The home page is the page that is loaded when MacMosaic is started and when the Home button is used. If this page is left with the default value, then MacMosaic attempts to load the MacMosaic home page at NCSA. We recommend that you point this to a local page.

3. Select the Misc Icon.

A window like that in Figure C-2 is displayed.

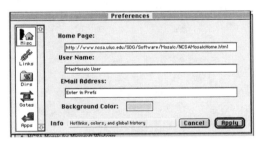

Figure C-2   Setting the Home Page in MacMosaic

4. Enter the URL that you want to use for a home page.

5. Enter your real name and email address.

6. Click on Apply.

Setting the Proxy

Proxy servers are primarily used as firewalls to protect clients. Some proxy servers also function as caching servers to store retrieved web pages and to minimize bandwidth impact.

7. Select the Gates icon.

A window like that in Figure C-3 is displayed.

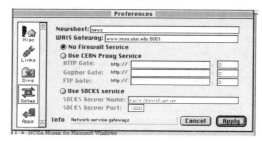

Figure C-3 Setting a Proxy in MacMosaic

8. Enter the system name and port for the proxy. Click on Apply.

Setting Auto-Loading of Images

When network speed is slow, image loading can be configured as on-demand only. Auto-Loading is turned off by default. Not Auto-Loading is the same as Delay Image Loading in Xmosaic.

9. Pull down the Options menu and select Auto-Load Images.

If this item is checked, images load automatically.

Installing Helpers

When MacMosaic receives a file of a type that it can't render internally, it checks its list of MIME type mappings to see if a helper is configured to render the file. Helpers are primarily used to output sound, pictures, and movies.

Note – Under Xmosaic and WinMosaic, helper programs are called viewers. The terms helper and viewer can be used interchangeably, but Mac convention calls them helpers.

Many vendors are making helper programs to integrate the output from their products with the Web. For example, the Adobe product, Acrobat, uses a file type of PDF. Adobe has released read-only versions of Acrobat, called Acroread, to display PDF files on the Web.

Since there are several different types of data and, in some cases, more than one helper can render a specific type of data, make a list of the helpers that you want to use for each type of data. That way, you won't miss covering a specific data type. Table C-1 lists MacMosaic helper programs.

Table C-1   Helper Programs for Various MIME Types

MIME Type	Helper Programs for MacMosaic
Sound/Au (Basic)	`sound-machine`

Image/Gif	`gif-converter`
	`graphic-converter`
	`jpeg-view`

Image/Jpeg	`gif-converter`
	`graphic-converter`
	`jpeg-view`

Image/Tiff	`gif-converter`
	`graphic-converter`
	`jpeg-view`

Video/Mpeg	`sparkle`
Video/Quicktime	`fast_player`

Obtaining Helpers

The source code for many helpers can be downloaded from NCSA at the same time MacMosaic is downloaded. Unfortunately, this means that you must compile the programs before using them. Use `archie`, an Internet tool for searching anonymous ftp sites, to find compiled versions of browsers. Use the ftp method shown previously to download the helper programs.

Installing a Helper

Each helper is installed differently. Read the README file that comes with the helper to obtain installation instructions. Rebuild your desktop after you have installed helpers.

C

Using MacMosaic

When you start up MacMosaic, it looks like the home page shown in Figure C-4.

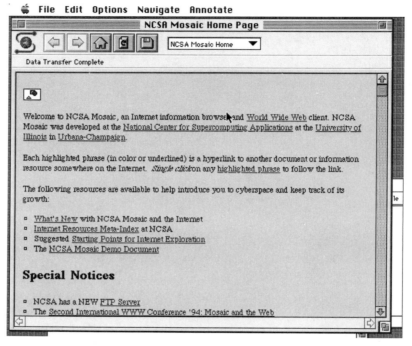

Figure C-4   MacMosaic Home Page

Menu Tour

Along the top of the screen is a row of these menus:

- **File** — Contains assorted items relating to the loading of a new page (file) and manipulating the current one, such as locating specific text, saving, mailing, and viewing the source of the page or file.

- **Edit** — Contains standard clipboard operations, such as cut and paste.

- **Options** — Deals with the configuration items. Since Auto-Loading is included here, other image item, such as Flush Cache, are also located here.

- **Navigate** — Offers several options for navigation, including hotlist maintenance.

- **Annotate** — Creates, deletes, and manipulates annotations. Refer to another book on Mosaic for more information on annotations.

Button Tour

At the top of the screen are these buttons:

- **The World** — A picture of the earth. When Mosaic is actively collecting information, the world spins, indicating that the application is doing something. However, the primary purpose of the world button is to allow the user to interrupt the process of information gathering. To stop a download, click on the world button.

- **Back (arrow pointing left)** — Redisplays the page previous to the current one.

- **Forward (arrow pointing right)** — If the Back button was used, the Forward button moves to the next page that you had already loaded.

- **Home (house)** — Loads the home page.

- **Reload (arrow in a circle)** — Reloads the current page. This button is useful when you have changed a document and want to redisplay the page.

- **Save As (disk)** — Saves the text of the current page to a file on disk.

Other Items on the Browser

There are a few other key areas on the screen:

- **Title** — On the right of the Save As (disk) button is a pull-down menu, which displays the title of the currently loaded web page. By pulling it down, you can select and move to a previous page.

- **URL** — Displays the URL of the currently loaded web page.

- **Status Line** — An area at the bottom of the screen that displays messages when pages are loading or when errors occur.

Navigating

There are several ways to navigate on the Web.

- **Clicking on links** — Links are displayed as underlined and colored text. Click on a link to load the page that the link points to. This is the method used to create kiosk display systems using the Web.

C

- **Using the preconfigured items in the Navigate menu** — Under the Navigate menu are four pointers: *Network Starting Points, Internet Resources Meta-Index, NCSA Demo Page*, and *NCSA What's New Page*. Use these pointers as starting points when surfing the Internet; they contain links to many other sites on the Internet.

- **Moving back and forth from page to page by using the** Back **and** Forward **buttons** — You can move between pages that you have already loaded with these buttons. The Back and Forward buttons won't take you any place new, but they will help you navigate among pages loaded during the current session.

- **Selecting items from a hotlist** — If you visit a site that is interesting or that you want to go back to, place it in your hotlist by selecting *Add Current to Hotlist* from the Navigate menu. To return, invoke the hotlist by selecting *Hotlist* from the Navigate menu and select the site that you want to revisit.

- **Entering URLs** — You can reach most places eventually by clicking on or following links that others have created. However, many new sites don't have links to them yet, and some older sites may require several hops to reach. In these cases, you can specify the URL that you want to load to go directly there. To do so, enter the URL in the URL field at the top of the page and press Return.

Reference

Appendix D lists the tags, environment variables, and special characters of HTML.

Tag Reference

Tags for formatting the following entities are tabulated:

- Documents
- Paragraphs
- Characters
- Lists
- Anchors
- Images
- Tables
- Server Includes
- Forms
- Input form elements
- Index pages

Document Formatting

Tag	Description
`<html>`	HTML document indicator
`<head>`	Document head
`<body>`	Document body
`<address>`	Owner/contact
`<h1>`...`<h6>`	Heading
`<title>`	Title
`<!-- -->`	Comment

D

Paragraph Formatting

Tag	Description
`<blockquote>`	Blockquote
`<p>`	Paragraph
` `	Line break
`<hr>`	Horizontal rule (horizontal line)
`<pre>`	Preformatted text

Character Formatting

Tag	Description
`<em>`	Emphasized
`<var>`	Variable
`<cite>`	Citation
`<i>`	Italics
`<strong>`	Strong
`<b>`	Bold
`<code>`	Code
`<samp>`	Sample
`<kbd>`	Keyboard entry
`<tt>`	Teletype
`<key>`	Keyword
`<dfn>`	dfm
`<strike>`	Strikethrough

List Formatting

Tag	Description
`<li>`	List item
`<ul>`	Unnumbered list
`<ol>`	Ordered list
`<menu>`	Menu list
`<dir>`	Directory list
`<dl>`	Description list
`<dt>`	Data term
`<dd>`	Data description

HTML for Fun and Profit

Anchor Formatting

Tag	Attribute	Description
`<A>`		Anchors hyperlink.
	`HREF`	Points to destination of link.
	`NAME`	Defines a named anchor so that a link can point to a place in a document, not just to the document itself.

Image Formatting

Tag	Attribute	Description and Notes
`<IMG>`		Incorporates images in a document.
	`SRC`	The href for the image.
	`ALIGN`	Aligns text, starting at the top, middle, or bottom of the side of an image.
	`ALT`	A name that can be displayed on browsers that don't have image capabilities.
	`ISMAP`	Activates the image so that the browser returns a set of x,y coordinates at which the image was clicked.

Table Formatting

Tag	Attribute	Description and Notes
`<TABLE>`		Defines the table.
	`BORDER`	Adds borders to separate rows and columns in tables.
`<TR>`		Marks the end/start of a table row.
`<TD>`		Encloses a cell of table data.
	`COLSPAN`	Modifies the number of columns a cell will span.
	`ROWSPAN`	Modifies the number of rows a cell will span.
	`ALIGN`	Defines the horizontal text alignment within a cell.
	`NOWRAP`	Declares that the cell text cannot be broken up to wrap from one line to the next.
`<TH>`		Encloses a cell of a table heading.
	`COLSPAN`	Modifies the number of columns a cell will span.
	`ROWSPAN`	Modifies the number of rows a cell will span.
	`ALIGN`	Defines the horizontal text alignment within a cell.
	`NOWRAP`	Declares that the cell text cannot be broken up to wrap from one line to the next.
`<CAPTION>`		Creates a title for the table, outside the table.

D

Server Include Formatting

Tag	Attribute	Description and Notes
`<!--#CONFIG>`		Used in conjunction with `<!--#FLASTMOD>` and `<!--#FSIZE>`, customizes time and date displays. It is also used alone to configure error messages.
	`ERRMSG`	Defines the error message string.
	`TIMEFMT`	Defines the date and time format returned.
	`SIZEFMT`	Defines the size format returned.
`<!--#ECHO>`		Returns a variable value.
	`VAR`	Defines the variable to return.
`<!--#EXEC>`		Executes a script or program.
	`CMD`	Defines the name of the program or script to be executed and that the program can be anywhere on the system.
	`CGI`	Defines the name of the program or script to be executed and that the program can only exist in an area defined as executable by the `access.conf` file.
`<!--#FLASTMOD>`		Displays the last modified date of a file.
	`FILE`	Defines the location of the document based on the calling document.
	`VIRTUAL`	Defines the location of the document based on the *DocRoot* variable.
`<!--#FSIZE>`		Displays the size of a file.
	`FILE`	Defines the location of the document based on the calling document.
	`VIRTUAL`	Defines the location of the document based on the *DocRoot* variable.
`<!--#INCLUDE>`		Adds the contents of a file to the document returned from the server.
	`FILE`	Defines the location of the document based on the calling document.
	`VIRTUAL`	Defines the location of the document based on the *DocRoot* variable.

Form Formatting

Tag	Attributes	Description and Comments
`<FORM>`		
	`ACTION`	Defines the `cgi-bin` script or program to execute with the incoming data.
	`METHOD`	Defines whether the incoming data will be stored in the environment variable `QUERY_STRING` or standard input.
`<INPUT>`		
	`TYPE`	Defines the type of input field.
`<TEXTAREA>`		
	`ROWS`	Defines the height of the text area.
	`COLS`	Defines the width of the text area.
	`NAME`	Defines the variable name.
`<SELECT>`		
	`NAME`	Defines the variable name.
	`SIZE`	Defines the number of items displayed.
	`MULTIPLE`	Indicates that more than one item can be selected.
`<OPTION>`		
	`SELECTED`	Makes the item selected by default.

D

Input Form Element Formatting

Input Type	Attributes	Description and Notes
submit		
	VALUE	Alters the text on the submit button.
reset		
	VALUE	Alters the text on the submit button.
image		
	SRC	Defines the URL for the image.
	NAME	Defines a variable name to be prepended to x and y when returning coordinates.
hidden		
	NAME	Defines the variable name.
	VALUE	Defines the value of the variable listed in NAME.
radio		
	NAME	Defines the variable name.
	VALUE	Defines the value of the variable listed in NAME.
	CHECKED	Indicates selected by default.
checkbox		
	NAME	Defines the variable name.
	VALUE	Defines the value of the variable listed in NAME.
	CHECKED	Indicates selected by default.
text		
	NAME	Defines the variable name.
	VALUE	Defines the value of the variable listed in NAME.
	SIZE	Defines the number of characters in the returned value.
	MAXLENGTH	Controls the display size of the text box.

Index Page Formatting

Tag	Attribute	Description
<ISINDEX>		Creates a prompt to gather a request for searching.
	ACTION	Defines the script or program called to complete the search.

HTML for Fun and Profit

Environment Variables

The following table is an alphabetical list of environment variables and their applicability to various browsers.

Variable Name	NCSA	CERN	https	MacHTTP
AUTH_TYPE	Yes	Yes	No	No
CONTENT_LENGTH	Yes	Yes	Yes	No
CONTENT_TYPE	*Yes*	Yes	Yes	Yes
DOCUMENT_NAME	Yes	No	No	No
DOCUMENT_ROOT	Yes	No	No	No
DOCUMENT_URI	Yes	No	No	No
DATE_GMT	Yes	No	No	No
DATE_LOCAL	Yes	No	No	No
GATEWAY_INTERFACE	Yes	Yes	Yes	No
HTTP_ACCEPT	No	Yes	Yes	No
LAST_MODIFIED	Yes	No	No	No
PATH	Yes	No	No	Yes
PATH_INFO	Yes	Yes	Yes	No
PATH_TRANSLATED	Yes	No	No	No
POST	No	No	No	Yes – equivalent to stdin
QUERY_STRING	Yes	Yes	Yes	No
QUERY_STRING_UNESCAPED	Yes	No	No	No
REMOTE_ADDR	Yes	Yes	Yes	address
REMOTE_HOST	Yes	Yes	No	No
REQUEST_METHOD	Yes	No	Yes	method
REMOTE_IDENT	Yes	Yes	No	No
REMOTE_USER	Yes	Yes	No	user
SEARCH	No	No	No	Yes
SERVER_PROTOCOL	Yes	Yes	Yes	No
SERVER_SOFTWARE	Yes	Yes	Yes	No
SERVER_NAME	Yes	Yes	Yes	Yes
SERVER_PORT	Yes	Yes	Yes	Yes
SERVER_ROOT	Yes	No	No	No
SCRIPT_NAME	Yes	Yes	Yes	Yes

D

8-bit ASCII Characters

The following table lists alphabetically, first by uppercase, then by lowercase, special characters used in Mosaic.

Character	Character Name	ANSI Number	Description
Æ	AElig	&#198;	capital AE diphthong (ligature)
Á	Aacute	&#193;	capital A, acute accent
Â	Acirc	&#194;	capital A, circumflex accent
À	Agrave	&#192;	capital A, grave accent
Å	Aring	&#197;	capital A, ring
Ã	Atilde	&#195;	capital A, tilde
Ä	Auml	&#196;	capital A, dieresis or umlaut mark
Ç	Ccedil	&#199;	capital C, cedilla
	ETH	&#208;	capital Eth, Icelandic
É	Eacute	&#201;	capital E, acute accent
Ê	Ecirc	&#202;	capital E, circumflex accent
È	Egrave	&#200;	capital E, grave accent
Ë	Euml	&#203;	capital E, dieresis or umlaut mark
Í	Iacute	&#205;	capital I, acute accent
Î	Icirc	&#206;	capital I, circumflex accent
Ì	Igrave	&#204;	capital I, grave accent
Ï	Iuml	&#207;	capital I, dieresis or umlaut mark
Ñ	Ntilde	&#209;	capital N, tilde
Ó	Oacute	&#211;	capital O, acute accent
Ô	Ocirc	&#212;	capital O, circumflex accent
Ò	Ograve	&#210;	capital O, grave accent
Ø	Oslash	&#216;	capital O, slash
Õ	Otilde	&#213;	capital O, tilde
Ö	Ouml	&#214;	capital O, dieresis or umlaut mark
	THORN	&#222;	capital THORN, Icelandic
Ú	Uacute	&#218;	capital U, acute accent
Û	Ucirc	&#219;	capital U, circumflex accent
Ù	Ugrave	&#217;	capital U, grave accent
Ü	Uuml	&#220;	capital U, dieresis or umlaut mark
	Yacute	&#221;	capital Y, acute accent
á	aacute	&#225;	small a, acute accent
â	acirc	&#226;	small a, circumflex accent
æ	aelig	&#230;	small ae diphthong (ligature)
à	agrave	&#224;	small a, grave accent
&	amp	&#038;	ampersand
å	aring	&#229;	small a, ring
ã	atilde	&#227;	small a, tilde
ä	auml	&#228;	small a, dieresis or umlaut mark

HTML for Fun and Profit

Character	Character Name	ANSI Number	Description
ç	ccedil	&#231;	small c, cedilla
é	eacute	&#233;	small e, acute accent
ê	ecirc	&#234;	small e, circumflex accent
è	egrave	&#232;	small e, grave accent
	eth	&#240;	small eth, Icelandic
ë	euml	&#235;	small e, dieresis or umlaut mark
>	gt	&#062;	greater than
í	iacute	&#237;	small i, acute accent
î	icirc	&#238;	small i, circumflex accent
ì	igrave	&#236;	small i, grave accent
ï	iuml	&#239;	small i, dieresis or umlaut mark
<	lt	&#060;	less than
	nbsp	&#032;	should be NON_BREAKING space - Not implemented in Mosaic
ñ	ntilde	&#241;	small n, tilde
ó	oacute	&#243;	small o, acute accent
ô	ocirc	&#244;	small o, circumflex accent
ò	ograve	&#242;	small o, grave accent
ø	oslash	&#248;	small o, slash
õ	otilde	&#245;	small o, tilde
ö	ouml	&#246;	small o, dieresis or umlaut mark
ß	szlig	&#223;	small sharp s, German (sz ligature)
	thorn	&#254;	small thorn, Icelandic
ú	uacute	&#250;	small u, acute accent
û	ucirc	&#251;	small u, circumflex accent
ù	ugrave	&#249;	small u, grave accent
ü	uuml	&#252;	small u, dieresis or umlaut mark
	yacute	&#253;	small y, acute accent
ÿ	yuml	&#255;	small y, dieresis or umlaut mark

D

HTML for Fun and Profit

More Information

The Web not only covers the Internet world, but it also encompasses many of the tools of the Internet. No single book can cover the diverse areas that web applications and web design can reach. This appendix lists sources of more information on the diverse tools and facets of the Web.

Perl

Perl is a scripting language that has become common across most platforms supporting web servers. This commonality makes Perl an ideal language for developing portable CGI interfaces without actually programming in C. Table E-1 lists sources for information about Perl.

Table E-1   For More Information About Perl and the Web ...

Source	Author or Subject	Title or Address
Books	▼ C. Dichter & M. Pease	• *Software Engineering with Perl*, PTR Prentice Hall, 1995.
	▼ E. Quigley	• *Perl by Example*, PTR Prentice Hall, 1995.
	▼ Schwartz, R.	• *Learning Perl*, OReilly & Associates, Inc., 1993.
	▼ L. Wall & R. Schwartz	• *Programming Perl*, OReilly & Associates, Inc., 1990.

Table E-1   For More Information About Perl and the Web ... (Continued)

Source	Author or Subject	Title or Address
FTP sites	▼ Source code	• `ftp://ftp.cis.ufl.edu/pub/perl/src`
	▼ Binaries	• `ftp://ftp.cis.ufl.edu/pub/perl/src /macperl` • `ftp://ftp.cis.ufl.edu/pub/perl/src /ntperl` • `ftp://ftp.cis.ufl.edu/pub/perl/src /msdosperl`
	▼ Scripts	• `ftp://ftp.cis.ufl.edu/pub/perl/scripts` • `http://www.seas.upenn.edu/~mengwong /perlhtml.html` (A web page pointing to more than a dozen sites that carry perl scripts) • `http://src.doc.ic.ac.uk/packages/perl/coombs- scripts` • `http://www.bio.cam.ac.uk/web/`
Netnews groups		• `comp.lang.perl`
WWW pointers	▼ Perl Programming Language Page	• `http://web.nexor.co.uk/public/perl /perl.html`
	▼ Univ. of Florida's Perl Archive Page	• `http://www.cis.ufl.edu/perl`
	▼ Index of Perl / HTML Archives Page	• `http://www.seas.upenn.edu/~mengwong /perlhtml.html`

Wide Area Information Servers (WAIS)

WAIS is a networked information retrieval system. Table E-2 describes email aliases concerned with WAIS; Table E-3 lists sources of general and specific information about WAIS.

Table E-2   Email Aliases for WAIS

Alias	Function	Contact
`wais-interest`	A moderated list that announces new releases for the Internet environment.	`wais-interest-request@think.com`
`wais-discussion`	A digested, moderated list on electronic-publishing issues in general and Wide Area Information Servers in particular. Postings every week or two.	`wais-discussion-request@think.com`
`wais-talk`	A technical, open list (interactive, not moderated) for implementors and developers. *Not a support list.*	`wais-talk-request@think.com`
`Z3950IW`	Z39.50-implementors list for low-level discussions of protocol details.	`LISTSERV@nervm.nerdc.ufl.edu`
`ZIP` (Z39.50-92 Information Project)	A mailing list for those interested in the development of the freeWAIS distribution from CNIDR.	`zip-request@kudzu.concert.net`
`SIG-WAIS`	A list for announcements of meetings and presentations of the WAIS Special Interest Group. These face-to-face conferences provide useful demonstrations and talks on WAIS and Z39.50.	`sig-wais-info@cnidr.org`

Table E-3   For More Information About WAIS and the Web …

Source	Address	Comments
General		
FTP sites	• `http://ewshp2.cso.uiuc.edu/`	Some perl scripts for WAIS interfaces, including `kidofwais.p`
Netnews groups	• `comp.infosystems.wais`	FAQ found at `ftp://rtfm.mit.edu/--/comp.infosystems.wais`
Specific		

Table E-3   For More Information About WAIS and the Web ... (Continued)

Source	Address	Comments
WAIS	• `http://www.wais.com/pub/freeware/`	• A professional WAIS index product offered by WAIS Inc.
freeWais	• `http://www.wais.com/pub/freeware/`	• The freeware version of WAIS Inc.'s professional WAIS product.
WWWWais	• `http://www.eit.com/software/ wwwwais/wwwwais.html`	• A program that acts as gateway between `waisq` and `waissearch` (programs that search WAIS indexes) and a forms-capable WWW browser. Works with freeWAIS.
freeWAIS-sf • freeWAIS-sf Home Page	• http://ls6-www.informatik.uni-dortmund.de/freeWAIS-sf/README-sf	Used to create an index of fields.
• SFgate	• `http://ls6-www.informatik.uni-dortmund.de/SFgate/SFgate`	• A CGI interface to WAIS databases without using `waisq` or `waissearch`.
• waistool	• `ftp://emwac.ed.ac.uk/pub/waistool`	• A Windows NT WAIS product

World Wide Web (WWW)

There are plenty of places to go to get information about the Web. The best way to proceed is as follows.

1. Start by reading the Netnews groups:

- `comp.infosystems.www.providers` — discusses WWW provider issues.
- `comp.infosystems.www.users` — discusses WWW user and user support issues.
- `comp.infosystems.www.misc` — includes general WWW discussions and discussions that don't fall into either of the above two groups.

2. Then, subscribe to the email aliases for specific items.

Note that most email aliases address a specific area. New-user or new-developer questions should not be taken there first. Table E-4 describes the aliases.

Table E-4   Email Aliases for WWW Information

Alias	Function	Send email to:
www-announce	Announces new web items, including new software and servers.	listserv@mail.w3.org with subscribe www-announce *firstname lastname* in the body.
www-html	Discusses current and future versions of HTML. *No newcomer questions.*	listserv@mail.w3.org with subscribe www-html *firstname lastname* in the body.
www-proxy	Discusses issues about proxies and caching.	listserv@mail.w3.org with subscribe www-proxy *firstname lastname* in the body.
www-talk	Discusses technical issues about current and future WWW software. *No newcomer questions.*	listserv@mail.w3.org with subscribe www-talk *firstname lastname* in the body.
www-rdb	Discusses relational database gateways to WWW.	listserv@mail.w3.org with subscribe www-rdb *firstname lastname* in the body.
www-mling	Discusses multilingual browsers. Archived at: http://www.ntt.jp/people/takada/ml/www-mling/	listserv@mail.w3.org with subscribe www-mling *firstname lastname* in the body.
www-security	Discusses the security aspects of web servers.	Majordomo@ns1.rutgers.edu with subscribe www-security *emailname* in the body.
www-buyinfo	Archived at: ftp://ftp.research.att.com/dist/www-buyinfo-archive/	www-buyinfo-request@allegra.att.com with subscribe www-buyinfo in the body.

3. Review the following areas of interest for pointers to information about:

- HTTP servers
- CGI scripts
- Browser clients
- Platform-specific information
- Filters and authoring tools
- HTML developments
- Web administration and issues

E

- Robots
- Security
- Professional associations and contacts

HTTP Servers

Table E-5 lists sources for information about HTTP servers.

Table E-5   WWW Pointers to HTTP Servers

Server	Pointer
CERN httpd	`http://www.w3.org/hypertext/WWW/Daemon/Status.html`
NCSA httpd	`http://hoohoo.ncsa.uiuc.edu/docs/Overview.html`
MacHTTP	`http://www.biap.com/machttp_info.html`
Windows NT https	`http://emwac.ed.ac.uk/html/internet_toolchest/https/`
Others	`http://www.w3.org/hypertext/WWW/Daemon /Overview.html`

CGI Scripts

For information about CGI scripts, see

- `ftp://ftp.ncsa.uiuc.edu/Web/httpd/Unix/ncsa_httpd/cgi/`

Browser Clients

Browser clients include:

- WinWeb and MacWeb
- Enhanced Mosaic
- NCSA Mosaic for UNIX, Microsoft Windows, and Macintosh
- Lynx
- Netscape
- Other

Table E-5 lists sources for information about these browsers.

Table E-6   Pointers to Browser Client Information

Browser Client	Pointer
WinWeb MacWeb	`http://galaxy.einet.net/EINet/WinWeb/WinWebHome.html` `http://galaxy.einet.net/EINet/MacWeb/MacWebHome.html`
Enhanced Mosaic	`http://www.spyglass.com/`
NCSA Mosaic for UNIX, MS Windows, and Macintosh	`http://www.ncsa.uiuc.edu/SDG/Software/Mosaic` `/NCSAMosaicHome.html`
NCSA Mosaic email alias	Send email to `listserv@uicvm.uic.edu` with subscribe mosaic-l *firstname lastname* in the body.
Lynx (text-mode)	`http://www.cc.ukans.edu/`
Netscape	`http://home.netscape.com/`
Netscape email alias	Send email to `listserv@irlearn.ucd.ie` with subscribe netscape *emailaddress* in the body.
Over a dozen others for specific platforms and uses.	`http://www.w3.org/hypertext/WWW/Clients` for most current information.

Machine-Specific Information

For information specific to Windows NT systems:

- Send email to `webserver-nt-request@mailserve.process.com` with subscribe webserver-nt in the body.

Filters and Authoring Tools

For overviews of filters and authoring tools, see

- `http://www.w3.org/hypertext/WWW/Tools/Filters.html`

- `http://www.w3.org/hypertext/WWW/Tools/Overview.html`

In addition to general HTML pointers (Table E-7), this section provides pointers to information about:

E

- FrameMaker/MIF — Table E-8
- Rich Text Format (RTF) — Table E-9
- WordPerfect — Table E-10
- Microsoft Word for Windows — Table E-11

Table E-7   Pointers to General HTML Information

Name	Function	Pointer
HTML Assistant	HTML editor for Windows	`ftp://ftp.cs.dal.ca/htmlasst` `/htmlafaq.html`
BBEdit Extensions	HTML extensions to the BBEdit editor on the Mac	`http://www.uji.es` `/bbedit-html-extensions.html`
HTML Editor	HTML Editor or the Mac by Rick Giles	`http://dragon.acadiau.ca:1667/~giles/` `HTML_Editor/Documentation.html`
BBEditLite	HTML Editor for the Mac	`ftp://ftp.std.com/pub/bbedit` `/bbedit-lite-30.hqx`
HTMLed	HTML editor for Windows	`http://pringle.mta.ca/~peterc` `/htmed11.zip`
HTML Writer	HTML editor for Windows	`http://wwf.et.byu.edu/~nosackk` `/html-writer/index.html`
HoTMetal & HoTMetal Pro	Editors for UNIX and Windows from SoftQuad	`ftp://ftp.ncsa.uiuc.edu/Mosaic` `/contrib/SoftQaud/hotmetal`
tkHTML	A UNIX editor based on `tk/tcl`	`ftp://ftp.u.washington.edu/public` `/roland/tkHTML`
S H E - Simple HTML Editor	An editor for the Mac using Hypercard	`ftp://ftp.lib.ncsu.edu/pub/software` `/mac/simple-html-editor.hqx`

FrameMaker/MIF

Here are pointers to FrameMaker information.

Table E-8   For More Information About FrameMaker and HTML ...

WebMaker — `http://www.cern.ch/WebMaker/`   Converts FrameMaker documents and books to a network of HTML files.   Contact: `webmaker@cern.ch` (Bertrand Rousseau et al.)
Frame2html - `ftp://bang.nta.no/pub/`
`Mif2html - http://www.quadralay.com/products/products.html`
`MifMucker - http://www.oac.uci.edu/indiv/ehood/mifmucker.doc.html`   Application for manipulating Frame documents and books. It contains a filter to   convert FrameMaker documents into HTML.

Table E-8   For More Information About FrameMaker and HTML ... (Continued)

`www_and_frame - ftp://ftp.w3.org/pub/www/contrib/`
`miftran - ftp://ftp.alumni.caltech.edu/pub/mcbeath/web/miftran` (A MIF-to-HTML converter written in C.)

mif.pl - `http://www.oac.uci.edu/indiv/ehood/mif.pl.doc.html`
    A perl library to parse Frame Maker Interchange Format (MIF), designed to be used by filters.
        Contact: `ehood@convex.com` (Earl Hood)

`edc2html - http://www.oac.uci.edu/indiv/ehood/edc2html.doc.html`
    A perl program that generates an HTML document to allow navigation through the structure of a FrameBuilder Element Catalog.
        Contact: `ehood@convex.com` (Earl Hood)

Rich Text Format (RTF)

Here are pointers to information about RTF and HTML

Table E-9   For More Information About RTF and HTML ...

	Pointer
`rtftohtml -ftp`	`ftp://ftp.cray.com/src/WWWstuff/RTF/rtftohtml_overview.html`
`rtftoweb - ftp`	`ftp://ftp.rrzn.uni-hannover.de/pub/unix-local/misc/rtftoweb/html/rtftoweb.html`
`rtf2html`	`http://www.w3.org/hypertext/WWW/Tools/HTMLGeneration/rtf2html.html`

WordPerfect

Here are pointers to WordPerfect information.

Table E-10 For More Information About WordPerfect and HTML ...

`WPTOHTML -`
`ftp://oak.oakland.edu/SimTel/msdos/wordperf/wpt51d10.zip`
   WordPerfect macros to convert from WP 5.1 to HTML
`ftp://oak.oakland.edu/SimTel/msdos/wordperf/wpt60d10.zip`
   WordPerfect macros to convert from WP 6.0 to HTML

`wpmacro - http://stoner.eps.mcgill.ca/wpmacro/wpmacro.html`
   WordPerfect 5.1 macro, now largely superseded by WPTOHTML
      Contact: `steeve@stoner.eps.mcgill.ca` (Steve McCauley)

E

Microsoft Word for Windows

Here are pointers to information about Word for Windows and HTML

Table E-11 For More Information About Word for Windows and HTML ...

	Pointer
HTML converters: latest list	`http://www.w3.org/hypertext/WWW/Tools /Filters.html`
CU_HTML.DOT	`http://www.cuhk.hk/csc/cu_html/cu_html.html`
ftp	`ftp://ftp.cuhk.hk/pub/www/windows/util/`
ANT_HTML.DOT	`http://www.w3.org/hypertext/WWW/Tools/Ant.html`
ftp	`ftp://ftp.einet.net/einet/pc/`
GU_HTML.DOT	`http://www.gatech.edu/word_html/release.htm`

HTML Developments

Virtual Reality Markup Language (VRML) is an evolving specification for a platform-independent definition of three-dimensional spaces within the World Wide Web.

To subscribe to its email alias, send email to
`infodroid@wired.com` with <u>subscribe www-vrml *emailaddress*</u> in the body

Web Administration and Issues

Table E-3 summarizes sources for information about various administration issues, including general administration and support, log file management, and HTML checking tools .

Table E-12 For More Information About Web Administration...

Source	Pointer
Administration and Support	
`web-support` email alias	To subscribe, send email to `web-support-request@mailbase.ac.uk` with <u>subscribe *email-address*</u> in the body.

Table E-12 For More Information About Web Administration... (Continued)

Source	Pointer
www-managers An email alias for WWW site setup and maintenance questions. Responses should be sent to the person asking the question, who in turn should summarize the answers and post to the list. *Not a discussion lis*t.	To subscribe, send email to `Majordomo@list.Stanford.EDU` with <u>subscribe www-managers *emailaddress*</u> in the body
Log File Management	
Getstats	`http://www.eit.com/software/getstats/getstats.html`
HTML Checking Tools	
Weblint	`http://www.khoros.unm.edu/staff/neilb` `ftp://ftp.khoros.unm.edu/pub/perl/www /weblint-1.000.tar.gz`
htmlchek.awk	`http://www.w3.org/hypertext/WWW/Tools /htmlchek.txt`
verify_links (*was* html_analyzer)	`http://wsk.eit.com/wsk/dist/doc/admin/webtest /verify_links.html`

Robots

For information about robots, consult the web page pointer and email aliases listed below.

WWW Pointers

- World Wide Web Robots, Wanderers, and Spiders Web Page
  `http://web.nexor.co.uk/mak/doc/robots/robots.html`

Email Aliases

- Lycos users
  To subscribe, send email to majordomo@mail.msen.com with <u>subscribe lycos-users *emailaddress*</u> in the body

- robots email alias
  To subscribe, send email to `robots-request@nexor.co.uk` with <u>subscribe robots *emailaddress*</u> in the body.

Security

Table E-13 lists email aliases concerned with security issues.

Table E-13 Security Email Aliases

Alias	To Subscribe:
First Virtual	Send email to `fv-users-request@fv.com` with <u>subscribe fv-users *emailaddress*</u> in the body.
SHttp	Send email to `Majordomo@OpenMarket.com` with <u>subscribe shttp-talk *emailaddress*</u> in the body.
www-security	Send email to `Majordomo@ns1.rutgers.edu` with <u>subscribe www-security</u> in the body.

Professional Associations and Contacts

- International Association of Independent Web Consultants

  email alias — `iaiwc@worldtel.com`

- Internet Developer's Association

  email alias — Send email to `association@presence.com` with <u>subscribe</u> in the body.

Glossary

absolute address

An address that identifies a storage location or a device without the use of any intermediate reference.

absolute pathname

For a file or directory, the list of directories from the *root directory* through the tree structure to the desired filename or directory name, each name in the series separated by a slash character (/).

access

To obtain entry to or to locate, read into memory, and make ready for some operation. Access is usually used with regard to disks, files, records, and network entry procedures.

access code

A unique combination of characters, usually letters or numbers, used in communications as identification for gaining access to a remote computer. On a network or an on-line service, the access code is generally referred to as *user name*, *user ID*, or *password*.

access control list

A list of user IDs and the specific access permission for specific files on the system.

account

See *user account*.

ACL

See *access control list*.

acronym

A word derived from the first or most important letters in a multiple word descriptive noun or other expression, often serving as a mnemonic to recall the words comprising the term. For example, HTML is short for "Hypertext Markup Language." Computer terminology is rife with acronyms.

address

In networking, a unique code that identifies a *node* to the *network*.

alias

An alternate label. For example, a label and one or more aliases may be used to refer to the same data element or point in a computer program.

American Standard Code for Information Interchange (ASCII)

The standard binary encoding of alphabetical characters, numbers, and other keyboard symbols.

anchor

A tag used to associate text with a hypertext link.

append

To attach to the end of; most often used in reference to writing a file (adding data to the end of the file) or adding to a string (adding characters to the end of a string of characters).

application

A software program specially designed for a particular task or the specific use of a software program. Graphics applications are usually designed to enable the user to manipulate data or images, or to create images from data or from a library of shapes.

architecture

The specific components of a computer system and the way they interact with one another.

arg

See *argument*.

arg list

Argument list.

argument

An item of information following a *command*. It may, for example, modify the command or identify a file to be affected.

ASCII

(Pronounced "as-kee.") See *American Standard Code for Information Interchange (ASCII)*.

attribute

Elements such as additional information stored with each tag.

base

A tag to define the portion of a URL to be used in indirect addressing.

baud rate

The rate at which information is transmitted between devices; for example, between a terminal and the computer. Often incorrectly assumed to indicate the number of bits per second (bps) transmitted, baud rate actually measures the number of events, or signal changes, that occur in 1 second. Because one event can actually encode more than one bit in high-speed digital communications, baud rate and bits per second are not always synonymous, and the latter is the more accurate term to apply to modems. For example, a so-called 9600-baud modem that encodes four bits per event actually operates at 2400 baud but transmits 9600 bits per second (2400 events times 4 bits per event) and thus should be called a 9600-bps modem.

bitmapped graphics

Computer graphics that are stored and held as collections of bits in memory locations corresponding to pixels on the screen. Bitmapped graphics are typical of paint programs, which treat images as collections of dots rather than as shapes. Within a computer's memory, a bitmapped graphic is represented as an array (group) of bits that describe the characteristics of the individual pixels making up the image. Bitmapped graphics displayed in color require several-to-many bits per pixel, each describing some aspect of the color of a single spot on the screen.

browser

A World Wide Web client tool. See also *World Wide Web*.

bullet

A character—typically a filled-in or open circle (•)—used to draw attention to an item in a list.

CD-ROM

Compact disc, read-only memory. A form of storage characterized by high capacity (roughly 600 megabytes) and the use of laser optics rather than magnetic means for reading data. See also *High Sierra specification*.

CGI

See *common gateway interface*.

checkbox

In the OPEN LOOK GUI, a nonexclusive setting that shows a checkmark in a square box when the setting is chosen.

click

To press a mouse button once and release it without moving the pointer.

clickable image

An inline image on a web page that the browser is monitoring for mouse input. If a point on the image is selected, the coordinates are returned to the web server defined in the <IMG> tag.

client

(1) In the client-server model for file systems, the client is a machine that remotely accesses resources of a compute server, such as compute power and large memory capacity.
(2) In the client-server model for window systems, the client is an *application* that accesses windowing services from a "server process." In this model, the client and the server can run on the same machine or on separate machines.

colormap

The color options in a graphics system, arranged by index number. Typically, the system has a default colormap. The index of colors in the colormap can be reallocated, however, depending on the application.

command

(1) An instruction to the computer. A command typically is a character string typed at a keyboard and is interpreted by the computer as a demand for a particular action.

(2) In a graphical user interface (GUI), a button or *menu item*.

common gateway interface

An interface between *World Wide Web* servers and scripts, utilities, and programs that generate custom responses to client requests.

container

A tag that has a start and end component. Containers enclose text.

control character

A character typed by pressing a key while the Control key is pressed. For instance, a Control-H is typed by pressing the H key while pressing the Control key.

daemon

A process that runs in the background, handling commands delivered for remote command execution. Typical daemons are the mailer daemon and the printer daemon.

default

An alternative value, attribute, or option assumed when none has been specified.

desktop publishing

To design, create, and print a document by using a personal computer or workstation and professional-grade word processing program.

dial-up connection

A connection between two machines through a phone line.

directory

A type of file that can contain other files and directories.

directory pathname

The complete name by which the directory is known. The pathname gives the sequence of directories by which the directory is linked to the *root directory*.

double-click

Clicking twice on a mouse button as an accelerator that performs a specific command.

drop site

A World Wide Web page that allows updates and additions to the links listed on the page. This is a common method of informally registering new web pages.

DTP

See *desktop publishing*.

echo

To repeat a stream of characters. For example, the commands the user types to the computer are displayed on the screen.

editor

A program to assist the user in creating and modifying written material to be stored in files.

email

Electronic mail. See also *mail*.

embedded

An adjective referring to items, such as program code or commands, that are built into their carriers rather than associated with or called by them when needed.

empty element

A tag that has only one component. An empty element indicates a display instruction that should occur only at that point in the document.

Encapsulated PostScript (EPS) format

A file format for graphics and text supported by several graphics drawing applications. An EPS file can contain two versions of an image: a bitmap used to display the image on the screen and a PostScript description used to print the image. See also *Encapsulated PostScript Interchange (EPSI) format*.

Encapsulated PostScript Interchange (EPSI) format

A version of the encapsulated PostScript format that describes an image, using a standard text file. See also *Encapsulated PostScript (EPS) format*.

environment

The conditions under which a user works while using the UNIX system. A user's environment includes those things that personalize the user's login and determine how the user interacts in specific ways with UNIX and the computer. For example, the shell environment includes such things as the shell prompt string, specifics for backspace and erase characters, and commands for sending output from the terminal to the computer.

environment variable

The UNIX C shell environment variables are similar to *shell variable*s, except that environment variables can be passed to every C shell that runs. Many applications use environment variables to set configuration directories, specify base directories for commands or data, and pass other information about the user environment to the program.

EPS

See *Encapsulated PostScript (EPS) format.*

EPSI

See *Encapsulated PostScript Interchange (EPSI) format.*

escape

To divest a special character of its special meaning by preceding it with a backslash (\) character. For example, the UNIX shell interprets ? to represent any single character, but a \? (an "escaped" question mark) is interpreted to be just a question-mark character.

executable file

A file that can be processed or executed by the computer without any further translation. When a user types in the filename, the commands in the file are executed.

extension

In reference to filenames, a set of characters added to a filename that serves to extend or modify the syntax and semantics of the language. The extension is usually the characters that follow the period in a filename. For example, in the file document.book, the characters book are the extension. The file-name extension can be assigned by the user or by (and have special meaning to) a program.

field

A subsection of a line. Programs such as `perl`, `sort`, and `awk` can look at individual fields within a line.

field separator

The character used to separate one field from the next; a string of one or more spaces is the usual field separator.

file

A sequence of bytes constituting a unit of text, data, or program. A file can be stored in the system memory or on an external medium such as tape or disk.

filename

The name of a file as it is stored in a directory on a disk. See also *pathname*.

file-name extension

See *extension*.

file permissions

A set of permissions assigned to each file and directory that determines which users have access to read, write, and execute its contents.

file system

In UNIX operating systems, a tree-structured network of files and directories through which the user can move to access the files and directories contained there.

file transfer protocol (FTP)

The Internet protocol (and program) used to transfer files between hosts.

filter

A command that reads the *standard input*, acts on it in some way, and then prints the results as *standard output*.

folder

A directory in a graphical user interface.

form

(1) A container tag to enclose form elements.
(2) An interactive web page to gather and return information to the server.

forms

HyperText Markup Language tags to generate interactive *World Wide Web* pages. Forms include buttons, menus, and text input areas.

FTP

See *file transfer protocol (FTP)*.

Gbyte

Abbreviation for *gigabyte (Gbyte)*; 1,073,741,824 bytes.

gigabyte (Gbyte)

One billion bytes. In reference to computers, bytes are often expressed in multiples of powers of two. Therefore, a gigabyte can also be 1024 megabytes, where a megabyte is considered to be 2^{20} (or 1,048,576) bytes.

graphical user interface (GUI)

A user interface, or GUI, that provides the user with a method of interacting with the computer and its special applications, usually via a mouse or other selection device. The GUI usually includes such things as windows, an intuitive method of manipulating directories and files, and *icon*s.

grayed

Term for *inactive* or not selectable.

GUI

See *graphical user interface (GUI)*.

heterogenous network

A network composed of systems of more than one *architecture*. Contrast with *homogeneous network*.

hidden character

One of a group of characters within the standard *ASCII* character set that are not printable.

hidden file

A special type of file, such as `.login`, that doesn't show up in normal file listings. Special files usually pertain to system configuration.

High Sierra specification

An industry-wide format specification for *CD-ROM* data. The High Sierra specification defines the logical structure, file structure, and record structures of a CD-ROM disc; it served as the basis for the ISO 9660, an international format standard for CD-ROM. High Sierra was named for the location of a seminal meeting on CD-ROM held near Lake Tahoe in November 1985.

home directory

The directory assigned to the user by the system administrator; usually the same as the *login directory*. Additional directories the user creates stem from the home directory.

homogeneous network

A network composed of systems of only one architecture. Contrast with *heterogenous network*.

horizontal rule

A horizontal line displayed when the `<HR>` tag is processed. Used to divide sections of a document.

hotlist

A list of URL links to click on. Hotlists are used to record the address of an interesting place and return quickly.

housekeeping

Keeping track of what files are where, of who is doing what, and the like.

href

See *hypertext reference*.

HSFS

High Sierra file system. See *High Sierra specification*.

HTML

See *HyperText Markup Language*.

http

See *HyperText Transfer Protocol*.

hypertext

A document that contains links to other documents, indicated by text in a nonstandard format. The linked document can be actively followed or referenced by clicking on the emphasized text.

hypertext reference

The address of the destination of a hypertext link. In WWW, hypertext references are given in URL format.

HyperText Markup Language

The document-formatting language used by WWW browsers.

HyperText Transfer Protocol

The Internet protocol used to transfer documents and other *MIME* data between systems. This is the protocol on which the World Wide Web is based.

icon

An on-screen symbol that simplifies access to a program, command, or data file.

image

A picture or graphic representation of an object.

inactive

Not accepting *input*. An inactive form item that is dimmed cannot accept input from the mouse or keyboard.

inline image

An image displayed in the browser display area, embedded within the text of the document.

input

Information fed to a command, a program, a terminal, a person, and so on.

interactive

Allowing the application and the user to carry on a dialog.

internet

    A collection of networks interconnected by a set of routers that enable them to function as a single, large virtual network.

Internet

    (Note the capital "I") The largest internet in the world consisting of large national backbone nets (such as MILNET, NSFNET, and CREN) and a myriad of regional and local campus networks all over the world. The Internet uses the Internet protocol suite. To be on the Internet, the user must have IP connectivity, that is, be able to access other systems via `telnet` or `ping`. Networks with only email connectivity are not actually classified as being on the Internet.

Internet address

    A 32-bit address assigned to hosts using *TCP/IP*.

IP address

    A unique number that identifies each host in a network.

items

    Menu controls that initiate actions. Also, choices found in a scrolling list.

Joint Photographic Experts Group (JPEG)

    A joint venture of the CCIT and International Organization for Standardization (ISO) that developed a standard for compressing gray-scale or color still images.

Kbyte

    Abbreviation for *kilobyte (Kbyte)* (1024 bytes).

kilobyte (Kbyte)

    A unit of measure equal to 1024 bytes.

link

    A hypertext reference to another document or another point in the same document.

login directory

    The directory that is current after the user logs in. Usually, the *home directory*.

login name

The name by which the computer system knows the user.

login shell

The name of the default *shell* used when a user logs in.

macro

A user-defined shortcut that types text or alters something, based on a sequence of commands.

mail

A computer system facility that enables the sending and holding of messages via the computer.

mailbox

A disk storage area assigned to a network user for receipt of electronic messages.

mailing list

(1) An electronic-mail address that is an alias for many other email addresses.
(2) The people who receive the email when a user sends it to such an address.

man pages

UNIX *on-line documentation.*

map

(1) To assign a new interpretation of a terminal key. For example, in vi, one can map, say, the @ key to represent the sequence a-Esc-j.
(2) A file used by NIS that holds information of a particular type, for example, the password entries of all users on a network or the names of all host machines on a network.

Mbyte

Abbreviation for megabyte; one million bytes.

megabyte (Mbyte)

A megabyte is 1,048,576 bytes or 1024 kilobytes; or roughly 1 million bytes or 1,000 kilobytes.

menu

A list of options from which a program user can select to perform a desired action. Many application programs use menus to provide the user with an easily understood alternative to memorizing program commands.

menu item

(1) The area of a menu that the user chooses to invoke a particular operation.
(2) An item on a *menu* with an arrow pointing to the right, used to display a *submenu*.

metacharacter

A character having a special meaning to UNIX. For example, the UNIX shell interprets the ? character to stand for any single character. See also *wildcard*.

MIDI

Pronounced "middy." Acronym for musical instrument digital interface. MIDI is a note-oriented control language for specifying music. MIDI data consists of codes specifying notes and timing. These codes can be generated by or output to MIDI-compatible devices, such as keyboards or synthesizers. MIDI applications are generally found in the computer music industry and are used for studio control and audio production.

MIME

See *Multipurpose Internet Mail Extensions (MIME)*.

modem

Short for modulator/demodulator. A device that enables a machine or terminal to establish a connection and transfer data through telephone lines. Because a computer is digital and a telephone line is analog, modems are needed to convert digital into analog, and vice versa. See also *baud rate*.

mount

The process of accessing a directory from a disk attached to a machine making the mount request or remote disk on a network. See also *unmount*.

mouse

An input device connected to the workstation that determines the location of the pointer. The basic features of a mouse are a casing with a flat bottom, designed to be gripped by one hand; one or more buttons on the top; a directional detection device on the bottom, such as a ball or optical sensor; and a cable that attaches the mouse to the workstation.

movie

A contiguous series of video frames (and optionally synchronized audio) that are displayed fast enough to provide the illusion of motion. A frame rate of 30 frames per second is a typical target for a smooth-running movie.

Moving Picture Experts Group (MPEG)

A group that developed standards for compressing moving pictures and audio data and for synchronizing video and audio datastreams.

Multipurpose Internet Mail Extensions (MIME)

Defines the format of the contents of Internet mail messages and provides for multipart textual and nontextual message bodies.

network

Technically, the hardware that connects various systems, enabling them to communicate. Informally, the systems so connected.

network administration

Tasks of the person who maintains a network, such as adding systems to a network or enabling sharing between systems.

network administrator

The person who maintains a network.

network operations center (NOC)

Any center tasked with the operational aspects of a production network. These tasks include monitoring and control, troubleshooting, user assistance, and so on.

newsgroups

Conglomerations of electronic mail messages sorted by topic, usually sent to thousands of users worldwide.

≡

NOC

See *network operations center (NOC)*.

node

An addressable point on a network. A node can connect a computing system, a terminal, or various other peripheral devices to the network.

nonexclusive scrolling list

A scrolling list from which users can choose one or more items at a given time.

on-line

Connected to the system and in operation.

on-line documentation

A disk-based form of documentation provided by many application programs, consisting of advice or instructions on using program features. On-line documentation can be accessed directly without the need to interrupt work in progress or leaf through a manual.

operating system

A collection of programs that monitor the use of the system and supervise the other programs executed by it.

optional argument

An argument accepted but not required by a command.

output

Information produced by a command, program, or such, and sent elsewhere; for example, to the terminal, to a file, or to a line printer.

output redirection

See *redirection*.

owner

(1) The person who created a file or directory.
(2) The attribute of a file or directory that specifies who has owner permissions.

page-description language (PDL)

A programming language, such as *PostScript*, that is used to describe output to a printer or a display device, which then uses the instructions from the page-description language to construct text and graphics to create the required page image.

parse

To break input into smaller chunks so that a program can act on the information. Compilers have parsers for translating the commands and structures entered by a programmer into machine language. A natural-language parser accepts text in a human language such as English, attempts to determine its sequence structure, and translates its terms into a form the program can use.

partition

The unit into which the disk space is divided by the software.

password

A security measure that restricts access to computer systems and sensitive files. A password is a unique string of characters that a user types in as an identification code. The system compares the code against a stored list of authorized passwords and users. If the code is legitimate, the system allows the user access, at whatever security level has been approved for the owner of the password.

password protection

The use of passwords as a means of allowing only authorized users access to a computer system or its files.

pathname

The location of a file or directory in the UNIX file system.

PDL

See *page-description language (PDL)*.

permissions

The attribute of a file or directory that specifies who has read, write, or execution access.

platform

The foundation technology of a computer system. Because computers are layered devices composed of a chip-level hardware layer, a firmware and operating-system layer, and an applications program layer, the bottom layer of a machine is often called a platform, as in "a SPARC® platform." However, designers of applications software view both the hardware and systems software as the platform, because both provide support for an application.

point-to-point protocol (PPP)

The successor to *SLIP*, PPP provides router-to-router and host-to-network connections over both synchronous and asynchronous circuits.

port

The abstraction used by Internet transport protocols to distinguish among multiple simultaneous connections to a single destination host.

port numbers

Numbers used by *TCP/IP* protocols to identify the end points of communication.

PostScript

A page-description language published by Adobe Systems Incorporated. PostScript describes the appearance of text and graphics on printed pages. The best-known page-description language, PostScript uses English-like commands to control page layout and to load and scale outline fonts. Because PostScript uses scalable outline fonts, it can create a font of any size, giving the user flexibility in creating documents. PostScript is used in many printers, either as the only print mode or as one alternative among several.

PPP

See *point-to-point protocol (PPP)*.

press

To push down and hold a mouse button.

program

A sequence of instructions telling a computer how to perform a task. A program can be in machine language or it can be in a higher-level language that is then translated into machine language.

proxy

The mechanism whereby one system "fronts for" another system in responding to protocol requests. Proxy systems are used in *network* management to avoid having to implement full protocol stacks in simple devices, such as *modem*s.

query

The process by which a web client asks a web server to return information, based on a character string passed to the server.

radio button

In graphical user interfaces, a means of selecting one of several mutually exclusive options, usually within an option-selection area such as a dialog box. The presence of radio buttons in a list of options means that only one of the options can be selected at any given time. Visually, a radio button is a small circle that, when selected, has a smaller, filled circle inside it.

readme file

A file containing information that the user either needs or will find informative and that might not have been included in the documentation. Readme files are placed on disk in plain-text form (such as *ASCII*) so that they can be read easily by word-processing programs.

recursive

A computer program that calls itself.

redirection

(1) The channeling of output to a file or device instead of to the *standard output*.
(2) The channeling of input from a file or device instead of from the *standard output*.

redirect output

To send to a file the information that the system would normally display on the screen as the result of a command. Basic output redirection requires use of the > or >> symbols. Also known as *redirection*.

regular expression

A pattern representing a class of character strings. For example, grep recognizes the regular expression h.t to mean any three-character string beginning with h and ending with t.

relative address

An address that uses a path relative to a certain point. See *relative pathname*.

relative pathname

A series of directory names separated by the slash (/) character that locates a file or directory with respect to the working directory. See also *absolute pathname*.

request for comments (RFC)

The document series, begun in 1969, that describes the *Internet* suite of protocols and related experiments. Not all (in fact very few) RFCs describe Internet standards, but all Internet standards are written up as RFCs.

RFC

See *request for comments (RFC)*.

RGB color

Short for red-green-blue. RGB color systems obtain their colors via a direct combination of red, green, and blue components. The range of colors that can be displayed depends on the number of bits that have been assigned to each pixel.

root

See *root file system*, *root directory*, and *root user name*.

root directory

The base directory from which all other directories stem, directly or indirectly.

root file system

> One file system residing on the root device (a device predefined by the system at initialization) designated to anchor the overall file system.

root user name

> UNIX user name that grants special privileges to the person who logs in with that ID. The user who can supply the correct password for the root user name is given superuser or administrator privileges for the particular machine.

screen editor

> An editing program in which text is operated on relative to the position of the cursor on the screen. Commands for entering, changing, and removing text involve moving the cursor to the area to be altered and performing the necessary operation. Changes are viewed on the screen as they are made. The UNIX vi program is an example of a screen editor.

script

> A type of program that consists of a set of instructions to an application or utility program. A script usually consists of instructions expressed using the application's or utility's rules and syntax, combined with simple control structures such as loops and if/then expressions.

scroll

> To shift text up or down one or more lines on the screen.

select

> To distinguish an object (or objects) on the screen so that they can be operated on.

selection

> A span of characters, highlighted in inverse video, underlining, or gray shading.

Serial-line Internet Protocol (SLIP)

> An Internet protocol that runs IP over serial lines such as telephone circuits or RS232 cables interconnecting two systems. SLIP is now being replaced by *point-to-point protocol (PPP)*.

server

(1) In the client-server model for file systems, the server is a machine with compute resources (and is sometimes called the compute server), and large memory capacity. Client machines can remotely access and make use of these resources. In the client-server model for window systems, the server is a process that provides windowing services to an application, or "client process." In this model, the client and the server can run on the same machine or on separate machines.

(2) A *daemon* that actually handles the providing of files.

server system

A system that is on a *network* and provides resources, such as disk space and file transfers, to other systems.

session

The time during which a program is running. With interactive programs typical of microcomputers, a session represents the time during which the program accepts input, processes information, and responds to user commands.

shell

A programmable command interpreter. The shell provides direct communication between the user and the operating system.

shell procedure

An executable file that is not a compiled program. A shell procedure calls the shell to read and execute commands contained in a file. This enables the user to store a sequence of commands in a file for repeated use. It is also called a "shell program" or "command file."

shell script

See *shell procedure*.

shell variable

UNIX shell variables affect how the shell runs and appears. For example, certain variables specify the list of arguments that are listed on the current command line or set the number of command lines saved in a command history.

SLIP

See *Serial-line Internet Protocol (SLIP)*.

HTML for Fun and Profit

source code

The uncompiled version of a program written in a language such as C or Pascal. The source code must be translated to machine language by a program known as the compiler before the computer can execute the program.

special character

See *metacharacter*.

specific address

See *absolute address*.

SQL

See *structured query language (SQL)*.

standard error

An open file normally connected directly to a primary output device, such as a terminal, printer, or screen. Error messages and other diagnostic output normally goes to this file and then to the output device. The user can redirect the standard error output into another file instead of to the printer or screen.

standard input

Short for "standard input device." The device from which a program or system normally takes its input. Usually a terminal or the keyboard.

standard output

Short for "standard output device." The device to which a program or system normally sends its output. Usually a terminal or the screen.

string

A connected sequence of characters, words, or other elements.

string variable

A sequence of characters that can be the value of a shell variable. See *variable*.

structured query language (SQL)

The international standard language for defining and accessing relational databases.

subdirectory

A directory that resides within another directory.

submenu ·

A menu that displays additional choices; a submenu is displayed through a menu item on a menu.

syntax error

An error in the use of language syntax; a statement that violates one or more of the grammatical rules of a language and is thus "not legal."

system

A computer that enables a user to run computer programs.

system administration

The tasks of a person who performs maintenance tasks on systems.

system administrator

The person who performs maintenance tasks on systems.

system name

The unique name assigned to a system on a network.

system type

The name that identifies a specific kind of system, such as a Sun-4™ or a Sun386i™.

system unit

The part of a workstation that contains the central processing unit (CPU), the disk, and other devices essential to operate the system.

table

A display of data in rows and columns.

tag

A sequence of characters starting with a < and ending with a >, used to mark up text with display instructions.

tag image file format (TIFF)

A standard file format commonly used for scanning, storage, and interchange of gray-scale graphic images.

HTML for Fun and Profit

TCP

> See *transport control protocol (TCP)*.

TCP/IP

> Acronym for transport control protocol/interface program. The protocol suite originally developed for the Internet. It is also called the *Internet* protocol suite. SunOS networks run on TCP/IP by default.

text editor

> Software for creating, changing, or removing text with the aid of a computer. Most text editors have two modes: an input mode for typing text and a command mode for moving or modifying text. Two examples are the UNIX system editors `ed` and `vi`. See also *screen editor*.

text field

> An area in a window into which users type text from the keyboard.

text formatter

> A program that prepares a file of text for printed output. To make use of a text formatter, a file must also contain some special commands for structuring the final copy. These special commands instruct the formatter to justify margins, start new paragraphs, set up lists and tables, place figures, and so on. Two text formatters available on the UNIX system are `nroff` and `troff`.

TIFF

> See *tag image file format (TIFF)*.

tool

> A package of compact, well-designed programs designed to do a specific task well. Several tools can be *link*ed to perform more complex tasks.

transmission control protocol (TCP)

> The major transport protocol in the Internet suite of protocols providing reliable, connection-oriented, full-duplex streams.

transport control protocol (TCP)

    The major transport protocol in the Internet suite of protocols providing reliable, connection- oriented, full-duplex streams. Uses IP for delivery. See *TCP/IP*.

tree structure

    A hierarchical calling sequence consisting of a root segment and one or more levels of segments called via the root segment.

Universal Resource Location

    An address that includes the protocol to reference the data, the system, path and data filename.

unmount

    The process of removing access to a directory on a disk attached to a machine or a remote disk on a network. See also *mount*.

URL

    See *Universal Resource Location*.

USENET

    A worldwide network of UNIX systems, with decentralized administration, used for electronic mail and transmission by special-interest discussion groups.

user account

    A record of essential user information that is stored on the system. Each user who accesses a system has a user account.

user ID

    A number that identifies a user to the system.

user name

    A combination of letters, and possibly numbers, that identifies a user to the system.

utility

    A standard program, usually furnished at no charge with the purchase of a computer, that performs housekeeping functions.

variable

A symbol with a value that may change. In the shell, the variable is a symbol representing some string of characters. Variables may be used in an interactive shell as well as within a *shell procedure*. Within a shell procedure, positional parameters and keyword parameters are two forms of variables.

whitespace

Characters that control the spacing, but do not show up in regular text. Whitespace includes tabs, spaces, carriage returns, and line feeds.

wildcard

A *metacharacter* used to represent a range of ordinary characters. Examples include the shell's use of * and ?.

wordwrap

The automatic continuation of text from the end of one line to the beginning of the next.

working directory

The directory in which the user's commands take place, given that no other directory is specified.

World Wide Web (WWW)

A network document publishing system that uses Hypertext Markup Language (HTML) as the authoring language and Hypertext Transport Protocol (HTTP) as the transport protocol. A variety of client and server products that support HTML and HTTP. See also *Hypertext Markup Language* and *Hypertext Transfer Protocol*.

WWW

See *World Wide Web (WWW)*.

HTML for Fun and Profit

Index

browser-client interactivity 215
browsers, pointers to client information 261
button
    (See also radio button)
    changing label 119
    check box type 125
    clear 139
    radio 122
    setting default value 126
    submit 119

C

CCI (See Common Client Interface)
CCMail 68
CELLPADDING attribute 206
CELLSPACING attribute 206
<CENTER> tag 49
centering text 49, 196
CERN
    developing HTML 3
    heading-level definition 37
    WebMaker 171
CERN httpd
    Document_Root 60
    httpd daemon 59, 60
    httpd server, making directory for
        executables 91
    rules variables 59
CGI
    environment variables for Server
        Includes 111
    environment variables set 156
    implementing clickable image 98
    operation overview 94
    passing information back 153
    passing variables or arguments to
        scripts 97
    preconfigured variables 102
    script information 260
CGI attribute 112
cgi-common directory 12
cgiparse 157
character formatting
    definition 27
    examples 42
    Netscape enhancements 201
    tags 41–45

check box
    fields 125
    use in forms 125
CHECKED attribute 126
CLEAR attribute 189
clickable image
    creating 99–102
    defined 98
    defining 101
    placing in form 120
    submitting a form 119
client connection
    home connections 165
    work connections 166
CMD attribute 112
color
    advice for planning 167
    listing current values 76
    Netscape enhancements 185–187
    specification 75
    transparent 76
    values defined by giftrans 75
COLS attribute of <TEXTAREA> tag 133
COLSPAN=*{number}* attribute 81
comment line, example 38
comment, hidden 38
Commercenet 213
Common Client Interface (CCI)
    NCSA feature 4
    proposal 215
<!--#CONFIG> tag 108, 110, 113
configuring for Server Includes 105–106
connection speed 165
contact.pl script 154
container in HTML 28
Content-type line 94, 95
creating searchable information 159
CU_HTML.DOT 172

D

daemon 15
    httpd 12
    inetd 12
    starting from a startup script 15
data
    description, in description list 47

≡

HTML for Fun and Profit

substitute syntax 152
physical formatting 41
<PLAINTEXT> formatting tag 35
port, URL component 52
POST data handling 151
POST, forms acceptance method 118
PostScript 69
PowerMac, version of Mosaic 237
.ppc extension 237
<pre>, preformatted 112
program execution 112
proxy server
    setting for MacMosaic 239
    setting for Xmosaic 219
    use 219
pull-down menu, definition 135

Q

query, imbedding in URL 52
query.pl script listing 150
QUERY_STRING environment variable 98,
    118
Quigley, E. 255

R

radio button
    attributes 123
    definition 122
    failure to return data 123
    fields 123
    in Macintosh browser 123
    in UNIX browser 123
    in Windows browser 123
    using more than one 124
    when used 122
reference anchor 52
restricted use licensing 11
Rich Text Format (RTF)
    filter for 170
    pointers to information 263
ROWS attribute of <TEXTAREA> tag 133
ROWSPAN={number} attribute 82
RSA 213
RTF-to-HTML filter, sources 171
rtftohtml2.7.5 filter 169

S

Schwartz, Randal 152, 255
script execution 112
ScriptAlias directive 91
scripting extensions, adding to Macintosh
    httpd 93
scripts
    contact.pl 154
    feedback.html 154
    installing 91–92
    query.pl 150
    running from https 92
    setenv.pl 156
    test-cgi.pl 147
scrolling list, creating in forms 135
search component, URL component 52
search tools 159
security
    access control list 212
    cable TV equipment 213
    digital wiretap equipment 213
    interoperability issues 214
SELECTED attribute to <OPTION> tag 137
server
    authentication 212
    connection speed 165
    http 9
    pointers to information about 260
    proposed improvements 215
    tools for creating 9
Server Include tags
    <!--#CONFIG> 108, 110, 113
    <!--#ECHO> 111
    <!--#EXEC> 112
    <!--#FLASTMOD> 109, 110
    <!--#FSIZE> 108
    <!--#INCLUDE> 106
Server Includes
    advantages 112
    configuring for 105–106
    defining directory trees for 106
    definition 105
    format of returned info 112
    permissions for 106
Server Side Includes (See Server Includes)
service provider charges
    disk space 179

URL
    components 51–52
    creating relative 55–57
    encoding 152
    for data processing from forms 118
    in clickable image anchor 101
    in navigating the Web 226
    partial, location for 57
    partial, pathname access 58
    passing variables 97
    relative 54
    specifying relative or partial 54

V

VALUE attribute 130
VAR attribute 111
variable pictures 157
viewer programs
    downloading 221
    for Xmosaic 221
viewer, adding 222
VIRTUAL attribute 106, 108, 109
Virtual Reality Markup Language (VRML)
        212, 264

W

W3 (See WWW)
WAIS
    email aliases 256
    information sources 257
    searches 179
    word location 4
Wall, Larry 152, 255
WAV, MIME format 69
Web
    administration information 264
    email aliases 259
    learning about 258–260
    navigating from WinMosaic 236
    navigating from XMosaic 225
web page
    aesthetic faux pas 167
    announcement 180, 181
    calling search tool 159
    created with HTML Assistant 173
    customizing (don't) 166
    designing for audience 73, 165

home page 163
images in 71
limiting execution permission 106
listing 180
maintaining 38
multimedia characteristics 67
Netscape-enhanced 185
Server Includes 106
storage 219
testing on multiple platforms 167
transparent background 75
unidentifiable 36
web site listings 181–183
webmaster 17
    defined 7
    maintaining web page 38
What's New
    announcements 182
    page 182
    page maintenance 106
whitespace formatting 39, 40
Wide Area Information Servers (See WAIS)
wildcard, in <!--#INCLUDE> 107
win32s subsystem, installing 229
Windows NT
    anchor to imagemap 102
    CD-ROM directories 10
    configuring for CGI 92
    configuring https 20
    converting long filenames for 10
    http service, https 9
    I/O in CGI scripts 94
    machine-specific email alias 261
    obtaining a list of services 21
    path for CGI scripts 96
    running perl scripts 90
    WinMosaic 227
winhttpd14 server 23
WinMosaic
    buttons 235
    configuring 229
    downloading 228
    home page example 234
    home page, defining 230
    latest version 227
    menus 234–235
    navigating on the Web 236
    versions 227
    viewer types 231

winsock.dll library 227
wiretap requirements 213
WordPerfect, pointer to information 263
World Button 224
World Wide Web Consortium (W3C) 211
World Wide Web Worm 182
WWW
    announcement starter 181
    archiving email messages 214
    creating exploration environments 214
    future security methods 213
    future uses 214
    interactivity 4
    new technology 211
    pronunciation 5
    security 212–214
    server authentication 212
    server improvements 215
    Service Providers list 180
    service types 52
    Virtual Library 181
WYSIWYG, HTML-equivalent formatting
       codes 27–28

X

.Xdefaults file 218
Xmosaic
    buttons 224
    configuring 218–221
    determination of system to use 35
    downloading 217
    home page example 223
    latest version 217
    menus 224
    navigating on the Web 225
    permissions 218
    viewer types 221

Z

.Z, file ending 217
.zip extension 227

Software Licenses

a) Accompany it with the complete corresponding machine-readable source code, which must be distributed under the terms of Sections 1 and 2 above on a medium customarily used for software interchange; or,

b) Accompany it with a written offer, valid for at least three years, to give any third party, for a charge no more than your cost of physically performing source distribution, a complete machine-readable copy of the corresponding source code, to be distributed under the terms of Sections 1 and 2 above on a medium customarily used for software interchange; or,

c) Accompany it with the information you received as to the offer to distribute corresponding source code. (This alternative is allowed only for noncommercial distribution and only if you received the program in object code or executable form with such an offer, in accord with Subsection b above.)

The source code for a work means the preferred form of the work for making modifications to it. For an executable work, complete source code means all the source code for all modules it contains, plus any associated interface definition files, plus the scripts used to control compilation and installation of the executable. However, as a special exception, the source code distributed need not include anything that is normally distributed (in either source or binary form) with the major components (compiler, kernel, and so on) of the operating system on which the executable runs, unless that component itself accompanies the executable.

If distribution of executable or object code is made by offering access to copy from a designated place, then offering equivalent access to copy the source code from the same place counts as distribution of the source code, even though third parties are not compelled to copy the source along with the object code.

4. You may not copy, modify, sublicense, or distribute the Program except as expressly provided under this License. Any attempt otherwise to copy, modify, sublicense or distribute the Program is void, and will automatically terminate your rights under this License. However, parties who have received copies, or rights, from you under this License will not have their licenses terminated so long as such parties remain in full compliance.

5. You are not required to accept this License, since you have not signed it. However, nothing else grants you permission to modify or distribute the Program or its derivative works. These actions are prohibited by law if you do not accept this License. Therefore, by modifying or distributing the Program (or any work based on the Program), you indicate your acceptance of this License to do so, and all its terms and conditions for copying, distributing or modifying the Program or works based on it.

6. Each time you redistribute the Program (or any work based on the Program), the recipient automatically receives a license from the original licensor to copy, distribute or modify the Program subject to these terms and conditions. You may not impose any further restrictions on the recipients' exercise of the rights granted herein. You are not responsible for enforcing compliance by third parties to this License.

7. If, as a consequence of a court judgment or allegation of patent infringement or for any other reason (not limited to patent issues), conditions are imposed on you (whether by court order, agreement or otherwise) that contradict the conditions of this License, they do not excuse you from the conditions of this License. If you cannot distribute so as to satisfy simultaneously your obligations under this License and any other pertinent obligations, then as a consequence you may not distribute the Program at all. For example, if a patent license would not permit royalty-free redistribution of the Program by all those who receive copies directly or indirectly through you, then the only way you could satisfy both it and this License would be to refrain entirely from distribution of the Program.

If any portion of this section is held invalid or unenforceable under any particular circumstance, the balance of the section is intended to apply and the section as a whole is intended to apply in other circumstances.

It is not the purpose of this section to induce you to infringe any patents or other property right claims or to contest validity of any such claims; this section has the sole purpose of protecting the integrity of the free software distribution system, which is implemented by public license practices. Many people have made generous contributions to the wide range of software distributed through that system in reliance on consistent application of that system; it is up to the author/donor to decide if he or she is willing to distribute software through any other system and a licensee cannot impose that choice.

This section is intended to make thoroughly clear what is believed to be a consequence of the rest of this License.

8. If the distribution and/or use of the Program is restricted in certain countries either by patents or by copyrighted interfaces, the original copyright holder who places the Program under this License may add an explicit geographical distribution limitation excluding those countries, so that distribution is permitted only in or among countries not thus excluded. In such case, this License incorporates the limitation as if written in the body of this License.

9. The Free Software Foundation may publish revised and/or new versions of the General Public License from time to time. Such new versions will be similar in spirit to the present version, but may differ in detail to address new problems or concerns.

Each version is given a distinguishing version number. If the Program specifies a version number of this License which applies to it and "any later version", you have the option of following the terms and conditions either of that version or of any later version published by the Free Software Foundation. If the Program does not specify a version number of this License, you may choose any version ever published by the Free Software Foundation.

10. If you wish to incorporate parts of the Program into other free programs whose distribution conditions are different, write to the author to ask for permission. For software which is copyrighted by the Free Software Foundation, write to the Free Software Foundation; we sometimes make exceptions for this. Our decision will be guided by the two goals of preserving the free status of all derivatives of our free software and of promoting the sharing and reuse of software generally.

NO WARRANTY

11. BECAUSE THE PROGRAM IS LICENSED FREE OF CHARGE, THERE IS NO WARRANTY FOR THE PROGRAM, TO THE EXTENT PERMITTED BY APPLICABLE LAW. EXCEPT WHEN OTHERWISE STATED IN WRITING THE COPYRIGHT HOLDERS AND/OR OTHER PARTIES PROVIDE THE PROGRAM "AS IS" WITHOUT WARRANTY OF ANY KIND, EITHER EXPRESSED OR IMPLIED, INCLUDING, BUT NOT LIMITED TO, THE IMPLIED WARRANTIES OF MERCHANTABILITY AND FITNESS FOR A PARTICULAR PURPOSE. THE ENTIRE RISK AS TO THE QUALITY AND PERFORMANCE OF THE PROGRAM IS WITH YOU. SHOULD THE PROGRAM PROVE DEFECTIVE, YOU ASSUME THE COST OF ALL NECESSARY SERVICING, REPAIR OR CORRECTION.

12. IN NO EVENT UNLESS REQUIRED BY APPLICABLE LAW OR AGREED TO IN WRITING WILL ANY COPYRIGHT HOLDER, OR ANY OTHER PARTY WHO MAY MODIFY AND/OR REDISTRIBUTE THE PROGRAM AS PERMITTED ABOVE, BE LIABLE TO YOU FOR DAMAGES, INCLUDING ANY GENERAL, SPECIAL, INCIDENTAL OR CONSEQUENTIAL DAMAGES ARISING OUT OF THE USE OR INABILITY TO USE THE PROGRAM (INCLUDING BUT NOT LIMITED TO LOSS OF DATA OR DATA BEING RENDERED INACCURATE OR LOSSES SUSTAINED BY YOU OR THIRD PARTIES OR A FAILURE OF THE PROGRAM TO OPERATE WITH ANY OTHER PROGRAMS), EVEN IF SUCH HOLDER OR OTHER PARTY HAS BEEN ADVISED OF THE POSSIBILITY OF SUCH DAMAGES.

END OF TERMS AND CONDITIONS

Appendix: How to Apply These Terms to Your New Programs

If you develop a new program, and you want it to be of the greatest possible use to the public, the best way to achieve this is to make it free software which everyone can redistribute and change under these terms.

To do so, attach the following notices to the program. It is safest to attach them to the start of each source file to most effectively convey the exclusion of warranty; and each file should have at least the "copyright" line and a pointer to where the full notice is found.

<one line to give the program's name and a brief idea of what it does.> Copyright (C) 19yy <name of author>

This program is free software; you can redistribute it and/or modify it under the terms of the GNU General Public License as published by the Free Software Foundation; either version 2 of the License, or (at your option) any later version.

This program is distributed in the hope that it will be useful, but WITHOUT ANY WARRANTY; without even the implied warranty of MERCHANTABILITY or FITNESS FOR A PARTICULAR PURPOSE. See the GNU General Public License for more details.

You should have received a copy of the GNU General Public License along with this program; if not, write to the Free Software Foundation, Inc., 675 Mass Ave, Cambridge, MA 02139, USA.

Also add information on how to contact you by electronic and paper mail.

If the program is interactive, make it output a short notice like this when it starts in an interactive mode:

Gnomovision version 69, Copyright (C) 19yy name of author Gnomovision comes with ABSOLUTELY NO WARRANTY; for details type 'show w'. This is free software, and you are welcome to redistribute it under certain conditions; type 'show c' for details.

The hypothetical commands 'show w' and 'show c' should show the appropriate parts of the General Public License. Of course, the commands you use may be called something other than 'show w' and 'show c'; they could even be mouse-clicks or menu items--whatever suits your program.

You should also get your employer (if you work as a programmer) or your school, if any, to sign a "copyright disclaimer" for the program, if necessary. Here is a sample; alter the names:

Yoyodyne, Inc., hereby disclaims all copyright interest in the program 'Gnomovision' (which makes passes at compilers) written by James Hacker.

<signature of Ty Coon>, 1 April 1989 Ty Coon, President of Vice

This General Public License does not permit incorporating your program into proprietary programs. If your program is a subroutine library, you may consider it more useful to permit linking proprietary applications with the library. If this is what you want to do, use the GNU Library General Public License instead of this License.